Beyond CLIL

If education is to prepare learners for lifelong learning, there needs to be a shift towards deeper learning: a focus on transferable knowledge and problem-solving skills alongside the development of a positive or growth mindset. In this book, a follow up to *CLIL* (2010), the authors review new developments in the understanding of the interface between language and learning and propose an original new 'pluriliteracies' approach which refines and develops current thinking in CLIL. It aims to facilitate deeper learning through an explicit focus on disciplinary literacies, guiding learners towards textual fluency, encouraging successful communication across cultures, and providing a key stepping stone towards becoming responsible global citizens. It both provides strong theoretical grounding, and shows how to put that understanding into practice. Engaging and practical, this book will be invaluable to both academics and education practitioners, and will enable conventional classrooms to be transformed into deeper learning ecologies.

Do Coyle is Chair in Languages Education and Classroom Pedagogy at the University of Edinburgh. **Oliver Meyer** is Head of the Department of Teaching English as a Foreign Language at the Johannes Gutenberg University of Mainz. Together, they have been working on a shared vision for deeper learning across subjects and languages. The pedagogic approach presented in this book is the result of extensive collaboration with expert practitioners and researchers around the world.

Beyond CLIL

Pluriliteracies Teaching for Deeper Learning

Do Coyle

University of Edinburgh

Oliver Meyer

Johannes Gutenberg University of Mainz

CAMBRIDGE
UNIVERSITY PRESS

CAMBRIDGE
UNIVERSITY PRESS

University Printing House, Cambridge CB2 8BS, United Kingdom

One Liberty Plaza, 20th Floor, New York, NY 10006, USA

477 Williamstown Road, Port Melbourne, VIC 3207, Australia

314–321, 3rd Floor, Plot 3, Splendor Forum, Jasola District Centre, New Delhi – 110025, India

103 Penang Road, #05-06/07, Visioncrest Commercial, Singapore 238467

Cambridge University Press is part of the University of Cambridge.

It furthers the University's mission by disseminating knowledge in the pursuit of education, learning, and research at the highest international levels of excellence.

www.cambridge.org
Information on this title: www.cambridge.org/9781108830904
DOI: 10.1017/9781108914505

© Do Coyle and Oliver Meyer 2021

First published 2021

Printed in the United Kingdom by TJ Books Limited, Padstow Cornwall

A catalogue record for this publication is available from the British Library.

Library of Congress Cataloging-in-Publication Data
Names: Coyle, Do, 1952– author. | Meyer, Oliver, (Professor of English) author.
Title: Beyond CLIL : pluriliteracies teaching for deeper learning / Do Coyle, University of Edinburgh ; Oliver Meyer, Johannes Gutenberg Universität Mainz, Germany.
Other titles: Beyond content and language integrated learning
Description: Cambridge, UK ; New York, NY : Cambridge University Press, [2022] | Includes bibliographical references and index.
Identifiers: LCCN 2020058409 (print) | LCCN 2020058410 (ebook) | ISBN 9781108830904 (hardback) | ISBN 9781108823722 (paperback) | ISBN 9781108914505 (ebook)
Subjects: LCSH: Language arts – Correlation with content subjects. | Language and languages – Study and teaching.
Classification: LCC P53.293 .C69 2021 (print) | LCC P53.293 (ebook) | DDC 418.0071–dc23
LC record available at https://lccn.loc.gov/2020058409
LC ebook record available at https://lccn.loc.gov/2020058410

ISBN 978-1-108–83090-4 Hardback
ISBN 978-1-108-82372-2 Paperback

Contents

Figures

Tables

Preface

Ask any educator what they would most like to achieve throughout their professional lives and the answer is likely to be 'to make a difference'. The drive to provide fair and inclusive opportunities to better prepare all young people for living fulfilling lives as citizens of the world, at any time and any age, is fundamental to the business of formal schooling. This is why teachers teach. This is what they do, whilst grappling with the 'unforgiving complexity' of teaching (Cochran-Smith, 2003, p. 4). Yet the educational world is in conflict. Fullan and Langworthy's white paper (2013) *Towards a New End: New Pedagogies for Deep Learning* opens by discussing the 'crisis' in schooling as a function of a push-pull dynamic. They describe push factors involving student dissatisfaction in terms of boredom and frustration with their educational experiences. The pull factors include emerging technology-rich environments with the potential to reach out. Their white paper acknowledges current moves in '*defining the what:* new goals for learning' relevant to the here and now and calls for 'immediate and urgent attempts *to innovate the how:* the processes of education' (2013, p. 1).

Educational literature is awash with perceived needs to bring about change across a broad range of learning contexts and systems. Fullan and Langworthy (2013, p. 4) define the need for school learning partnerships grounded in 'purposeful learning by doing'; Claxton (2013) calls for 'epistemic apprenticeship' which focusses on cultivating habits of mind such as resilience, imagination and curiosity; the OECD promotes the Learning Compass 2030 – a future-oriented visionary framework for learning in a world of uncertainty and rapid change, to help students navigate towards the future they want, where 'the new normal' is founded on a sense of wellbeing; and the Slow Education Movement encourages deeper learning as real learning – learning through 'curiosity, passion and interest' (Harrison-Greaves, 2016). However, such positioning is important, since big ideas such as these act as triggers for critical reflection, deep thinking, exploration and decision making, acceptance and rejection, determination and drive, in the quest to 'make a difference'.

Our own inspiration can be summarised by Stigler and Hiebert's (1999) claim, made over two decades ago, that to improve the quality of education for our young people, change has to take place in the classroom, where 'the challenge now becomes that of identifying the kinds of changes that will improve learning for all students... of sharing this knowledge with other teachers'. In essence, we know this is where it matters. This is where the 'what' becomes not only the 'how', but fundamentally the 'why' and 'for whom'. This is what has driven the writing of this book. We are not looking for answers, for formulas and fixes, but we are looking for better ways of understanding the complexities of learning in general, and bilingual learning in particular, which need to be critiqued and shared, to be practised and evaluated, to be adapted and owned.

Since its authors were part of the early, trans-national, pioneering Content and Language Integrated Learning (CLIL) community of language and subject educators and researchers over three decades ago, the thinking underpinning this book is rooted in a patchwork of experiences gained over a prolonged period of time, including work in classrooms with teachers and learners across linguistic and cultural boundaries, as well as a growing body of robust research in the field. Contrary to early publications, which tended to cast a positive light on bilingual learning, studies published in the early 2000s indicated that subject learners often struggled to express their understanding adequately (Volmer, 2011). These findings were consistent across both L1 and L2 contexts, which suggest a troubling possibility of a more general educational problem that extends far beyond bilingual classrooms. Put simply, we began to realise that we weren't doing enough to promote deeper understanding in our classrooms. Figuring out what it really means for learners to 'understand' and how to promote that understanding in the classroom has informed our professional quest ever since: the Pluriliteracies Initiative was funded by the Council of Europe through the ECML (European Centre for Modern Languages) and led to the formation of the Graz Group – a trans-European group of teachers, teacher educators, researchers and academics. Given the changing demographics of our classrooms, and the need to enable learners to have equitable access to purposeful bilingual experiences, the Graz Group focussed on unravelling the potential of literacies development as the conduit for deeper learning. As emergent thinking evolved into new understanding in dialogue among disciplines, through practices of social negotiation and in creative collaboration with peers and experts, so too did the realisation that we had to go beyond seeing CLIL as bounded by subject learning and language learning, as in current practices. Instead, a critical holistic look at *how* deeper learning can be fostered across the curriculum was needed. Indeed, the more attention we paid to understanding the far-reaching implications of integrated learning, the more the essential role of learners deepening their understanding through *languaging* was reinforced. Moreover, this was not limited to L2 or L3, but also included L1. An increasing awareness of learning identified pathways leading to embracing a multi-perspective view of language and content (Dalton-Puffer et al., 2010, p. 280) that goes beyond CLIL. We believe this has the potential to advance the earlier conceptualisations of CLIL. If we accept that deeper learning puts language as central to the process of knowledge construction, then attention needs to be paid to what is known as 'epistemic functioning', involving the cognitive processing of language as well as its social, cultural and linguistic functions (Reitbauer et al., 2018).

Motivated by what Balsamo et al. (2010, p. 430) refer to as ecological shifts that challenge what *is*, and by bringing together pedagogic experiences, a broad range of theoretical constructs and critical frameworks, this volume charts a carefully constructed contribution to Nikula et al.'s (2016b, p. 12) call for 'well-developed, research-based conceptualisations and models as tools for practitioners to make better sense content and language integration'. This we frame as *Pluriliteracies Teaching for Deeper Learning* – a concept which we will develop throughout this volume.

The book is in three parts. Part I focusses on stages in the developments of CLIL, charting the changes and challenges in terms of principle and practices. Given the impact of technological advancements, movement of peoples and societal needs on what happens in classrooms, we use the lens of 'curriculum-making' and theories of practice to critically examine the framing of CLIL classroom pedagogies within broader and deeper educational demands. Building on the issues raised in Part I, Part II takes the reader through a theoretical paradigm shift from integrated learning to pluriliteracies. Throughout these chapters, our understanding of pluriliteracies is not only defined, but is used to shape a holistic model of *Pluriliteracies Teaching for Deeper Learning*. The construction of the model seeks to address deeper learning from different perspectives. The *mechanics* and trajectories of deeper learning are unravelled and analysed, alongside the *drivers* that enable individual learners to engage and the essential role of the teacher in mentoring learning. Part III focusses on implications for applying the pluriliteracies model in practice. As design principles for a more coherent pedagogical approach to deeper learning emerge, guiding questions for teachers position its underlying thinking firmly in the classroom. However, it was at this point in the development of our thinking that we became aware of an increasingly urgent gap that was not being addressed – the role of language teachers as subject experts. We debated the positioning of this chapter within the book but decided that its rightful place was the final chapter. We realised that we needed to develop our ideas using subject disciplines first in order to understand better how language teachers are not only part of the pluriliteracies movement, but are essentially fundamental to its development. We hope that the insights we present will contribute to debate and discussion. We also hope that the challenges and insights might lead in some way to 'making a difference', not only for learners but also, and especially, for educators.

PART I
CLIL: Moving On

1 Understanding the CLIL Phenomenon: Developments and Directions

This chapter provides an overview of content and language integrated learning as a constantly evolving approach to learning and teaching in our multilingual and multicultural classrooms. Bilingual education was described by Cazden and Snow several decades ago (1990) as a 'simple label for a complex phenomenon'. This complexity is evidenced by the different models that bilingual education encompasses on a global scale – for example, Garcia (2009) identified at least thirty-three different designations. Moreover, given the unprecedented movement of peoples, classrooms as multilingual and multicultural spaces are changing rapidly, with resulting 'super-diversity', (Vertovec, 2007, p. 1024) impacting at all levels on learning practices.

> Classrooms the world over are full of people who, for different reasons, are learning additional languages and/or are studying through languages that are not their first. Gaining insights into such contexts is complicated for researcher and practitioners alike by the myriad of contextual variables that come with the different implementations and make comparison and generalisation a tricky business. (Dalton-Puffer et al., 2014)

It is against this backdrop that the CLIL phenomenon can be considered as part of the bilingual education movement. CLIL has become increasingly piloted and practised over the last decades across very different contexts and places of learning on a global scale (Doiz et al., 2014; Knapp & Aguado, 2015). The trend is heterogeneous, and occurs due to a wide range of complex reasons – sometimes as a result of strong political priorities; sometimes to build educational opportunities as a means of addressing increasing social demands; sometimes to provide equitable pathways for diverse learners to access curricula; sometimes to grow economic capital; and sometimes to enhance national profiles, taking into account international comparators as well as social and cultural exigencies. As CLIL programmes have exponentially expanded, so too have different interpretations, models, frameworks, points of reference and theoretical underpinnings across national, regional and local boundaries. Whilst this diversity is inevitable – due to the nature of educational trends and cultural traditions inherent in formal schooling and tertiary education systems across the world – academic debates and practical discussions have contributed to some confusion and disagreement about the very nature of CLIL.

There has been particular emphasis on defining what is meant by CLIL and how it relates to other forms of learning, especially those that involve more than one language. Debates have encompassed the distribution of time spent in CLIL, the professional demands of adopting and adapting integrated approaches to learning, the linguistic competence required by both teachers and learners to maximise benefits, the associated pedagogic processes and assessments, and the constant plea for more research and classroom data. More recently, concerns have been expressed about the quality of learning in the subject or thematic discipline and the linguistic competence of learners in terms of the projected outcomes. Few longitudinal empirical research studies have been published to date.

It is timely, therefore, to take account of the development of the CLIL movement, to reiterate that the phenomenon is not in a static state – 'this is what you do if you do CLIL' – but is dynamic in terms of its potential for building an expansive yet rigorous theoretical basis and a fundamental value system reflecting social justice and equitable opportunities for all learners to experience their own successes. This is a 'big' statement, which requires careful and detailed analysis of different factors to understand in more nuanced terms how CLIL potential might become a reality in different classrooms and in different ways.

1.1   Unravelling Key Questions

Taking an overview of studies, documents, policies and debates over several decades relating to the development of bilingual education (Coyle, 2018), we observe a constant plea for greater emphasis on interpreting CLIL; more detailed understanding of the learning processes which lead to quality learning outcomes; and research evidence in terms of classroom data, especially of a longitudinal nature.

What is understood by Content and Language Integrated Learning has become increasingly debated, at times contentiously, as the global expansion of programmes and pedagogic approaches that use the term accrues. This is an inevitability – increasingly diverse interpretations of the phenomenon working with and across increasingly complex contextual variables lead to ambiguities and adaptations. Whilst Cenoz et al. (2014) believe that 'coherent evolution' is dependent on a common understanding of the nature of CLIL, the speed of socio-cultural and political change suggests that educational and pedagogic developments within education systems are dynamic and in a state of flux. Evolution is messy. It is a given that understanding and experiencing the affordances and constraints of new or alternative modes of working will lead to differences in (re)conceptualising, rationalising and realising the ways in which learners learn and teachers teach. CLIL is not and cannot be formulaic, with pre-defined procedures and learning outcomes, but is a multifaceted, theoretically sound, contextually embedded phenomenon, which has to address the complementary and at times conflicting pedagogies associated with language learning and subject or thematic learning. Integrating these practices, which are steeped in their own cultural discursive traditions, requires a different lens on learning based on 'organic pedagogic practices' (Sadovnik, 2001, p. 689).

CLIL can be described as:

> a dual-focused educational approach in which an additional language is used for the learning and teaching of both content and language. That is, in the teaching and learning process, there is a focus not only on content and not only on language. Each is interwoven even if the emphasis is greater on one or the other at a given time. (Coyle et al., 2010, p. 1)

We would argue that whilst this has become known usefully as an umbrella term, the fact that in the last two decades CLIL experiences 'have burgeoned throughout Europe' (Merino and Lasagabaster's term, 2018, p. 17) has led to a wide variety of interpretations and pedagogic labelling, due to the contextual variables inherent in regional, national and international educational settings. Cenoz et al. concluded that:

> Our examination of the definition and the scope of the term CLIL both internally, as used by CLIL advocates in Europe, and externally, as compared with immersion education in and outside Europe, indicates that the core characteristics of CLIL are understood in different ways with respect to: the balance between language and content instruction, the nature of the target language involved, instructional goals, defining characteristics of student participants and pedagogic approaches to integrating language and content instruction. (2014, p. 255)

Distinctions and convergences concerning the definition of CLIL have been well argued in the literature (e.g. Garcia, 2009; Lasagabaster & Sierra, 2010; Cenoz et al., 2014; Dalton-Puffer et al., 2014). However, the challenges lie not in arriving at one definition of CLIL – labels are meaningless if the quality of the learning process is not fit for purpose – but in the positioning of a shared understanding of fundamental principles of plurilingual learning which inspire educators to define, design, enact and evaluate with their learners the conditions for learning that are of the highest possible quality and relevant to the communities they serve. Harrop's critique (2012) levelled at CLIL 'literature' as having an 'unmistakable evangelical tone' in our view describes the earlier phases of exploring alternative learning pathways, where an understanding of the potential of CLIL served to uncover the increasing intricacies of learning a language and subject content simultaneously. This stage has now been succeeded by a phase of rigorous investigations and critical reflections, which look into as well as beyond the immediacies of the classroom. Garcia (2009, p. 6) emphasised that bilingual programmes, including CLIL, need to provide experiences that guide learners to become 'global and responsible citizens as they learn to function across cultures and worlds, that is beyond the cultural borders in which traditional schooling often operates'.

The need, therefore, to ensure that the CLIL phenomenon embraces the macro and micro, the broad values-driven educational agenda and the hybridity of classroom conditions for learning which will motivate, engage and prepare students, is an enormous task. As was argued in The Place of CLIL in (Bilingual) Education (Coyle, 2018), bridging the gap between political rhetoric and teacher discourse, between theoretical constructs and professional beliefs, does not depend on one established set of rules or pedagogic trends. Neither is it a case of adding thematic references in language lessons or translation in subject lessons – minor adjustments cannot equate with the enormity and pedagogic impact of the change processes required. The pedagogic and theoretical substance of CLIL needs to be clearly articulated and substantiated. It requires time. It requires critical reflection. And yet there is an increasing moral urgency – the rights for all learners to access a quality education are at the core of the global Millennium Development Goals (United Nations, 2000). Therefore, in order to provide a reliable contribution to those goals, the need to conceptualise the rigorous dynamic of the breadth and depth of CLIL is paramount.

Regardless of positive and negative rhetoric about the potential of CLIL, there is no single approach – one size does not fit all. However, the corollary that an 'anything goes' approach allows for flexibility and diversity is equally unacceptable. CLIL, as with all educational thinking, has to be carefully analysed, critiqued, experimented and evidenced. It has to evolve and grow whilst continually being scrutinised from different perspectives. Moreover, however challenging the task, arguments need to be substantiated by evidence. This growth – which is at times contentious and uncomfortable and at others reassuring and encouraging – depends on an openness to scientific and rigorous research, enquiry, exploration, analysis and evaluation. It also depends on a preparedness to activate stakeholders to support the necessary changes that will inevitably be required to optimise conditions for authentic learning. Emerging from such growth leads us towards what Hornberger describes as an 'ecological heuristic' (2002, p. 27) – an inclusive blueprint for integrated learning, which embraces the overarching goals of education; where there is 'a focus not only on content and not only on language'; and which constantly explores ways of engaging and enabling (preparing) all learners through high-quality, relevant, real-world experiences. There will be some readers who immediately raise questions: what do we understand by *quality* learning? What is meant by inclusive? What is integrated learning? How might overarching goals of education be defined? And how might these differ across cultures and nations? What about plurilingual and pluricultural classrooms? How does this attune with goals of education in existence? What about learner dispositions and abilities? And teacher support for constantly reflecting on learning? These are all good questions and ones which, in our view, can only be answered by bringing together a range of perspectives, to map out and clarify alternative pathways. Taking this stance, we understand it to be the responsibility of those who design and organise formal learning to involve school leaders, teachers and learners in identifying and making transparent the specificities of 'integrated learning' in their own contexts, including the theoretical and moral principles upon which it is built, alongside the pedagogic exigencies that guide classroom practices and student learning. This is not passing the buck! Throughout this volume we seek to raise and consider many of these questions in greater depth.

The increasingly extensive ramifications of globalisation, especially over the last decade, should not be underestimated in terms of their impact on classroom learning, which is in the process of irreversible change in terms of the linguistic profiles and cultural roots of learners and teachers. The plurilingual nature of learners grouped together in education settings, alongside advances in accessibility and use of digital technologies, have amplified two contradictory forces – uniformity (e.g. national norms, especially in terms of measurable and comparable outcomes) and diversity (reflecting what May (2014) refers to as the 'multilingual turn'); underpinned by ideological drives towards equality, inclusion and social justice.

> The ever-fast evolving cultural landscape is characterised by an intensified diversity of peoples, communities and individuals, who live more and more closely. The increasing diversity of cultures, which is fluid, dynamic and transformative, implies specific competences and capacities for individuals and societies to learn, re-learn and unlearn so as to meet personal fulfilment and social harmony. (UNESCO, 2013, p. 4)

A significant drawing together of the role of 'languages in schooling' (Schleppegrell, 2004) has, supported by Council of Europe initiatives over the past thirty years, brought into question the dominance of monolingual curricula, implicating not only language teachers but educators responsible for enabling all learners to access national curricula using different languages for different purposes (Commission of the European Communities, 1996). Discussions about the medium of instruction, literacies and the language of the classroom are starting to merge, creating the potential to bridge existing disciplinary divides, with (foreign) language teachers, language teachers, EAL teachers (English as an Additional Language) or equivalent teachers (e.g. in countries where acquiring the language of schooling is a priority for immigrant or mobile learners) and subject specialists all engaging in ways of understanding and enacting the broader yet crucial role of language for learning. However, this also raises the issue of what Dalton-Puffer notes as the 'overwhelming prevalence of English' as the vehicular language that effectively leads to Content and English Integrated Learning (CEIL) (Dalton-Puffer, 2011).

> Despite the fact that CLIL's original objective was to spread multilingualism, there is little doubt that in the European context English is the predominant language. (Merino & Lasagabaster, 2018, p. 79)

Whilst this is inevitable, given the role of 'global Englishes', it could be argued that it has led to the marginalising of LOTE (languages other than English) contexts, especially those where English is the national language and those which are predominantly trilingual, such as in the Basque Autonomous Community (Merino & Lasagabaster, 2018).

Uniting language and subject educators involves not only a shared understanding of known practices, but also a co-construction of new integrated pathways to guide meaning making through connecting language domains. Such integration, according to de Graaff, 'is more than just a combination of two elements: real fusion asks for an understanding of the characteristics and interplay of both' (Nikula et al., 2016a, p. xiii). De Graaff goes on to argue that whilst this may appear to suggest a reconceptualisation of learning, integrating content learning with language learning may not be 'new', and as such:

> We may just not have had the lens to understand (or the language to express) the full teaching, learning or research potential of an integrated perspective on content and language. (2016a, p. xiii)

De Graaff's position is very helpful in suggesting that an alternative lens may assist educators in the task ahead. An emphasis on alternative interpretations, and in particular an ecological perspective, is what has driven us to write this book. We wish to share our concerns and our vision to provide readers with alternative pathways for conceptualising learning – not as an answer to current CLIL challenges but rather as a means to identifying emergent 'invisible barriers' and unravelling possible ways of breaking through them, whether our readers are experienced CLIL educators or starting out on building learning partnerships and laying foundations for CLIL. There is clearly some way to go before such links are transparently connected and made visible and accessible for teachers and learners – the 'wider conversation has just begun' (May, 2014, p. 217).

The arguments presented thus far are not meant to confuse readers, nor are they intended to complicate an already multi-faceted phenomenon. Rather they are intended to problematise in a realistic way the range of factors stakeholders have to take into account when considering, planning, developing and evaluating bilingual integrated approaches to learning in their schools and universities (Merino & Lasagabaster, 2018). This is summarised by Garcia when she states:

> What recent European investigations have taught us is to move away from the unilingual frame of reference in bilingual programs by underlining that bilingualism is never an all-or-nothing phenomenon, that the outcome of bilingual education is not a reduplication of monolingualism, but a 'more or less' proficiency in more than one language. (2009, p. 212)

Garcia argues that this positions Content and Language Integrated Learning within the broad field of bilingual education, illustrated by a particularly strong visual image of an 'all-terrain vehicle in its heteroglossic potential' rather than a 'bicycle with two balanced wheels' (2009, p. 17):

> We believe that monolingual education is no longer adequate in the twenty-first century, and that every society needs some form of bilingual education. Our view of bilingual education is complex, like the banyan tree, allowing for growth in different directions at the same time and grounded in the diverse social realities from which it merges. (Garcia, 2009, p. 17)

1.2 Developmental Stages towards Integrated Learning

Three broad stages in the growth of CLIL have emerged over the last few decades, which position the related arguments and concerns, as well as claims for success and achievement, in a wider international agenda. The stages can be described as follows: first, the content and language stage; second, the integration of content and language; and third, the focus on inclusive learning and the quality of learning experiences. Of course, it could be argued undisputedly that quality learning, for example, has always been at the core of CLIL and that the different focusses involving CLIL merge with no clear distinction. Yet what is understood as 'quality learning' differs considerably across cultural and social boundaries. However, we believe it is useful to loosely identify the ways in which CLIL has developed in rapidly changing educational contexts in order to understand the ebbs and flows, the important milestones and reiterations that change processes bring. This will essentially enable us to look forwards, and to interpret constantly emergent thinking – again an inevitability in trying to capture optimal conditions for human learning.

1.2.1 Content and Language

It is now well documented how, in the 1990s, a pioneering European group, supported by and in line with fundamental principles for developing skills and experiences for European citizens, set out to establish an alternative way of developing linguistic competence across school systems. It is not our intention to revisit in detail the early stages of CLIL in Europe – readers can find these summarised in the literature (e.g. Coyle, 2007; Coyle et al., 2010; Harrop, 2012; Pérez Cañado, 2016) – but to reflect on how the concept of CLIL has developed, deepened and transformed over significant periods of time. The teaching and learning of subjects through a language other than the learner's first was certainly not new, and can be traced back for centuries. However, the key principle promoted by CLIL suggested that the learning of a language at the same time as learning new knowledge and skills associated with 'non-language' subject disciplines or thematic studies in the school curriculum had the potential to raise linguistic competence and subject discipline knowledge, skills and understanding. This approach also suggested economies of time spent on learning, moving towards a multilingual, multicultural Europe, whilst significantly contributing to raising national linguistic capital. It was also an attempt to offer an appropriate alternative that built on the shared experiences of other models of bilingual learning which had been pioneered and were well established in other parts of the world.

Throughout this mainly European-oriented period, concerns emerged regarding the relative balance of importance between the subject and the language, and the significant impact on teacher professionalism and teacher education. This resulted in perceived threats to teacher identity, teacher confidence and learner and teacher linguistic competence, as well as questions about where CLIL might be positioned within the curriculum. The big questions focussed on issues such as: was the subject or the language more important? Was the planning of the learning driven by language learning principles or subject learning principles, or both? Who was best suited to teach CLIL – language specialists or subject experts? These questions are examples of concerns raised about CLIL, and improvements in the provision of professional development and teacher education were often identified as being key to wider adoption.

Of course, throughout CLIL's development there have always been examples of outstanding practice, mainly due to specific variables that have enabled, encouraged and supported CLIL classroom practices. However, such practices were often not replicable on a larger scale: few teachers had an in-depth understanding of how an additional language functions as a learning tool as well as a communicative tool in specific subject areas, or had the confidence in creating tasks and activities which targeted progression in subject disciplines. These did not lie in the pedagogic repertoires of the majority of subject teachers. Equally, language teachers whose clear goal was to increase linguistic proficiency in their learners had traditionally been tasked with ensuring learners could communicate effectively and accurately in a particular language, and in some contexts with expanding learner skills into accessing literature and other cultural references associated with target language and cultures. Language teachers were not usually required to teach non-language subject disciplines and skills. The notion, therefore, of learning both a subject discipline and a language at the same time had by its very definition to evolve over time. It had to develop its own transdisciplinary discourse.

Early pedagogic frameworks began to emerge, with the 4 Cs Framework considered to be one of the most useful in terms of large-scale adoption. There was an urgent need to look at ways of ensuring that subject discipline was not a re-enactment of what would have happened in the first-language classroom, but in a different language, with both teachers and learners resorting to translation to access resources and texts. In the same vein, there was expediency around ensuring that thematic or subject discipline studies were not oversimplified or a repetition of what had already been covered in subject studies in the first-language classroom. At all costs, the cognitive level of any learner could not be compromised due to potential linguistic 'barriers'. And yet the two pathways for language learning and content learning did not easily fuse. Language teachers were focussed on developing linguistic competence in the form of communicative skills and grammatical understanding. Subject teachers and generalist teachers were focussed on ensuring the subject content learning led to appropriate competences, associated ways of learning within the subject discipline and knowledge-based 'measurable' outcomes. None of this is surprising. Few teachers considered themselves CLIL teachers and instead brought with them particular views and beliefs about learning, depending on their orientation. However, awareness was raised in terms of the implications of enabling learners to use language for learning purposes whilst processing and developing the same vehicular language.

1.2.2   Towards Integrating Content and Language

In an analysis of developments in CLIL throughout the last three decades, Cenoz et al. (2014) conclude that careful theoretical, empirical and pedagogic attention needs to be paid to understanding how best to integrate language and content in terms of classroom practices and institution-based policy.

> The integrated approach to language and content teaching espoused by CLIL had the potential to better integrate foreign language/L2 instruction and the teacher responsible for that instruction with the mainstream curriculum and teachers. (Cenoz et al., 2014, p. 256)

Some decades ago, Van Lier (1996, p. 203) warned of being 'trapped inside a dichotomy between focus on form and a focus on meaning', suggesting instead a focus on language, since 'in practice it becomes impossible to separate out form and function neatly in the interactional work that is being carried out'. Byrnes (2005) states that separating language(s) from learning is an illusion – a position which will be explored more in subsequent chapters. The move away from the 'either-or' debate was critically informed by Lyster's work (2007) in immersion classrooms, where he suggested that in order to support optimal conditions for learning across different forms of content-based teaching, a balance between focus on meaning and focus on form is fundamental. Lyster refers to this as a 'counter-balanced approach'. The subsequent strategies and guidance developed for immersion teachers (Lyster, 2018) are based on the premise that in content-oriented classrooms, learners need to 'notice' language forms explicitly – either directly or indirectly – according to different task forms and dialogic processing, including through the nature of feedback (such as recasts) within the learning environment.

The purpose and enactment of 'balance' in Content and Language Integrated Learning contexts, however, lie at the core of constant debate about what is meant by CLIL and the nature of integration. Whilst it could be argued that balancing focus on form and meaning goes some way towards bringing together the demands of subject learning and language learning, it does not address how integration could be reconceptualised using a different lens.

The work of Llinares et al. (2012, p. 13) focusses on the roles of language in CLIL, where they argue that:

> It is possible to bring about a genuine integration of content and language by helping CLIL learners to attend to language features which are essential for the construction of knowledge in the classroom.

They detail how data from classroom research demonstrates both proactive and reactive teaching and learning strategies for authentic meaning making in CLIL classrooms. Using an overarching socio-cultural perspective which unites a Vygotskian theory of learning with a social-semiotic theory of language (Halliday's systemic functional linguistics), alongside sociocultural theories of second-language acquisition, the researchers found a means to make visible a 'more principled integration of content and language' (2012, p. 20). Their reasoning unites theories of language with theories of learning in order to enable integrated pedagogies to emerge. In describing the linguistic features of key types of text (genres) which learners require in order to construct their conceptual understanding, an alternative to grammatical chronology as the determinant of linguistic progression was emphasised. A three-part framework that brings together the different roles of languages focusses on the convergence of subject literacies, classroom interaction and language development to inform design for learning in CLIL contexts. Such an approach, the authors suggest, reinforces the need to make more explicit the kinds of language that learners need to construct meaning. We will return to the role of subject literacies subsequently.

Calls for shared responsibility for language development across the school curriculum, as well as with language specialists, are already very familiar. According to Genesee and Hamayan (2016), CLIL planning frameworks are designed to integrate language objectives 'alongside and entwined' within content and learning objectives. This resonates with the concept of language-rich curricula in any language, including the main language of schooling. For this goal to be achieved, attention has to be paid to developing learners' linguistic resources to construct, use and refine their knowledge base across the curriculum by subject teachers (Department of Education and Science, 1975). Similarly, Mohan's Knowledge Framework (1986) provided a systematic way of integrating content objectives and language objectives that applies across the curriculum. Whilst such examples may seem to belong to a previous era, it could be argued that the principles they promote, and as such their legacy, provide a rich basis for recycling and reiterating fundamental ways of conceptualising classroom learning. These principles will be explored in greater depth in the following chapters.

The seminal work of Nikula et al. (2016a) investigates a conceptual framework for CLIL that focusses on unravelling the complexities of integration as a shared concern 'for all forms of education that have simultaneous content and language learning objectives' (Nikula et al., 2016a, p. 1). In it, they seek to redress the dominance of research carried out from a more language-oriented perspective in CLIL settings. They challenge views on what language learning is and address how there needs to be a shift in its role as the medium both of and for learning. Davison and Williams (2001) suggest that a continuum from a curricular focus on content learning to a curricular focus on language learning, whilst being conceptually realistic, reveals an urgent need for comprehensive theory building. They underline the importance of making transparent in each context the implications of and for more integrated approaches to language and content learning that inform teaching and learning practices. However, the challenge of realising integrated pedagogies is all the greater, since subject pedagogies and language pedagogies 'form their own largely independent universes of discourse, both in the daily life of educational institutions and in the world of academic research' (Dalton-Puffer, 2018) – what Lin (2016) refers to as 'intercurricular disconnect'.

Conceptualising the integration of subject learning goals with language learning goals is therefore especially challenging if one accepts that there is an inherent interrelationship between the two that is relevant not only to classrooms where more than one language may be used, but in any learning context. The need to extend thinking to ensure that 'language-aware' subject pedagogies intersect with content-aware language pedagogies becomes fundamental to achieving more realistic learning outcomes. Yet arriving at this intersection is problematic. It is clear that what drives a language teacher will not necessarily resonate with what drives a history teacher – neither is a CLIL teacher per se. Shared understanding through collaborative and guided in-depth discussions of the roles of language in learning and their impact on meaning making, alongside the extent to which pedagogic approaches embrace much broader educational values, including social justice and civic responsibilities, require time and professional space. As Nikula et al. emphasise, the essential nature of:

> the remit of the term 'integration' that any educational institution offering CLIL or other forms of bilingual education needs to address, for example, integration of different types of teacher expertise and teacher identities involved, integration as the use of and merging of different languages in classroom practices, as well as the whole enterprise of integrating content and language as a meeting place for different, sometimes conflicting discourses, processes and practices. (2016a, p. 4)

Such positioning identifies three very broad perspectives for analysing integration: multi-level curriculum, pedagogy and planning; participant perspectives, including the roles of teacher cognition, beliefs and identities as well as learners' fluctuating and stable attitudes, motivations and self-efficacy; and classroom practices. All of these impact on the what, the why and the how of CLIL. Leung and Morton's (2016, p. 237 as cited in Nikula et al. 2016a) conceptual framework for integration, using two intersecting axes to plot disciplinary orientation and language pedagogy (see Figure 1.1), provides an extremely useful planning heuristic to guide more longitudinal moves and shifts towards developing and nurturing integration.

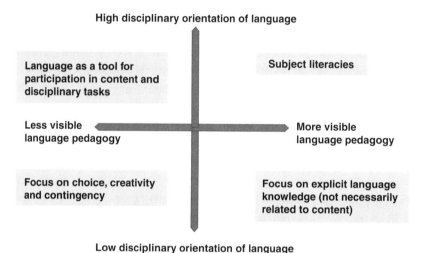

Figure 1.1 Adapted from Leung and Morton (2016)

However, caution must be exercised in (mis)interpreting such frameworks as having hidden messages about what is desirable and 'good' and the converse. Similarly, labels such as 'hard CLIL' and 'soft CLIL', whilst describing the extent of language or content orientations, might suggest a hierarchy of importance rather than descriptors of how integrated content learning and language learning can be developed in different contexts. Morton and Llinares (2017, p. 1) suggest that rather than as a label for specific programme types, 'CLIL is best seen as a way of bringing together a range of pedagogical or methodological principles and perspectives for the integration of content and language'.

Therefore, as more attention focussed on uncovering increasingly intricate, multifaceted yet interconnected elements of the integration of subject content and language learning in the classroom, emergent analyses from a range of perspectives served to underscore, for example, its cognitive (e.g. Lyster, 2007), functional (e.g. Llinares et al. 2012) and discursive (e.g. Nikula, 2010; Barwell, 2016) nature.

Despite significant progress in this respect, developing an understanding of 'integration' that is sufficiently fine-grained to be meaningful on the level of classroom pedagogy as well as substantially linked to both language education and specific frames of reference of history, science, or arts education continues to be a challenge. Such an understanding, though, is essential as approaches to language-aware subject teaching that are exclusively anchored in the world of linguistics and language education are in danger of being experienced as transgressive or even meaningless by content-subject educators. (Dalton-Puffer, 2018, p. 6)

1.2.3 Making Connections: Convergence and Divergence for Integrated Learning

Increasingly, an urgency to go beyond a 'balancing' of content and language forms towards a much 'deeper integration' (Morton, 2018, p. 57), which embraces a broader perspective on the goals and processes involved in formal learning, is becoming apparent. This resonates with Barwell's position (2005, p. 208) that the language-content dichotomy remains problematic (see also Davison & Williams, 2001, p. 63). Despite acknowledgement that they are inseparable (Mohan et al., 2001, Byrnes, 2002), the continued use of these terms by researchers and practitioners leads to their conceptual separation. Whilst acknowledging the importance of this distinction in designing and organising learning, Barwell suggests that this shapes our thinking in particular ways and comments that 'it would be illuminating to find new ways of talking about language and content that avoids that distinction'.

Current trends in the development of CLIL, therefore, set out to 'dig deeper' into the implications of integrated learning, with an increasing emphasis on broadening perspectives in order to 'transcend such an understanding that conceptualizes language and curricular content as separate reified entities and instead think of them as one process' (Dalton-Puffer, 2011, p. 96). Moreover, the need to connect with wider pressing educational issues that impact learning, such as the changing demographic of classrooms, alongside a growing perception that content and language integrated learning may favour more able learners, have to be addressed. As has already been noted, some research findings bring the gains of CLIL into question (e.g. Bruton, 2013; Vollmer, 2008), whilst others reveal gaps in our collective understanding. Ways in which alternative curricular approaches might contribute to national policies and priorities are under the microscope. Furthermore, attention to the role literacies can play in supporting and guiding CLIL is proliferating, thereby providing a bridge for exploring the wealth of accumulative professional and academic practices across the curriculum. As Morton (2018, p. 57) points out, 'A recent trend in CLIL pedagogy has been to add a focus on subject-literacy to that on content and language'. We content that subject literacies are much more than a 'focus' but are fundamental to the evolution of CLIL in our plurilingual, pluricultural classrooms. Indeed, such thinking takes us beyond CLIL, and will be analysed in detail in Parts II and III.

In reality, we know there are no quick-fix solutions. Yet increasing awareness – resulting from the convergence of distinct fields (Becher and Trowler's 'academic tribes', 2001) with varied classroom learning practices and interconnected synergies (professional experts and their practices) and the accounts of those who learn in those spaces – suggest principled divergence from the established 'norms' of language learning and subject learning towards a 'quality learning' agenda that takes into account the 'big issues' discussed in this chapter and translates them into pedagogic practices. These can be summarised as focussing on multilingual and multicultural learners, the roles of language(s) across the curriculum, successful learning for all learners and learner-teacher partnerships. We celebrate the outstanding work that many CLIL teachers and educators have achieved over the last few decades to ensure appropriate, effective and successful experiences for learners, as well as their contribution to informing thinking as it develops and practices as they grow. We also acknowledge the challenges and critiques: boundary-breaking change requires time, continual critical analysis and reflection. To refer, as previously, to the 'messiness' of pedagogic adjustment and innovation is not to reduce the serious nature of concerns, nor to dismiss the drive for improving the quality of learning experiences for all learners. It indicates the need for a broader lens, as de Graaff suggests, through which to understand more the potential of how classroom practices and spaces interconnect with the individuals who create them and the overarching curriculum and policy drivers which dominate (Dalton-Puffer, 2016). This is particularly pertinent in current times, as Fullan and Langworthy (2014) maintain that the 'present past' as the dominant model of education is in the process of change and subsequent transformation. The evolution of classroom norms, particular structures and collaborations requires 'new learning partnerships' built on principles of 'equity, transparency, reciprocal accountability and mutual benefit' (Fullan & Langworthy, 2014, p. 12).

This chapter set out to provide an overview of the development of CLIL over three decades, with particular reference to shifts in the conceptualisation of integrated learning. The intention, therefore, was to provide the reader with context not only for critical reflection but also for both the expansion and deepening of thinking beyond integrating content and language issues towards addressing developments in and contributions to the broader educational agenda. In order to challenge what on some levels seems like an obsession with focussing on and implementing an integrated approach to learning and teaching in CLIL classrooms, more inclusive and holistic thinking draws us towards exploring ways of maximising learning experiences for all learners everywhere. Chapter 2 will look inside CLIL classrooms from a multidimensional perspective to critically – yet constructively – contribute further to this evolution.

2 Problematising CLIL: Bringing the Outside In and Inside Out

Chapter 1 considered some of the milestones in the development of CLIL over several decades. It acknowledged the CLIL phenomenon as diverse and dynamic in developing theoretical principles and constructs that guide and situate classroom teaching and learning across different contexts. However, we suggest that the nature of 'intercurricular disconnect' (Lin, 2016) and the independent universes of language and curricular content as 'reified entities' (Dalton-Puffer, 2011, p. 196) should neither be underestimated nor seen as impermeable barriers with regard to changing classroom practices.

Perhaps it is useful to pause and reflect on those purposes by taking a critical view of developments in CLIL from the classroom perspective. It explores the challenges and necessity for CLIL to not only be context embedded – taking account of local, regional and/or national demands of educational 'systems' – but also to be curriculum embedded, alongside a growing awareness that integrated learning must be sustainable, equitable and of perceived value by societies and members of communities within them. Curriculum embeddedness relates to what is taught and learned, and why. It is situated within subject disciplines and the broader sense of educational values and purposes – all 'wrapped up' in the language of education. Abstract terms such as 'effective', 'high-quality' and 'excellence' permeate policy documents describing learning goals. Biesta (2015, p. 76) differentiates between what he calls 'good education', which is purposeful and values based, and 'effective education', which is often interpreted as quantifiable, measurable and comparable across nations. He emphasises that the point of education is *not* that students learn but that they learn *something* and for a *reason,* and that they learn it from *someone*. He problematises the 'language of education', seeing it as insufficient for expressing what matters in schooling in the same ways that theories of learning are insufficient to capture what education is all about.

> The problem with the language of learning, both learning the language itself and the ways in which it is used and contextualised in research, policy and practice – is that it tends to prevent people from asking the key educational questions of content, purpose and relationships. (Biesta, 2015, p. 76)

We may describe our goal as a desire for 'quality learning' or 'effective learning', but in the sense of the rights, values and meanings it holds for all those engaged in classroom learning enacted through inclusion and social justice. We seek to address these evolving tensions and challenges throughout the book, in which design for learning is explicit and purposeful. Purpose is very different from learning outcomes or aims and objectives of lessons. The 'why' of learning is at the core. The 'what' and the 'how' follow. We are mindful of tensions between policy demands, theoretical principles and their 'translation' into classroom realities, all of which impact on the quality of the experiences of both teachers and learners. In essence, the phenomenon of CLIL, with its potential as a contributory, transformative element of the regular curriculum, requires pedagogic enquiry, critique and confidence which is not only dynamic but within the realms of possibilities for practitioners across all areas of the curriculum.

> Curriculum-making is a job that never ends and lies at the heart of good teaching. When educators talk about curriculum-making, we refer to the creation of interesting, engaging and challenging *educational encounters* which draw upon teacher knowledge and skills, the experiences of students and the valuable subject resources of the subject. Curriculum-making is concerned with holding all of this in balance (Lambert, 2016).

It is exactly such 'educational encounters' and sustaining 'the balance' that require analysis and review of everyday practices. This is not to criticise what many CLIL teachers do and constantly strive to achieve. Instead we take a hard look at the drivers which shape those practices and in Lambert's words focus on 'curriculum-making' as a more holistic approach to integrated learning.

2.1   The 4 Cs Framework as a Planning Tool

In order to frame curriculum making in CLIL classroom practices, reference will be made to one widely used pedagogic tool: the 4 Cs Framework (Coyle, 2008). Published in detail in Coyle, Hood and Marsh (2010), it originated as a principled planning heuristic developed by teachers and researchers working together in the early stages of CLIL to support ways of conceptualising CLIL classroom practices. Over a decade later, the 4 Cs Framework has encouraged adaptation and critical debate of some key 'components' of CLIL, with Content, Cognition, Communication and Culture (Figure 2.1) identified as requiring explicit attention. Whilst in reality these four constructs are inherently interconnected, separating them at the initial planning phase made sense in terms of making visible the distinctiveness of designing integrated learning within a CLIL context. It could be argued of course that teachers have always intuitively considered these elements in their teaching, but there was a need to ensure that these were *explicit* in defining and planning tasks and activities. It was through encouraging debate and critique of the 'Cs' that a deeper understanding of their interconnectedness could be charted and gaps in pedagogic thinking could be identified. Increasingly, as thinking evolved and practices were analysed and evaluated, the need to transcend boundaries, as reflected in subject and language thinking, signified a shift towards integration as inclusive, pluricultural curriculum making.

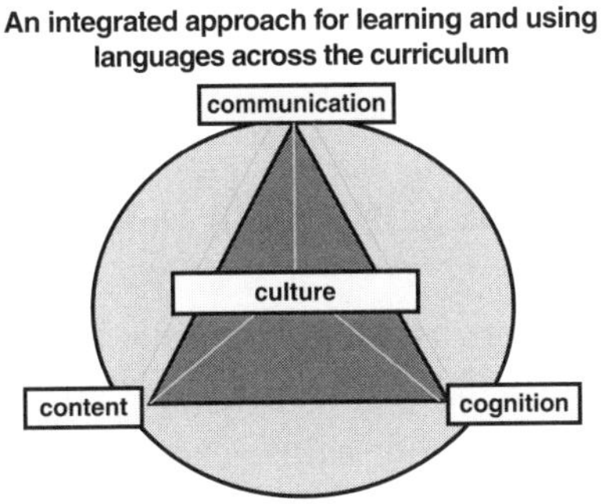

Figure 2.1 The 4 Cs Framework (Coyle, Hood & Marsh, 2010)

Given the extensive use of the 4 Cs Framework on a global scale over the past decade, we look briefly yet critically at how the tool contributes to *preparing* for the way learning happens in our classrooms. We know this is complex and 'messy'. We also know there are no fixed answers – but there are principles that can guide our own decision making. We also know this doesn't take us far enough in terms of asking difficult questions about ways in which learners and teachers interact in a classroom environment.

We start by considering the nature of content in CLIL and suggest that too little attention has been paid to the far-reaching implications of defining the nature of content across different educational contexts. It could be argued that CLIL has been disconnected from broader educational debate, which takes account of curriculum and pedagogic purpose. In 2010, Coyle, Hood and Marsh situated C-Content in CLIL contexts as the '*point de départ*' and suggested that the very nature of Content itself drives how the other Cs are conceptualised, in terms of underlying values and theoretical principles. Yet very little has been written in CLIL research about subject or thematic content in comparison with language-related issues. As we know, CLIL embodies learning – not only content learning and not only language learning. Research into CLIL content teaching and learning has tended to focus on measuring the quality of the learning outcomes when using other languages in comparison with those achieved through the main language of schooling. This is clearly a concern for CLIL teachers. However, we suggest that CLIL provides teachers with multifaceted opportunities for enhancing learning experiences for all learners, not only in the CLIL vehicular language but also in first-language learning contexts under clearly defined conditions. These opportunities are not explicitly written in official documents. Instead they lie in the design of classroom learning by teachers, in everyday dialogic practices and in the 'balance' of planning, evaluation, inquiry and reflection with and for learners. Throughout this chapter, we suggest issues for debate and reflection, leading to what might be termed the construction of a *Theory of Practice*, which educators can (co-)construct to guide future thinking and planning. We will return to this point subsequently.

2.2   Revisiting Content as Curriculum Matter

So, what do CLIL educators means when they talk about content? There are currently three general ways of looking at content in CLIL. The first is where content is determined by the established and regular curriculum – usually, but not always subject-oriented in both primary, secondary and tertiary educational contexts. The second is where the content is more flexible and is constructed according to project-based or phenomenon-based frameworks for learning. In these instances, inter- and trans-disciplinary learning is encouraged across subject disciplines. The third is non-specified content, where the teacher, sometimes with learners, decides the nature of the theme or topic to be studied; often this type of content is related to more language-oriented classrooms, with the teacher as 'language expert' rather than 'subject discipline expert'.

Whatever the content matter or the orientation of the CLIL teacher, C-Content demands CLIL teachers to position their own thinking about the nature and potential of integrated learning as an approach to curriculum which, within the boundaries of formal learning, has to be accessible for all learners. Such strong reasoning is based on several principles but fundamental is the values-driven tenet referred to in Chapter 1: CLIL must provide a *quality curriculum experience* for *all* learners. We know that limiting the *level* of the content learning to match the linguistic level of learners is not appropriate. Yet finding ways of enabling the learning of appropriate-level content through scaffolding the language for conceptual knowledge building remains a fundamental challenge for teachers.

First, the concept of C-Content cannot be separated from its positioning within the situated curriculum and how this is interpreted across different education systems. Making transparent and analysing the purposes and nature of learning of subjects, themes and topics is fundamental to the C-Content of CLIL. However, we posit that this thinking has been absent from CLIL discussions and that content is often seen as syllabus. In addition, there remains a strong professional focus on the identification of language elements related to accessing and assessing the content to be taught and learned. In our view, this omits one very crucial preparatory element in the process of planning for CLIL. When C-Content is analysed in terms of specific subject or thematic *concepts* and inherent skills and behaviours (i.e. the cultures which determine the very essence of a subject discipline), what follows does not depend solely on acquiring related language structures and lexis. Neither does it depend on teacher-led notions of 'delivering' the content separate from making visible related skills, attitudes and values. Designing tasks that provide learners with a transparent range of opportunities to *demonstrate* their understanding in different ways creates coherent pathways for progressing individual learning. Whilst a syllabus or textbook may list concepts to be covered, this does not necessarily address the nature and demands of subject disciplines, including how experts in a particular subject area think, communicate and behave (these issues are detailed in Chapter 3). For this reason, for content to be situated and embedded in the curriculum, CLIL teachers need to engage in discussion, clarification, analysis and shared understanding of the interconnected nature of subject concepts and discourses, skills, attitudes and values – the hermetically sealed CLIL bubble bursts.

The second consideration with regards to C-Content refers to projects, initiative or topics that are integral to specific subject knowledge and are more likely to involve broader explorations of phenomena that are interdisciplinary in nature and often enquiry based. There is a wealth of literature on project-based (language) learning – for example, where projects are designed to 'build knowledge and develop skills, to incorporate language learning and intercultural understanding and to connect learning to the real-world' (Cooney, n.d., para 2). At the core of this definition is 'sustained inquiry' driven by teachers and learners raising challenging questions for problem solving using a wide range of human, digital, public and educational resources. In a similar vein, phenomenon-based learning embraces the study of holistic real-world phenomena generating the 'right' questions to foster scientific enquiry as a necessary foundation for knowledge building and making sense of the world. Typical phenomena for study often include issues such as the study of rain, soil erosion and poverty, which trigger the design of trans-disciplinary *educational encounters*. This approach to content builds tangible connections between school curricula and the outside world and provides a nexus for interdisciplinary learning and teaching. A study of the Egyptian pyramids can include an understanding of engineering and physics, whilst a study of fossils and sedimented craters can involve geography and science, which together throw light on the Earth's biodiversity millions of years ago. Whilst there could be many examples, the point we wish to emphasise here is that thematic, project or phenomenon-based approaches to content, when modelled on enquiry-based learning, require systematic and explicit development of enquiry processes to encourage curiosity and communication *as they relate* to the issues under investigation. This interconnectedness signals that if learners engage in 'thinking' and developing enquiry skills (C-Cognition) that are *isolated* from the specific knowledge domains being studied (C-Content), it is not conducive to effective learning and appropriate knowledge 'ownership'. This is particularly critical in interdisciplinary learning, which provides an authentic context for making visible different ways of thinking and behaving based on both substantive (evolving from the subject) and syntactic (about the nature of the subject) demands. This way of thinking also involves making explicit the cultural roots (C-Culture) and references of academic disciplines and phenomena within, across and outside the curriculum.

The third approach to C-Content lies in areas of study which are determined by the teachers and learners. These themes usually do not lie in traditional curriculum-defined subjects or interdisciplinary projects at the school level and are more likely to develop in more language-oriented classrooms. Whilst language learning per se involves some kind of content, usually driven by textbooks (typically topics about family, house and home, transport, hobbies and pastimes – especially in the earlier stages) this content is often used as a means for learning language and simulated communication skills. It less serves the purpose of a vehicle for knowledge building and facilitating enquiry into authentic dialogue (e.g. about relevant and/or real-world issues, creative texts or the arts). It could be argued that this type of 'surface' content is there as a *convenience*. It is not a means to enable learners to meaningfully access and use the kind of language needed to engage in purposeful knowledge building at a cognitive level appropriate for the age and experiences of the learners.

The key point here underscores the need for CLIL teachers to broaden and deepen the value of topics or projects by offering learners involvement in selection and choice, especially those that deal with real-world issues. The topic of transport, for example, can challenge learner perceptions when it involves learners in undertaking scientific enquiry into the advantages and disadvantages of free bike schemes in cities, car-shares, electric cars or big data mining, focussing on pollution in big cities, transport issues in rural areas, healthy living, space travel and so on. Challenges such as these foster 'good' questions raised by learners and encourages critical investigation. In other words, for language-oriented contexts to embrace integrated learning, rethinking topics as C-Content is critical in order to provide creative, relevant problem-solving challenges. There is of course the question of literature, which often populates syllabi for more advanced language learners. However, its potential remains untapped in terms of contributing to authentic and inspiring text to inform thematic or literary studies for less advanced or younger learners. This is an area for urgent development in CLIL contexts and is revisited in Chapter 9.

Tedick and Camarata (2012) suggest that the need to rethink the language learning curriculum in ways which support bilingual education by language teachers remains hidden, as does the broader role of language teachers in CLIL classrooms and the specific role they can play, not only as language experts but in developing integrated curricula. A review into the pedagogic and collaborative practices of language teachers in bilingual streams conducted by Dale et al. (2018a) acknowledged that little is known about the role of language teachers in bilingual streams and their collaboration with subject specialists. Using a lineage metaphor, the study captures several lines of thinking about language teaching and learning, bringing together 'foreign language' teaching, second-language teaching and mother-tongue or first-language teaching. As Dalton-Puffer (2018) suggests, all three lineages provide insights into how language teachers can develop their own 'legitimised' contribution to bilingual education, and specifically into suggesting alternative perspectives of (re-conceptualising) content for the language classroom. This signals that C-Content in CLIL contexts is as significant for language teachers as it is for subject teachers. It crucially provides curriculum 'space' for shifting and extending teaching and learning across all disciplines, including language lessons of very different kinds.

It should also be noted that in the 4 Cs Framework, C-Content refers not only to 'subject' content but also the language content *of* and *for* learning. This point will be commented on further when discussing the Language Triptych tool.

2.3   Cultures, Concepts and Discourses for Knowledge Building

The previous section raised fundamental questions concerning the relationship between the nature of content in CLIL and its place within a teaching and learning curriculum. Assuming that C-Content involves more than 'surface-level' knowledge building and understanding, the boundaries are blurred in relation to national curricula or norms and subsequent enactment in the classroom. The need to define C-Content as 'knowledge' or 'knowledges' (Anderson & Krathwohl, 2001), according to epistemological and ontological understandings associated with specific curriculum subjects, is not recognised. An immediate challenge arises, however, if we consider current trends in national curricula on a global scale (Nieveen & Van der Hoeven, 2011; Sinnema & Aitken, 2013), which signify an overt shift from knowledge to competencies as the focus of curricula. Anderson and Krathwohl (2001), in drawing attention to four kinds of 'knowledges' and their relation to the cognitive dimension of Bloom's taxonomy of thinking skills conflate C-Cognition and C-Content. They refer to factual, conceptual, procedural and metacognitive knowledge. For example, procedural knowledge is described as knowledge of subject-specific skills, techniques and methods. The multi-dimensional structure of knowledge draws attention to connecting knowledge-based and competence-based ways of prioritising learning. In a similar vein, Counsell (2018) differentiates between substantive knowledge (i.e. content based on established facts, such as imperialism or the Treaty of Versailles) and disciplinary knowledge involving ways in which that knowledge is constructed, revised and interpreted, using subject-related skills such as enquiry, reasoning and argumentation. In other words, since different kinds of 'knowledges' require different kinds of language for exploration, analysis and explanation, we are once again reminded that without clear definition and visibility of the kind of conceptual demands and related skills required by the subject content, deeper quality learning will not happen.

Whitty (2010, p. 34), also usefully reminds us that 'knowledge is not the same as school subjects and school subjects are not the same thing as academic disciplines'. This simple statement reminds us of the importance of taking into account inherent behaviours and ways of seeing the world through the lens of an academic discipline, through trans-disciplinary studies or through specific subjects and topics (from multiple perspectives) as fundamental for effective learning for everyone. It is fundamental because it refocuses the *cultural exigencies* of those disciplines or interpretations of curriculum content 'knowledges' to be learned. We argue, therefore, that C-Culture needs repurposing. At the macro level it must take account of the social, political, spiritual, aesthetic, ecological and economic domains associated with seeing the world through other sociolinguistic communities. At the micro or classroom level, C-Culture has to address the ontological demands of learning and subject disciplines or thematic studies, as well as the textual demands of different pedagogic and social media. Connecting the macro with the micro and vice versa is fundamental for purposeful learning (Lorenzo & Dalton-Puffer, 2016). Simply put, C-Culture becomes *C-Cultures*. Alexander summarises 'cultures' and their related complexity as follows:

> classroom cultures, values and interactions are variously shaped by collective, communitarian and individualist emphases in accounts of social relations and by culturally located stances on human development, the nature and acquisition of knowledge and the act of teaching. (2017, p. 562)

Applying Alexander's arguments to a CLIL context, where C-Cultures particularly focuses on 'the nature and acquisition of knowledge' and C-Content mediates discipline- or thematic-related learning and engagement, then questions about developing language as an integral part of those disciplines emerge:

> Learners need to have the linguistic means to define, classify, report, evaluate etc in their L2. These may be picked up implicitly for their teachers (and/or by reading) but for this to happen, the teachers need to be able to provide rich and repeated modelling (Dalton-Puffer, 2016, p. 52).

Knowledge building and understanding, therefore, involves not only integrating cognitive processes (C-Cognition) with C-Content (knowledges), but also the discourses needed and used to express meaning (C-Communication and C-Cultures). We are familiar with seminal work from Alexander (2005), Mercer (2000) and Wells (1999), for example, which, whilst focussing on first-language classrooms, promotes the need for teachers to broaden their own and their learners' repertoire of talk-based skills and strategies. They emphasise the need to:

> expand and refine the talk repertoires and capacities of their students. Acknowledging the uniqueness of each classroom's personalities and circumstances it gives the teacher the responsibility for deciding how the repertoire should be applied. This responsibility is progressively shared with students, the development and autonomous deployment of whose own talk repertoires is the ultimate goal. This commitment to repertoire combined with teacher and student agency is fundamental. (Alexander, 2018, p. 563)

In similar vein, Skidmore (2000) distinguishes between pedagogic dialogue and dialogic pedagogy – the former tending to be 'teacher-controlled closed interaction with limited opportunities for participation' focussing on question-answer-feedback routines common across all classrooms. Dialogic pedagogy he describes as participatory and fundamental for learning and interaction that encourages learners to voice their understanding and make evaluative judgements. In terms of language boundaries, extensive classroom research indicates that closed questions, recall answers and minimal feedback remains the pedagogical default, despite abundant evidence that it wastes much of the cognitive and educational potential that dialogic communication offers (Mortimer & Scott 2003; Smith et al., 2004; Galton 2008; Mehan & Cazden 2015; Resnick & Schantz., 2015). These scholars challenge ways in which language is learned, developed and used in the (CLIL) classroom by highlighting the importance of developing patterns of classroom interaction (C-Communication). In essence, dialogic pedagogy is built on the ways of opening up opportunities to engage socially and cognitively in classroom learning, and 'by actively treating students as *thinkers* and *reasoners*, thereby modifying the ways in which they engage with content... gives students opportunities to explain their ideas' (Resnick 2015, p. 446). Furthermore, Resnick expands on what is described as a 'culture of argumentation' that has the potential to go beyond any individual student's power of reasoning. 'The students challenge one another, call for evidence, change their minds and restate their claims, just as adults do in virtually every discipline of knowledge in the world outside of school.' (Resnick, 2015, p. 446).

Understanding of the roles of languages in CLIL has significantly developed and will be explored in depth in Part II (Llinares et al., 2012; Nikula et al., 2016a). For CLIL practitioners, dialogic learning requires creating opportunities for learners to be questioners, to behave like thinkers and reasoners according to specific learning contexts. It also requires learning and using the language needed to become a thinker and reasoner in that context. In other words, 'dialogic learning' (Wells, 1999) requires learners to knowingly develop appropriate subject-related or thematic discourses as well as the social communication needed to learn effectively with others in a classroom.

This position resonates with the Language Triptych (Coyle et al., 2010), where language *of*, *for* and *through* learning acts as a planning tool which focusses on the language demands of knowledge building (Figure 2.2). Whilst knowledge *of* and *for* learning provide a way of planning for the kinds of language needed for C-Content and concept-building C-Cognition, *through* learning is less predictable and lies in enabling learners to be thinkers, their own knowledge builders and reasoners. It brings together all Cs. To recap, language *of* learning includes terminology and discourse-specific phrases embedded in appropriate language 'chunks', including 'language specific to subject and thematic content; for example, the language of science, or curriculum discourse' (Coyle et al., 2010, p. 37), as well as functional elements of language such as 'social activity in a particular culture, the linguistic realisations of which make up register' (Llinares & Whittaker, 2006, p. 28). Language *for* learning is related to classroom activities guiding learners how to conduct themselves and their learning through honing strategies and skills development (e.g. interacting with others, asking questions, developing cooperative and group skills). It is based on the principle that effective learning cannot take place without language and thinking: learning *is* language and thinking. 'When learners are encouraged to articulate their understanding, then a deeper level of learning takes place' (Coyle et al, 2010, p. 37).

However, it is language *through* learning that enables knowledge building to happen when it is driven by C-Cultures, connected to C-Content and C-Cognition. This implies that 'discourse creates meaning… as we acquire new areas of knowledge, we acquire new areas of meaning' (Mohan and van Naerssen, 1997, p. 2). Language *through* learning is the language which learners use to express their understanding, which becomes increasingly more refined as knowledge building grows and becomes internalised. Although language *through* learning remains less tangible, unpredictable and enigmatic, more recent thinking suggests that *through* learning is fundamental to learner agency in determining what is to be learned, developed, internalised and applied. The ways in which individual learners activate

Figure 2.2 The Language Triptych (adapted from Coyle et al., 2010)

C-Communication *through* learning relies heavily on the language tools they can access, interpret, manipulate and use, as well as those which they need but don't yet know. It embodies C-Cultures.

There is broad consensus about the importance of classroom talk (Mercer, 2000), as previously discussed. Dalton-Puffer (2016, p. 30) acknowledges talk as 'the chief locus of knowledge construction' where subjects are 'talked into being'. The process of *talking into being*, however, requires specific 'visible' attention. It has to be transparent in ways of equipping learners with the linguistic tools they need to engage in 'knowledge-oriented communication, patterns and schemata of a discursive, lexical and grammatical nature... where knowledge is being constructed and made intersubjectively accessible' (Dalton-Puffer, 2016, p. 31). In the same vein, Hood and Tobutt (2015) provide an interesting, powerful alternative to the commonly practised formulaic 'presentation, practice and production' approach in language classrooms. Underpinned by dialogic principles, learners are involved in *meeting* new language for knowledge building, *manipulating* that language by developing, practising and using the language needed to engage in knowledge construction and skills development, and *making the language their own* – that is, where learners demonstrate agency in using the different learning tools to achieve their own deeper understanding, the exact nature of which is largely unpredictable by teachers. This is a simple yet rich concept. It implies a clear stance that learners need to 'own' their learning, and within that the language they use to learn.

This section set out to examine the complexities of understanding, analysing and reflecting on the 'what' of CLIL. It also raised the awkward question of the 'why' of CLIL in terms of purposefulness. The intention was not to engage in pedagogic analysis of CLIL theories and practices – rapidly growing literature in the field already provides readers with extensive and somewhat controversial evidence (see Chapter 1). Instead, given the ethical, social and educational urgency to provide fit-for-purpose education, we felt taking a critical exploratory look at commonly used planning tools would provide opportunities for educators to explore their own practices. Using the 4 Cs Framework and the Language Triptych as examples, the objective was to emphasise that interconnectedness is not only crucial, complex and non-sequential, it impacts significantly on both the processes and outcomes of CLIL as an educational phenomenon, regardless of the age and stage of learners. It also emphasises that without a more holistic approach to learning, key elements of a pedagogic and human nature (e.g. motivation, assessment, resilience and feedback) can easily disconnect from being part of founding CLIL principles. The overarching goal is built on the adage that the sum of the parts is greater than the whole. It requires alternative ways of conceptualising and designing those *educational encounters* suggested in the opening of this chapter.

2.4   Theories of (Disruptive) Practice

The final section of the chapter suggests that when educators engage in construct-ing their own (guided) Theories of Practice, meaningful pathways for learning are created and reflected upon. For practitioners to become agentic educators, where they make visible and evidence their own thinking, principles and values, requires understanding scientific research, engaging in its translation through 'close-to-practice enquiry', and developing transformational practices through persistent, realistic (yet visionary) and increasingly confident thinking.

> What it takes to teach cannot be determined directly from what it takes to learn, which means that teachers must be willing to treat the process as essentially problematic, iterative, and always improvable; we must stop assuming that teaching can be theorized like a natural science, and treat it as a design science. (Laurillard, 2013, p. 82)

Laurillard's idea of teaching as a design science aligns with Van Lier's (1996, p. 24) proposal of a 'practical philosophy of education' where theory, research and prac-tice are 'dynamic ingredients' and where implicit theories and new ideas are made explicit, practised and evaluated. According to Van Lier (1996, p. 24), constructing a Theory of Practice envisions teacher development as pedagogic development, involving practising, theorising and researching.

> Our growing understanding of this process determines the relevance of information from different sources and disciplines [as] a mode of professional conduct which in some respects differs from traditional ways of doing theory, research or practice. In other respects, however, it is no different than any other thoughtful approach to work. (Van Lier, 1996, p. 24)

We suggest that when Theories of Practice and the research, reflection and explor-atory practices inherent in their iteration and reiteration – referred to by Rodgers (2006, p. 217) as small 't' theories (sometimes requiring the implicit to become explicit) – are co-constructed alongside large 'T' theories – developed by 'those who spend their time creating such theories', – a potentially transformational dialectical relationship emerges that looks for meaning between them. This has powerful connectivity, and echoes Lantolf and Poehners' (2014, p. 27) view that practice is not predicated on the application of theory but rather is 'drawn into the scientific enterprise in a profound way'.

Theories of Practice can act as the trigger for discussion, as the bridge, as the connection for growing a genuinely co-constructed and shared understanding be-tween teachers and between teachers and students of the 'why' and the 'what' of CLIL. The ongoing construction and reconstruction of Theories of Practice pro-motes professional enquiry by raising challenges and problematising how CLIL can be enacted appropriately and effectively in the classroom. Such teacher-owned thinking facilitates ways in which theoretical constructs can be 'translated' into agreed principles, which are then 'transformed' into classroom practices – and, crucially, vice versa.

Theories of Practice begin with practitioners constructing their own vision of classroom learning by identifying key tenets which matter to them, built on beliefs about practices both established and new, built on research and evidence in the field which challenge thinking. These processes can be uncomfortable and disruptive, challenging and critical, visionary and realistic. Documenting emergent principles, prioritising them and selecting a focus for development or enquiry is collaborative work that is ongoing. However, we believe working with Theories of Practice provides a nexus for ideas and a forum for sharing with others. They raise questions and are practical and tangible. They also emphasise teaching as well as learning and go some way towards redressing what Biesta (2015) calls the 'learnification' of education, where a persistent focus has been on learning and the learner, with much less consideration on teaching and the teacher. Shires summarises Theories of Practice as follows:

> Theory helps us address the 'how' and 'why' questions that arise by operating as a set of ideas that explain something; as a set of key concepts to shape practice and how those concepts relate to each other. My own position is that the activity of theorising one's own (that is to say, planning what and how I teach through the lens of pedagogic and curriculum theory) deepens my pedagogy because the epistemological basis at the centre of theory and practice are brought together. (2018, p. 1)

In education, we are familiar with trends, turns and shifts. Tensions emerge. Dichotomies prevail. Models, frameworks and taxonomies evolve. The time when CLIL positioned itself as 'different' from the regular curriculum has passed. It is now the period of transition on a global scale, bringing together broader societal and educational priorities into a practice-oriented frame. This requires dealing with challenges, problematising learning in authentic contexts, and making the familiar strange and the over-familiar visible. Engaging in critical re-visioning supports teachers, motivates change and disrupts 'this is what we do' to promote 'this is what we are exploring together'. It provides space for busy professionals to explore the tacit and make visible and accessible ways in which they enable their learners to think, behave and learn like 'experts'. Asking 'curriculum' questions is a fundamental prerequisite for informing pedagogic decisions regarding the implications of curriculum making. These have been absent from the CLIL agenda.

For example, Dann and Hanley (2019, p. 11) suggest an emergent curriculum 'turn' as 'the consequences of promoting curriculum *outcomes* over curriculum breadth, balance and experiences are increasingly realised'. We have drawn on Young and Muller's (2010) stance that subject knowledge is not something that is fixed or demarcated or can be 'delivered' to learners; neither is it limited to a competence-based and learning skills approach. They propose a pendulum swing towards a more subject knowledge-based curriculum, recognising that:

> specialist theoretical knowledge has been created by the disciplines, which are not entirely arbitrary. This knowledge exists outside the direct experience of the student and is powerful, *because* it is derived in part by the specialist communities and the disciplined procedures that produce and verify it. It is powerful also because acquiring such disciplinary knowledge provides access (via the examinations system and selection) to influence, through the professions for example. It is therefore a matter of social justice that all young people have access to powerful knowledge. (Lambert & Biddulph, 2015, p. 216)

The notion of 'powerful knowledge' sees teachers and learners as curriculum makers as they engage in processes that require creative boundary work and focus on what knowledge building and skills in the classroom fundamentally entail. 'Curriculum-making' (Lambert & Biddulph, 2015) or 'recontextualisation' (Young, 2019, p. 15) involves actively transforming expert disciplinary knowledge, discourse and behaviours into meaningful disciplinary understanding. This starts with the experiential 'knowledges' that all learners bring with them. Young highlights the dynamic two-way relationship between the social, economic and cultural lives of learners and the potential of constantly evolving disciplinary ways of thinking and being which serve to educate young people. He also proposes that this bridging process, this recontextualisation, is significantly different from focussing on making content 'accessible' or differentiating learning activities. Instead, it requires an *induction* into disciplinary concepts and specific, systems-oriented ways of thinking and dialoguing that enable all learners to understand and question conceptual knowledge through opportunities to enquire the world.

> Curriculum does not replace knowledge that pupils bring to school: it challenges it and enables pupil to transform and extend it by engaging with new and often troubling ideas with a teacher who they have learned to trust. (Young, 2019, p. 15)

These principles not only impact on all the Cs – they go beyond. They embrace a broader learning agenda, challenging interpretations of curriculum by asking awkward questions and foregrounding the contribution of teachers and learners to curriculum-making processes. They demonstrate that interconnectedness is fundamental to 'curriculum-making' and demands epistemological change. This, we believe, provides a lens through which to shift from the 'what' of CLIL to the 'how', by constructing a Theory of Practice underpinned by critical questions. These questions are part of an ongoing 'itinerary of ideas and the generation and appropriation of knowledge within the professional community' (Dalton-Puffer, 2018, p. 386), which demand significant shifts in thinking. Therefore – when C-Content is defined by different kinds of subject or thematic knowledges and customs and ways of being enacted in our multilingual, multicultural class-rooms (C-Cultures), those knowledges involve specific concept-building skills, and processes and strategies appropriate for enabling learners to access disciplinary domains (C-Cognitive) activated by using the 'linguistic switchboard' (Lorenzo & Dalton-Puffer, 2016, p. 61) and developed through discourse and dialogic activity (C-Communication) to be processed, internalised and externalised.[1] According to Biggs (2003), constructive alignment starts as learners construct their own learning through engagement in activities designed for the purposes of achieving learning goals, enacted through clearly articulated pedagogic principles which frame teaching and learning. For Biggs, the key lies in ensuring that:

> all components in the teaching system – the curriculum and its intended outcomes, the teaching method used, the assessment tasks – are all aligned to each other. All are tuned to learning activities addressed in the desired learning outcomes. The learner finds it difficult to escape without learning appropriately. (Biggs, 2003, p. 1)

Whilst these messages are familiar to educators everywhere, the realities of what is aligned and ways in which this multi-faceted alignment is operationalised in the everyday classroom are open to critical debate. It is not in the regular port-folio of teachers' work. Yet, herein lie significant and often hidden implications for developing CLIL practices. They reiterate that the 'how' of CLIL needs to focus on diverse, dynamic conditions that are conducive to 'good' teaching and learning, which involve: curriculum making, in the sense described in this chapter; making visible social and discipline-specific literacies and cultures for learning; promoting and using the cultural and linguistic diversity of learners to normalise plurilingual and pluricultural learning agendas; fostering learner attitudes, beliefs, motivation and self-esteem; and addressing social justice and inclusion through induction into subject disciplines.

In Part I of this volume, we have acknowledged the complexities of the 'fire and fog' of CLIL (Gonzalez, 2016) over the last two decades, noting changes and developments in thinking that have impacted on the growing global and diverse community of CLIL teachers and learners. Given our rapidly changing educational landscapes, we are now driven towards what we believe to be a significant shift in the evolution of CLIL – the 'flow' of CLIL into purposeful *educational encounters* which transcend mono- and plurilingual boundaries. Using a holistic ecological

---

[1] 'Constructive alignment' starts with the notion that the learner constructs his or her own learning through relevant learning activities. The teacher's job is to create a learning environment that supports the learning activities appropriate to achieving the desired learning outcomes. The key is that all components in the teaching system – the curriculum and its intended outcomes, the teaching methods used, the assessment tasks – are aligned to each other. All are tuned to learning activities addressed in the desired learning outcomes. The learner finds it difficult to escape without learning appropriately (Biggs, 2003).

compass to chart critical and formative pedagogic perspectives which impact on the everyday lives of learners and teachers in classrooms, we suggest that recent 'turns' in educational thinking (May, 2014) have resulted in 'ontological disruption' (Nicol & Sangster, 2019), which offers a critical space to bring 'the outside in and the inside out'. In Part II we explore how an evolving Pluriliteracies Model maps out a new trajectory towards more inclusive, aligned, purposeful learning experiences. Fundamentally, this demands a focus on understanding, designing and constructing meaningful, balanced *educational encounters* for all learners, whatever social, cultural, linguistic and cognitive skills and experiences they bring with them. It sets the scene for moving beyond CLIL driven by the fourth letter of the acronym and embracing *education* in the broadest sense.

'Would you tell me, please, which way I ought to go from here?'
'That depends a good deal on where you want to get to.'

(Alice and The Cheshire Cat, *Alice in Wonderland* by Lewis Carroll)

PART II
Pluriliteracies: Building a Pedagogical Approach for Deeper Learning

Part II of this book plots the co-construction of the Pluriliteracies Teaching for Deeper Learning (PTDL) model. It takes the reader through the stages in its development, from identifying basic tenets at its inception to pulling together multiple facets of learning so that the current model frames a holistic, inclusive approach to learning. Through each of the chapters, we seek to represent ways in which our model takes on the challenges of current thinking, not only in CLIL but in the broader sense of education and learning, which culminates in the model itself and next-steps development. Part III will explore the implications for applying PTDL to classroom practices. The construct of Pluriliteracies for Deeper Learning encompasses not only the 'what', but also the 'who' and the 'why' of learning in order to respond to some of the increasingly complex challenges raised in Part I.

3   Moving towards Pluriliteracies

3.1   Unpicking Literacies

> Literacy is more essential than ever before. In societies dominated by the written word, it is a fundamental requirement for citizens of all ages in modern Europe. Literacy empowers the individual to develop capacities of reflection, critique and empathy, leading to a sense of self-efficacy, identity and full participation in society.
>
> (European Commission, & Directorate-General for
Education and Culture [DG EAC], 2012, p. 21)

In today's globalised economy, we are told that the successful transfer of knowledge is more important than ever. Economic success largely depends on the skills of so-called knowledge workers to transfer knowledge successfully through acquiring, assimilating and processing a constant stream of information in ways which are contextually relevant, meaningful and appropriate (Kale & Little, 2011; Eppler & Burkhard, 2004). Since these processes and trends not only affect an ever increasing part of the workforce but have spread pervasively across all aspects of life, it has become vital for societies to prepare all learners adequately for the challenges of living in a globalised and digitised economy of unprecedented levels of interconnectedness, and to help them become creative, responsible global citizens. However, in our current world, the chasms between societies on a global scale appear to be widening, with increasing numbers of people moving across national, cultural and social boundaries. It is therefore imperative that diversity is factored into our education approaches, not as a problem per se but as means of disrupting thinking and enriching what happens in our classrooms.

We must also take into account one of the major challenges brought about by the rapid and ubiquitous processes of digitisation – sometimes cited as one of the key reasons why literacy is gaining in importance. There is much more to it than that. Digitisation not only changes the way we communicate; it is changing the very nature of literacy.

> [T]he digital world requires higher-order problem-solving skills. Reading print on paper and reading online share many core characteristics but reading online demands a greater ability to evaluate information critically within the context of a seemingly infinite universe of available options. Likewise, there is an increasing need for the ability to extract and use knowledge from an ever-growing number of online resources. (DG EAC, 2012, p. 23)

Becoming digitally literate enables individuals to participate more fully in a knowledge society. As the above-quoted *EU High Level Group of Experts on Literacy* report (DG EAC, 2012) suggests, being a knowledge worker encompasses far more than using software and digital means of communication. First and foremost, it is about being able to use existing knowledge to solve new problems and develop new products or services (Chiriac & Ghitiup Bratescu, 2011). Growing demands for expert problem-solving skills requires a critical re-evaluation of what is meant by communicative competence. General reading and writing skills are not enough to enable individuals to carry out non-routine problem solving and engage in sensitive interactive and context-appropriate communication. The call for a focus on competencies that include expert thinking and complex communication (Levy & Murnane, 2004), whilst not new, is gaining momentum.

There is clearly a need for education systems to develop pedagogies which equip citizens to construct, critically analyse and communicate knowledge adequately and successfully across cultures, languages and disciplines. Moreover, returning to the urgent need to build on diversity and hybridity in our schools by creating inclusive learning environments relevant for all learners, whatever their background, the multilingual and inclusive dimension of literacy becomes critical. Pedagogic approaches designed to develop and improve literacies for every student in regular classroom contexts are fundamental for a just society. Inclusive literacy education is:

> the provision of age-appropriate curriculum, using explicit, sequential, differentiated instruction that includes learning activities in oral language, reading, viewing, writing and creating a range of texts in traditional digital formats. (Milton, 2017, p. 8)

Terms such as 'literacies', which are evident in many educational and curriculum documents, are open to very wide interpretation, driven by cultural norms, policy directives and contextual specificities. That is why we will now briefly summarise current trends in the field of literacies research as indicated in Part I, which are characterised by a move from multi- to pluriliteracies and from generic skills to disciplinary literacies.

3.2   The Role of Disciplinary Literacies

The Australian curriculum provides a useful definition of what it is to be literate, which resonates with our own thinking.

> Students become literate as they develop the knowledge, skills and dispositions to interpret and use language confidently for learning and communicating in and out of school and for participating effectively in society. Literacy involves students listening to, reading, viewing, speaking, writing and creating oral, print, visual and digital

texts, and using and modifying language for different purposes in a range of contexts. (Australian Curriculum, Assessment and Reporting Authority, 2012, p. 16)

The idea that literacies are embedded in different channels or multiple modes of communication led the New London Group to propose a multiliteracies pedagogy which focusses on how literacy practices have been influenced by local and global, social, cultural, and technological change (Cazden et al., 1996).

Garcia, Bartlett and Kleifgen (2007) introduce the term *pluriliteracies* to capture and reflect the sociolinguistic realities of our increasingly plurilingual societies. Their pluriliteracies approach not only acknowledges:

> the integrated, hybrid nature of plurilingual literacy practices but also values all plurilingual practices equally. In so doing, the interplay between multiple languages, discourses, dialects and registers is promoted with particular attention paid to multilingual literacies reliant upon multiples modes and channels of communication and semiotic systems. (Garcia et al., 2007, pp. 12–13)

The concept of pluriliteracies, therefore, is a highly dynamic one. It is open to enabling learners to understand and develop ways in which cultural and linguistic contexts and social relations influence and impact literacy practices within and beyond schooling.

Building on these ideas, we chart the growth of a pedagogic approach to pluriliteracies developed by the Graz Group (see the Preface). This approach is ambitious and focusses on supporting *all* learners in acquiring a pluriliterate repertoire that will empower them to successfully and appropriately communicate knowledge across cultures and languages in a wide variety of analogue and digital modes, in order to become creative and responsible global citizens (Meyer et al., 2015). This not only resonates with the notion of 'powerful knowledge' (Young, 2019, p. 14) and curriculum-building explored in Chapter 2, it seeks to bring together the collective knowledge and understanding of researchers, educators, learners and communities into a coherent whole.

A growing move in pedagogic thinking towards emphasising the increasingly important role of disciplinary or subject-specific literacies for deeper learning across secondary and tertiary settings, is predicated on actively and transparently building on the growth and transition of basic literacies usually acquired in primary education. Taken from a range of contexts, the following quotations illustrate the pedagogic, subject-specific nature of literacies.

> 'Historical literacy requires a degree of fluency in the disciplinary language of history and, more broadly, requires fluency in historical ways of knowing.' (N. Mandell)
> 'Geography develops spatial literacy (the ability to understand and make effective use of spatial information) that has breadth, depth and scope. Students gain an in-depth understanding of essential geographic – and spatial – concepts such as location,

distribution, scale, spatial association, spatial interaction and spatial interdependence.' (D. Miles & M. Ward)

'I strongly believe that if school math classrooms presented the true nature of the discipline, we would not have this nationwide dislike of math and widespread math underachievement.' (J. Boaler)

'It seems, in general, that the practice of science instruction is still significantly focussed on teaching and learning science concepts and principles and neglecting competencies providing insight into science inquiry and views of the nature of science – which are given a major emphasis in more recent standards of science education. As a result, science instruction usually seems to provide a somewhat limited scientific literacy.' (R. Duit & M. Tesch)

These ideas challenge widely held assumptions about how we build knowledge and develop problem-solving skills by refuting the notion that knowledge can be accessed and constructed through a set of *generic* skills; that learning is quasi-independent of the underlying subject matter; or that such skills can transfer across different tasks and content areas and will enable learners to solve whatever set of problems they may encounter in their future lives.

Experts agree that skills such as problem-solving or critical thinking are dependent on 'large bodies of domain-specific knowledge' (Christodoulou, 2017, p. 33). After a comprehensive review of available research, Hilton & Pellegrino conclude that transfer of learning, or, more specifically, 'specific transfer of general principles' (National Research Council [NRC], 2012, p. 72) is dependent on 'the way in which the individual and the community structures and organizes the intertwined knowledge and skills' (NRC, 2012, p. 6) and that it is 'inextricably linked with subject matter domains' (NRC, 2012, p. 78).

In other words, it is through mastering subject-specific ways of generating and communicating knowledge (i.e. subject-specific literacies) that individuals develop transferable knowledge. The 'process through which an individual becomes capable of taking what is learning in one situation and applying it to a new situation' (NRC, 2012, p. 5) has been coined *deeper learning*. Accordingly, deeper learning is essential to acquiring appropriate skills and competencies which are 'situated within, and emerge from, the practices in different settings and communities… with their own cultures, languages, tools, and modes of discourse' (NRC, 2012, p. 74).

This, again, reminds us of the need to be actively inclusive. For example, when focussing on reading skills, research (e.g. Goldman et al., 2016) indicates that disciplinary experts not only read differently from novices in their field but, crucially, also very differently from experts in other areas. Shanahan and Shanahan (2012) reject the idea that basic reading skills automatically evolve into more advanced skills over time. Instead, they make a case for transparently teaching disciplinary literacies that highlight the differences in the language required and ways in which it is used in different disciplines. This draws attention to tools used by experts in those disciplines to construct and communicate knowledge and to the ways that individual disciplines construct and interpret texts.

Equipping learners with appropriate literacy skills within and across subject disciplines demands conceptualising their development over time. In other words, Shanahan & Shanahan (2008) suggest a move from basic literacy (including skills of decoding and increasing knowledge of high-frequency words) through more intermediate literacy (like generic comprehension strategies) to disciplinary literacy specific to subject areas (Figure 3.1).

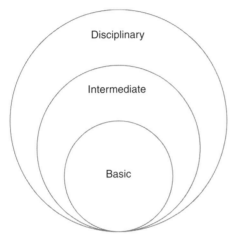

Figure 3.1 Literacy development (adapted from Shanahan & Shanahan, 2008)

For Shanahan & Shanahan, *literacy development* means learning increasingly more and more sophisticated but less generalisable skills and routines. They point out that these specialised literacies are challenging to learn because they do not necessarily share many parallels in oral language use and that they have to be applied to authentic and difficult texts.

So, what exactly do we mean by disciplinary literacy and what are the implications of a shared understanding of the concept in the context of primary and secondary education? According to McConachie, disciplinary literacy 'involves the use of reading, reasoning, investigating, speaking and writing required to learn and form complex content knowledge appropriate to a particular discipline' (2009, p. 16). For Putra and Tang, disciplinary literacy refers to 'the ability to use specialised language and practices valued and used in a given discipline to navigate and participate in the discipline'. Embedded in pedagogic approaches, disciplinary literacy 'aims to nurture students to be literate in the discipline they are pursuing'. The main idea of disciplinary literacy pedagogy, therefore, is 'to have students to be apprentice disciplinarians and practise what disciplinarians do' (2016, p. 569).

Taking science as an example, Beacco et al. (2016) scrutinised the concept of scientific literacy and applied it to a school context. Subject literacy is interpreted as a 'path towards critical thinking and knowledge application as well as towards social participation' (2016, p. 26) and comprised of domain-specific knowledge, skills and attitudes. More specifically, subject literacy consists of six dimensions, which are interdependent and build on one another:

1. Comprehending/understanding in depth
2. Communicating and negotiating knowledge
3. Reflecting on the acquisitional process, the learning outcomes and their personal as well as social uses
4. Applying knowledge to and within other contexts
5. Participating in the socio-scientific world
6. Transferring generalisable knowledge, skills and attitudes

(Beacco et al., 2016, p. 27)

Beacco et al. are very much aware of the expansive and transformative potential of such an understanding of literacies, given that the teaching of most subjects in the school context is not informed by an understanding of 'learning as apprenticeship' into the discipline. Nevertheless, they argue that education should first and foremost be concerned with furthering understanding and skills. This includes the ability to adequately communicate and negotiate knowledge, as well as the ability to apply knowledge and skills not only in different subject contexts but also to real world issues – that is, to 'any future problem in life and any new learning situation' (Beacco et al., 2016, p. 27).

3.2.1 Summing Up

If education is to prepare learners to cope with the challenges of learning throughout their lives, there needs to be a shift towards deeper learning. We posit that it is through the process of deeper learning that learners acquire those lifelong learning competencies. The concept of pluriliteracies which we define, discuss and demonstrate throughout the second part of this book will align education with the notion of deeper learning. This step will also take us beyond CLIL and into the mainstream of education because the principles of deeper learning apply to the teaching and learning of any subject in any language. Pluriliteracies was the defining term which emerged from work by the Graz Group (Coyle et al., 2018). It seeks to represent an ecological conceptualisation of dynamic, complex yet sustainable literacies across subjects, languages, values, cultures and our digitised world. As such, our use of the term pluriliteracies refers to:

1. **An explicit focus on disciplinary literacies in all subjects of schooling:** Since deeper learning is a domain-specific process, education needs to find ways

of promoting subject literacies in all subjects of schooling by focussing on subject-specific ways of constructing and communicating knowledge, so that learners can become pluriliterate in the sense of acquiring subject literacies in several subjects of schooling.

2. **Pluriliterate language use:** In a global world, learners need to be able to successfully and adequately communicate knowledge across cultures and languages. Therefore, an equally important facet of the 'pluri-' in pluriliteracies embraces and extends to being literate in several subjects and languages.

3. **Textual fluency:** Communication is increasingly plurimodal or hybrid in nature and reliant on multiple analogue and digital channels of communication and semiotic systems. Being able to critically evaluate sources is key to global citizenship and will prepare young learners for the world they will inhabit through understanding the need for social justice and democratic cultural competence. Therefore, being pluriliterate also entails the ability to critically navigate, evaluate and produce a wide variety of plurimodal texts and text types.

As a pedagogic approach, Pluriliteracies Teaching for Deeper Learning (PTDL) aims to facilitate deeper learning through an explicit focus on disciplinary literacies. By extending the concept across languages and all subjects of schooling, learners will be guided towards textual fluency. This will encourage successful communication across cultures and provide a key stepping stone towards becoming responsible global citizens.

Making disciplinary literacies development a reality will require us to rethink and reconceptualise the way we think about learning and teaching. When subject-specific or disciplinary practices transparently value multiple languages, cultures, modes of communication and semiotic systems, they develop into pluriliteracies. Pluriliteracies impact what educators do. They not only affect the way we design, evaluate and assess learning but, more importantly, require us to redefine our roles as teachers. Teachers who want to embark on that journey will first and foremost require an in-depth understanding of the process of deeper learning, especially with regards to the fundamental role of language in any kind of learning. It is appropriate now to move on to consider the mechanics – the principles and processes which underlie deeper learning.

Throughout the remainder of the book, we will demonstrate how these principles challenged us – and continue to do so – to co-construct a pluriliteracies model that is coherent, transparent and adaptable. Crucially, any such model must speak to educators and support them in experimenting and adapting the model across different learning environments, critiquing it in the light of experience and collaborating constantly to ensure it is fit for purpose. The following chapters analyse and discuss in turn the different elements of the model in order to arrive at a coherent and shared understanding.

4 The Mechanics of Deeper Learning

A basic tenet of our pluriliteracies model is that deeper learning is fundamental for an individual's learning progression and development. This is not new. However, closer investigation reveals the complex and dynamic nature of the processes involved. Whilst a great deal has been written about deeper learning and its importance for engaging learners 'through discovering and mastering existing knowledge and then creating new knowledge', (Fullan & Langworthy, 2014, p. 2), there is little to guide in-depth understanding of the nature of those processes – that is, what it means to master existing knowledge and create new knowledge which can then be 'translated' into pedagogic practices to support and 'grow' classroom learning. In seeking to understand better the nature of deeper learning and its implications for learning and teaching, two strands have emerged: the *mechanics* or cognitive-linguistic processes through which deeper learning evolves, and the *drivers* of and for deeper learning. We define drivers as those factors that promote or inhibit the processes or mechanics of deeper learning, such as student and teacher engagement.

Articulating the *mechanics* or processes allows the trajectories or pathways for deeper learning to emerge. The *drivers* focus on the learners and, subsequently, the role of teachers in mentoring learning. In this chapter, we focus on the mechanics, followed by the roles of strategy instruction, practice and transfer.

Defining the competencies and skills that learners require to succeed in their personal and professional lives is essential, complex and multi-faceted. Developing teaching and learning approaches that create learning environments in which learners can safely and successfully acquire those competencies is the key challenge of contemporary education.

Learning and innovation skills are increasingly being recognised as the key differentiators between those who will be ready for increasingly complex life and work environments and those who won't. This particular blend of knowledge and skills has been termed *twenty-first century competencies*, and can be defined as knowledge that can be transferred or applied in new situations (NRC, 2012). Transferable knowledge includes content knowledge and skills in a specific domain or subject, as well as an understanding of how, why and when to apply these to answer questions and solve problems. Hilton and Pellegrino describe twenty-first century skills as clusters of competencies from the cognitive, intrapersonal and interpersonal domains.

Deeper learning, therefore, is how we acquire those fundamental competencies. It is 'the process through which an individual becomes capable of taking what was learned in one situation and applying it to a new situation' (NRC, 2012, p. 5).

Table 4.1 clearly shows that a pedagogical approach to deeper learning cannot and must not focus on cognitive skill sets alone. If the goal of education is to enable learners to become critical, highly informed and reflective citizens with the ability to evaluate situations and take informed decisions and who act responsibly, educators are faced with the challenge of designing environments from a more holistic perspective. In this sense, design processes involve much more than planning lessons, yet they are rarely brought into professional learning programmes to encourage teachers to understand how learning happens. In short, in order to foster deeper learning, the mechanics have to take into account personal growth for both learners and educators. In other words, they must address intra- as well as interpersonal competencies, as outlined in Table 4.1.

Consequently, our vision for constructing a holistic and accessible pedagogic model built on pluriliteracies development has to incorporate aspects such as learner engagement and self-efficacy, as well as personal beliefs and values that emphasise the impact of well-being, mindset, motivation and self-regulation on deeper learning. Moreover, we firmly believe that deeper learning and personal growth involve a highly proactive role by teachers, one which transcends the traditional understanding of teachers as 'guide on the side' or facilitator of learning. Therefore, we propose a revised understanding of the teacher's role as one which encapsulates ways of doing, knowing, enabling and being through integrated inclusive processes of mentoring learning, in what we call 'partnerships for deeper learning'. Such partnerships evolve where mentors and mentees are engaged in processes of constructing and communicating knowledge 'that go beyond the information given and shape unique episodes of knowledge productive interaction' (Tillema et al., 2015, p. 16). In fact, throughout the book,

Table 4.1 Twenty-first century competencies by domain (NRC, 2012)

Cognitive domain	Intrapersonal domain	Interpersonal domain
Cognitive processes & strategies Knowledge Creativity	Intellectual openness Work ethic & conscientiousness Positive core self-evaluation	Teamwork & collaboration Leadership
Associated skills Critical thinking Information literacy Reasoning Innovation	Associated skills Metacognition Flexibility Initiative Appreciation for diversity	Associated skills Communication Responsibility Conflict resolution

we refer constantly to learning partnerships, which, as mentioned in Chapter 1, involve teachers and learners working together in meaningful, reciprocal ways for 'equity, transparency, reciprocal accountability and mutual benefit' (Fullan & Langworthy, 2014, p. 12). Such partnerships are built on dialogic ways of being, built on finding practical, realistic ways of co-designing tasks and activities, learning pathways and spaces for demonstrating learning valued by peers and teachers alike. Such learning partnerships are fundamental to growth and a sense of belonging in learning ecologies. Reflecting on learning partnerships will close the volume in Part III.

We will now briefly consider how different types of knowledge are stored in long-term memory (LTM) and introduce the key processes through which knowledge is committed to LTM.

4.1 How Knowledge Is Stored in Long-Term Memory

The mechanics of deeper learning involve re-examining how and where deeper knowledge and understanding are 'stored'. Ormrod (2011) defines learning as long-term change in behaviour, in terms of both achievement and mental representations, including attitudes resulting from experiences. Therefore, for learning to be successfully internalised, knowledge must be committed to long-term memory (LTM). LTM can be represented in the following way.

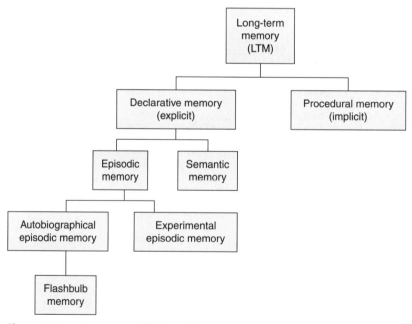

Figure 4.1 Long-term memory (LTM) model

Drawing on this representation, different types of knowledge are stored in different parts of the LTM. Procedural memory stores information on how to do something (our skills and habits). The process through which skills are committed to procedural memory via practice is called proceduralisation or *automatisation.*

Declarative memory is widely considered to consist of episodic and semantic memory. Episodic memory allows us to remember past events from our lives (autobiographical episodic memory) or what we were doing when we learned certain facts (experimental episodic memory). Semantic memory contains our factual and conceptual knowledge, and processes, ideas and concepts which are not drawn from personal experience. These information-processing systems receive information from perceptual systems, retain aspects of this information and, if necessary, transmit specific information to other systems (Tulving, 1972 and 2002). Both systems store different types of information and react differently to retrieval. Crucially, semantic memory is also the memory system for the use of language. Tulving referred to it as a 'mental thesaurus, organised knowledge a person possesses about words and other verbal symbols, their meanings and referents, about relations among them, and about rules, formulas, and algorithms for the manipulation of these symbols, concepts and relations' (Tulving, 1972, p. 386).

However, more recent studies (i.e. Renoult et al., 2012 and 2016; Greenberg & Verfaellie, 2010) propose that the distinction between semantic memory and episodic memory is not as clear-cut as previously suggested. They indicate that these two memory forms are interdependent, and that *personal semantics* may act as an intermediary between both semantic and episodic systems – that is, they may share a neural base. This idea leads Renoult et al. (2012) to formulate a continuum perspective for declarative memory, where so-called *autobiographically significant concepts* share features of semantic and episodic memory. This new type of conceptual knowledge may be especially relevant for the design of deeper learning tasks and will be explored later.

It seems, however, that the role of memory in learning is overlooked in terms of the conditions which impact effectively on classroom learning. For our purposes and as a useful reminder, it is vital to understand that committing information to long-term memory alone does not equal deeper learning. Teaching which focusses predominantly on factual information and which fails to provide learners with opportunities for using and applying that knowledge will lead to so-called 'inert knowledge' (Gentner et al., 2009; Hoa & Huong, 2015; Iran-Nejad & Stewart, 2010), which cannot be accessed for problem-solving. In order to really understand, learners need to connect new information with prior knowledge, assign it to superior contexts and understand its relevance both for the discipline and for their daily lives. They need to engage in decision-making or problem-solving activities, through experimentation or investigation (Irvine, 2017; Marzano & Kendall, 2008). This leads on to a review of concept building and the internalisation.

4.2   Internalisation of Conceptual Knowledge

As has been discussed above, we are operating on the premise that deeper learning is essential for knowledge transfer. This of course raises questions about how learners actually construct understanding. We have argued before that transferable knowledge is based on conceptual understanding, which leads to the formation of increasingly complex mental models, patterns, schemata or concepts. The process through which such concepts are formed and stored is called internalisation and is one of the key mechanisms of deeper learning.

Concepts are 'perceived regularities in events or objects, or records of events or objects designated by a label' (Novak, 2002, p. 550). They are hierarchically structured and represent the building blocks of organised knowledge. Concepts are the foundation of interconnected propositions or units of meaning, which are built using cognitive structures, as represented below (Figure 4.2).

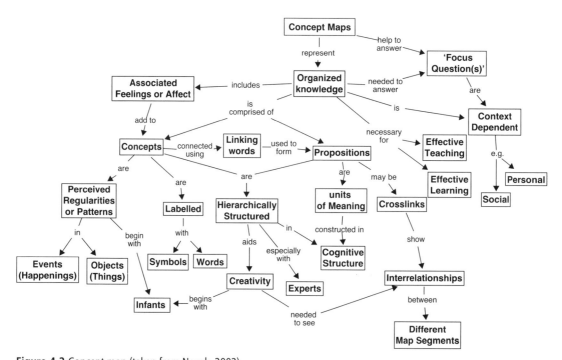

Figure 4.2 Concept map (taken from Novak, 2002)

According to Novak, learning happens and develops 'when a new regularity is perceived… leading to concept formation and/or the construction of new propositions' (Novak, 2002, p. 550). Gowin's Vee illustrates how twelve elements involved in the process of constructing new knowledge or meanings (Figure 4.3) interact in the development of conceptual thinking.

Figure 4.3 Gowin's Vee: twelve epistemological elements operating in the construction of knowledge (adapted)

In a similar vein, Lantolf argues that 'scientific concepts are the foundation of the process of developmental education... concepts are relevant for the formation of consciousness because they shape how we perceive, understand, and act in and on the world' (Lantolf and Poehner 2014, p. 59). Given the interconnectedness of processes involved in concept building, it becomes increasingly apparent from research studies that understanding and knowing require the successful *internalisation of conceptual knowledge*. Internalisation, however, is dependent on several stages of development. The four stages below plot development from surface learning to abstraction to consolidation to internalisation (see Figure 4.4).

All learning starts at the surface level, with learners encountering new content. In order to understand that content, learners need to find and connect the dots or, more specifically, determine how events, facts and observations are connected. This information is then distilled into meaningful patterns called concepts (i.e.

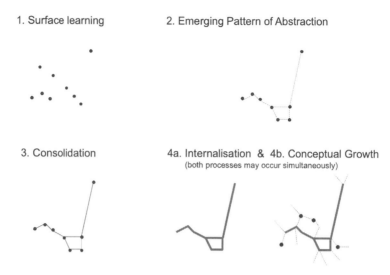

Figure 4.4 Visualising internalisation of conceptual knowledge

mental models). Lantolf and Poehner argue that at this stage, which they call the *material stage*, initial understanding develops best if learners have opportunities to experience new content in a 'hands-on' fashion in action-oriented approaches – for example, by investigating or experimenting, or by interacting with material objects or charts, diagrams or models (see Figure 4.5).

To reach the next stage, however, students need to *communicate* their growing conceptual understanding either to each other (social communication) or to themselves (private speech). This step is crucial because learners gain control over a concept and its use through language. Therefore, they need opportunities to share and deepen their conceptual understanding appropriately.

Such 'languaging' activities support the abstraction of the concept – a fundamental step – to make use of a concept in a wide array of different contexts. This is called the *verbal phase*. Deliberate practice, reflection and spaced repetition will help learners consolidate and internalise conceptual knowledge. As learners gain mastery over a concept, the process becomes a purely mental one (i.e. understanding and using a concept becomes internalised). An individual is now able to use the concept appropriately in different contexts and in creative ways. Moreover, progression occurs when the concept is expanded, extended or deepened, or when opportunities for transfer are increased and complex. Transfer of conceptual knowledge is only possible when concepts have been fully internalised. Transfer is discussed further in Section 4.3.

Thus far, we have explored the role of memory and concept building and the importance of the internalisation of conceptual knowledge and the automatisation of procedural knowledge and skills. According to Christodoulou (2017), analysing the importance of conceptual understanding in learning and its effect on

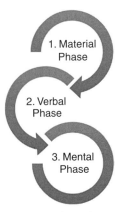

Figure 4.5 Three phases
in processing concepts

actual performance reveals a critical flaw in current educational thinking and competences-based approaches: the idea that performing a complex task (such as writing an article) will effectively increase the target competences. Christodoulou explains that this widely held assumption is problematic because complex tasks require a set of subject-specific competences, not generic ones:

> Experts in every field depend on rich and detailed structures of knowledge stored in
> their long-term memory. These structures – often called schema or mental models –
> are what allows the expert to encounter new problems and solve them with such ease.
> (Christodoulou, 2017, p. 34).

Christodoulou further argues that we have to distinguish between learning tasks and tasks. Since performance depends on the 'detailed, knowledge-rich mental models stored in long-term memory', learners depend on learning tasks that help them create those mental models in the first place. This entails a basic understanding of related facts and concepts so that learners will be able to 'connect the dots' by identifying new knowledge elements and discovering how they are related to each other. Also, learners need to know how to proceed – that is, which steps to take to solve a problem or complete a task (i.e. strategic knowledge).

Learners who are asked to solve complex problems without access to previously established mental models in long-term memory are forced to rely on problem-solving searches in working memory. This will overburden working memory and waste resources on activities unrelated to learning. As a result, a student may be thinking hard and struggling without learning anything. This is why competences-based approaches that do not strike a careful balance between learning and performance tasks, may ultimately fail to meet the needs of learners.

Theories about the formation of conceptual knowledge have significantly impacted the development of our pluriliteracies model, including our understanding of the nature of 'content', 'language' and how they are related to deeper learning. We propose that *content learning first and foremost needs to be about furthering learners' conceptual understanding.* That is, deeper learning requires the successful internalisation of conceptual knowledge. We posit that language – or more precisely, 'languaging', 'the process of making meaning and shaping knowledge and experience through language' (Swain, 2006) – is the key to deeper learning because it mediates conceptual development. The attention drawn to languaging provides us with a pedagogic lens through which to revisit the role of language in concept formation.

Building on the evidence of the role of language in learning, it is imperative that educators factor this two-fold function into the design of classroom learning:

- language(s) serve to make learners' understanding and thinking accessible or visible; and
- language is the tool that allows teachers to mediate their learners' thinking and understanding by reconfiguring their internal conceptual structures through pedagogic intervention and scaffolding.

In this way, language can be used to strengthen the general patterns underlying the epistemological or the meaning-making elements involved in the process of knowledge construction. This is why *languaging* is so powerful. In fact, it is the profound effects of languaging on cognitive development that have led Lantolf and Pohner to formulate a *pedagogical imperative* demanding that education should focus on maximising the developmental potential of students, especially those from disadvantaged backgrounds.

> If a function such as WM [working memory] significantly contributes to successful educational outcomes then short of eliminating poverty... the macro cultural institution of education must make a commitment to enhance this capacity for individuals and members of socioeconomic groups who enter the institution in a disadvantageous position. This would comprise a far better and equitable solution to the problem than to place students into instructional programs according to their WM capacity and where they would receive instruction "tailored to their cognitive abilities". (Lantolf and Poehner, 2014, p. 36)

4.2.1   Language and Knowledge Construction: A First Look

In order to summarise our thinking with regards to enabling learners to language their understanding, we provide a distillation which defines the nature of the interplay between language and thinking, based on the theories and assumptions of conceptual development introduced so far. These are as follows.

4.2.2　Language and Knowledge Construction

Guiding principles for meaningful practice

1. Concepts and propositions are cognitive patterns of varying complexity.
2. The 'shape' of those patterns is determined by the way individual items of knowledge are connected (causal, temporal etc.).
3. The mind is a constantly shifting system, so patterns aren't static. They are meaningful and dynamic. This is summarised by Kelso: 'In nature's pattern-forming systems, contents aren't contained anywhere but are revealed only by the dynamics. Form and content are thus inextricably connected and can't ever be separated' (Kelso, 1995, p. 1).
4. Conceptual growth is the result of the complexification of the patterns underlying concepts and propositions.
5. Learning new concepts or complex skills depends on practice, which creates specific neural wiring that supports schema or skills formation (Jackson, 2011, p. 96).

These considerations may help to clarify why functional linguists consider language to be the 'primary evidence of learning' (Mohan et al., 2010): language can make thinking and learning visible by revealing the level of conceptual understanding as reflected in the state/shape of the pattern used to express thinking/understanding (Figure 4.6). Brown demonstrates how such an understanding of conceptual development can be used to develop a flexible model of cognition. His model is built on a continuum of understanding ranging from intuition to expertise, where 'learning is conceived as a progress toward higher levels of sophistication and competence as new knowledge is linked to existing knowledge and deeper understandings are developed' (Brown, 2011, p. 225).

In addition to making thinking and learning visible, a functional understanding of language considers language as 'social semiotic' (Coffin & Donohue, 2014, p. 23), as 'a tool that enables conceptual development'. This perspective links language with the notion of social mediation, the process by which teachers and learners employ semiotic tools to mediate meaning – that is, positioning language as the mediator of meaning making for individual learner understanding.

A more detailed analysis of the fundamental functions of the role of language in learning (see Section 4.5) will allow us to examine what lies at the interface between thinking and language and the cognitive learning goals that are ever-present in classrooms. This brings us to underline the linguistic evidence of learning, building on cognitive strategies that for each individual constitute their own learning.

Level		Description of Person	Description of Response
5 Emergent	B ↑ A₁ ↔ A₂	The phenomenon is seen as an emergent property of a system, made up of interacting components. The system evolves over time, eventually producing the observed effect.	A1 and A2 happen. Over time they interact and evolve, until eventually B happens. Meanwhile, A_1 and A_2 continue to happen.
4 Multiple	A_1 → B A_2	The phenomenon is seen as an effect produced by multiple causal elements. All are necessary; if one is removed the effect is not Produced.	A_1 and A_2 cause B when they both happen at the same time.
3 Justified	A → B	The phenomenon is seen as an effect produced by a single causal element. Justification or a mechanism is necessary.	A causes B, and this is how.
2 Elemental	A → B	The phenomenon is seen as an effect produced by a single causal element. Justification or a mechanism is not necessary.	A causes B.
1 Acausal	B	The phenomenon is seen as an instantiation of reality. No cause is necessary.	B happens because that's the way things are.
0 Absent	B ?!?	The phenomenon is surprising. No explanation seems possible.	I can't explain why B happens.

Figure 4.6 A model of cognition (Brown, N. & Wilson, M., 2011, p. 228)

4.2.3   Summing Up

Throughout the first part of the chapter, two of the fundamental elements of deeper learning were analysed alongside the role of language in concept building. The need to find accessible and transparent ways for learners to both internalise their learning and automatise it constitute crucial stages. The role language plays in activating those processes is fundamental – that is, it emphasises the role of languaging as key to deeper learning.

4.3   Re-evaluating the Role of Practice

Continuing with the mechanics of deeper learning, we now explore the role of practice and transfer as requisites for deeper learning. What we mean by practice needs careful analysis, since how educators encourage and enable their learners to 'practice' in ways which are truly beneficial is open to wide interpretation. It also requires reassessing the meaning of automatisation, since the two are linked yet rarely discussed together in pedagogic literature.

4.3.1   Strategy Instruction and Practice: Key to Automatisation

Anderson's Adaptive Control of Thought model (ACT, Anderson, 1983) considers skill acquisition to be the result of the proceduralisation or automatisation of rule-bound declarative knowledge through practice and feedback. Macaro (2006) argues that the process of automatisation is governed by learner strategies. From this perspective, instruction which promotes appropriate awareness, use and development of learner strategies is fundamental to enabling individual learners to automatise specific skills, thereby opening up pathways for deeper learning.

Therefore, teachers need to 'set up contexts in which these skills can be displayed, monitored, and appropriate feedback given to the shape of their acquisition' (Anderson et al., 1995 p. 71). Additionally, they need to 'incorporate activities that promote automaticity into the… learning situation in a manner that respects transfer-appropriate processing' (Segalowitz, 2003, p. 402). In other words, learning episodes need to provide ample opportunities for learners to *practise* and reflect on the use of specific strategies in order to develop and hone the desired skills.

The question as to which specific strategies learners make use of whilst learning and using second languages has attracted a considerable amount of research since the late 1970s and led to parallel research efforts in language learner strategy instruction (for a comprehensive review see Hassan, Macaro et al., 2005; Cohen & Macaro, 2007; Chamot & Harris, 2019). Despite claims that learner strategies are key to learner autonomy and knowledge construction in CLIL (Wolff, 2009), research on the effect of learner strategies on successful CLIL learning and performance is very sparse. There are only a few intervention studies (Azkarai & Agirre, 2016; Jaekel, 2015; Lorenzo et al., 2010; Ruiz de Zarobe & Zenotz, 2015) published to date.

However, there seems to be a growing consensus that what is needed to assess the effect of instructed strategy use on learner performance is a reconceptualisation of how learner strategies can be taught and learned, and how they can be made accessible for reflection and subsequent modification by the learners and thus become individualised (Schmenk, 2009, pp. 84–5).

Macaro's revised theoretical framework (2006, Figure 4.7) is based on research from the fields of second-language acquisition, cognitive psychology and neuroscience. Disposing of many of the terminological and conceptual incongruities of earlier works in the field, the framework offers a plausible explanation for the interaction of learner strategies and the underlying mental processes and language skills (Macaro, 2006; Cohen & Macaro, 2007; Macaro, 2010).

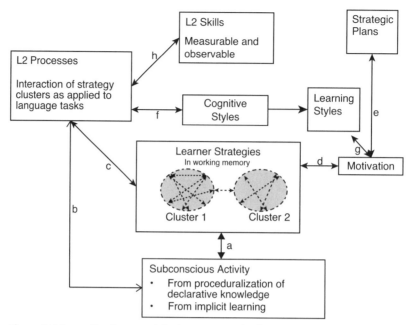

Figure 4.7 A cognitive framework for learner strategies (Macaro, 2006, p. 326)

According to Macaro, learners employ clusters of strategies to perform specific tasks. These strategies in turn trigger a variety of processes, which become manifest in language skills. These processes can be automatised, but only if or when those strategies have been evaluated by the learner and considered to be useful to them: 'It may be that, through repeated practice and confirmation of effectiveness, a particular action Z becomes automatic in learning situation X.' (Macaro, 2006, p. 329). We propose that these principles apply to any skill in any subject of schooling. Learner involvement in these processes is of paramount importance.

Another important aspect of the model is that strategies can be transferred to similar tasks through pattern matching procedures. Moreover, Macaro proposes that strategies can still become subject to modification after they have been automatised and that the successful development of skills encompasses the complex relationship between processes, skills and strategies:

> The automatisation of strategies, through the continual deployment of clusters of strategies during L2 processes, leads to the development of skilful behaviour. In the field of L2 acquisition, as in the field of experimental psychology, skills increase their efficiency the more their underlying cognitive processes become proceduralised. (Macaro, 2006, p. 331)

With regards to the development of subject-specific literacies, we propose that it is primarily through subject-specific strategies that learners develop subject-specific skills and thus literacies. This suggests identifying instructed strategy use as a

key variable for teaching and lesson/materials design because the cognitive processes underlying the targeted skills can be automatised through a wide range of
carefully balanced subject-specific tasks and practice activities. This requires very
careful analysis and design by the teacher in terms of the nature of the tasks and
the types of activities designed.

4.3.2 Practice: Key to Skill Development

Practice is a complex issue and one which is seldom analysed for its distinct properties – for example, in differentiating between practice and repetition. Moreover,
the successful automatisation of skills is further complicated by the assumption of
the existence of dual coding systems that learners tap into for language production: an analytic rule-based system and a memory-driven exemplar-based system
(Skehan, 1998; Lyster, 2007). Both systems feed on different types of practice:
controlled practice activities or exercises, on the one hand, are cognitively unde-
manding and context reduced and engage the learner's awareness of rule-based
representations. *Communicative practice activities,* on the other hand, are rich in
context and engage learners in more open-ended and meaning-focussed tasks
(Lyster, 2007).

So, to help learners develop certain skills or skill sets, teachers need to offer
their learners a carefully balanced array of activities and tasks which promote the
automatisation of the processes underlying the use of specific strategies. Purposeful selection and ordering of activities and tasks according to these principles are
unlikely to be in the regular planning practices of teachers.

What we mean by practice needs careful analysis, however, since how educators
encourage and enable their learners to 'practice' in ways that are truly beneficial
is arguably open to wide interpretation.

4.3.3 Key Components of Strategy Instruction

1. **Noticing and controlled practising:** Learners need to be taught when to apply
   subject-specific strategies in specific contexts and how to adopt and adapt
   these appropriately to complete a given task. Awareness-raising or 'noticing'
   activities coupled with controlled practice activities serve to strengthen the
   rule-based system (Lyster, 2007).
2. **Communicative practising:** Communicative practice activities (i.e. complex
   learning tasks that require the application of the desired strategies in authentic
   contexts) serve to strengthen the memory-based system and will promote the
   quick retrieval of the linguistic components of a strategy through the process
   of *chunking* – that is, breaking down tasks into smaller units which can be
   practised and automatised (DeKeyser, 2008, p. 292).
3. **Providing feedback and reflecting on learning:** Instructed strategy use ap-
   pears to be especially effective in promoting deeper learning if it is carried out

over lengthy periods of time and includes a focus on metacognition (Hassan et al., 2005; Macaro, 2006). In other words, learners need opportunities to critically reflect on their individual strategy use and receive feedback that supports the automatisation of the target features.

4.3.4   Rethinking and Re-evaluating Practice

Daniel Coyle offers a fascinating neurological explanation for how skills are developed: 'Skill is a cellular insulation that wraps neural circuits and that grows in response to certain signals.' (Daniel Coyle, 2009, p. 5). He argues that all skills are made of living circuits which grow according to certain rules. When these circuits fire in the right way, myelin responds by wrapping insulation around that specific neural circuit. The thicker the layer of myelin, the better the insulation of the nerve fibres, the 'faster and more accurate our movements and thoughts become' (Daniel Coyle, 2009, p. 4).

The myelin sheath is an electrically insulating layer wrapped around the axon of a nerve cell. It increases the speed of electric conduction. Learning is about the formation of neural networks. According to Coyle and others, deep practice can increase the thickness of the myelin layer, increase the speed of electric conduction within a neural network and thus boost performance.

For Coyle, the discovery of the role of myelin in the way the brain functions amounts to a Copernican-style revolution in a field which had predominantly focussed on the formation of neural networks. This has largely been made possible by new imaging technology (so-called diffusion tensor imaging), which allows neurologists to measure and map myelin inside living people. Coyle further reports that in 2005, Fredrik Ullend scanned the brains of concert pianists and found a connection between hours of practice and myelin growth. In 2000, he had already linked reading skills to white matter or myelin increase. In 2006, Pujol was able to establish similar links between myelinated white matter growth and vocabulary increase.

The reason why Coyle considers the discovery of the role myelin so groundbreaking is that it clearly implies that the role of *focussed practice* may be much more important in shaping skills than that of genes or intelligence. In fact, the idea that talents or skills can be built and developed like muscles requires a big shift in thinking, but one which may lead to rethinking certain practices:

> Deep practice is strange concept for two reasons. The first reason is that it cuts against our intuition about talent. Our intuition tells us that practise relates to talent in the same way that a whetstone relates to a knife: it's vital but useless without a solid blade of so-called natural ability. *Deep practice raises an intriguing possibility: that practice might be the way to forge the blade itself.* (Daniel Coyle, 2010, p. 18)

However, it's important to note that myelin growth does not occur automatically. Coyle proposes that myelin growth results from *specific types of practice*. This resonates with the points previously made concerning the type of practice that is beneficial for learners and the type that wastes time. Coyle emphasises three important features of *deep practice.*

First, in order to practise a certain task or action efficiently, it needs to be '*chunked up*'. This means that complex tasks need to be broken down into smaller units that can then be practised and automatised. Deep practice usually means slowing down the pace of the action. Repeating a movement slowly allows the individual to 'perform' it more accurately and to identify mistakes that need to be fixed. Coyle writes about a visit to a New York music school where sheet music was cut up in such a way that pieces had to be practised slowly and in a random order first. When the musicians finally played the piece in its correct order, they had gained a much deeper understanding of each element of the musical piece.

Second, deep practice requires time, since enhancing skills demands a lot of *repetition.* The more often we repeat a task, targeting perfection or improvement, the more precise and quicker the action will become, because the myelin layer surrounding the relevant circuit thickens. However, it is the third feature which is critical, since engaging in deep practice means making things a little more difficult during practising activities. We know that simply repeating something we already know how to do well will not improve our skills or lead to deeper learning. Instead, deep practice demands that we always practise just beyond the limits of our abilities.

> Struggle is not optional – it's neurologically required: in order to get your skills circuit to fire optimally, you must by definition fire the circuit sub-optimally, you must make mistakes and pay attention to those mistakes, you must slowly teach your circuit. You must also keep firing that circuit – i.e., practising – in order to keep myelin functioning properly. After all, myelin is a living tissue. (Daniel Coyle, 2009, p. 42)

Therefore, deep practice is a highly focussed and reflective activity. It involves a number of distinct actions: choosing a target, reaching for it, evaluating the gap between the target and the reach, and returning to step one. Deep practice requires deep engagement and long-term commitment and motivation. One such motivator Coyle describes as *ignition*, which acts as an external cue to instil in us a desire to become skilled at something. It convinces us that we can achieve that goal if we work hard for it. Or, as Coyle puts it, ignition supplies the energy, whilst deep practice translates that energy over time into forward progress or wraps of myelin.

Interestingly, even though the concept of task repetition and its positive effects on language learning are fairly well documented (Bygate, 2018), practice still seems to get a 'raw deal' in education. This may be due to ways in which many teachers still associate practice with mindless, repetitive pattern drills. It has become clear that deep practice is very different from pattern drills in terms of skills development; meaningful and mindful repetition will make all the difference.

The way these ideas relate to deeper learning is this: we posit that deep understanding, or the internalisation of conceptual knowledge, will lead to the formation of neural networks in the brain. The same is true for new skills or skillsets. The more often these networks are activated through deep practice, the thicker the myelin layer and the faster signals can travel. This will affect understanding and performance. In other words, if learning creates new networks in the brain, deeper understanding will increase the complexity of these networks and deep practice will increase the speed at which these networks operate effectively.

Thus far, the emphasis has been on deeper learning and the necessary processes that support its development. However, one of our challenges is that many of the key constructs used to describe these processes are open to very wide interpretation. The point we wish to make here is that careful attention needs to be paid to the meaning and implications of key concepts. They quickly become part of common educational rhetoric without there being a shared understanding of what they mean in specific learning contexts and how they contribute explicitly to deepening learning. The idea that education should enable learners to use and adapt their knowledge successfully in new situations is at the heart of every contemporary approach to teaching and learning.

4.4   Transfer of Learning Revisited

Many pedagogic approaches are astonishingly vague on what exactly is meant by transfer and how to best to promote it in actual classroom situations. Although research on transfer of learning has advanced considerably since its beginnings in the 1980s, different perspectives and research foci have naturally caused the field to branch out significantly. In considering the nature of transfer and the concerns expressed, it is quite a challenge to find positions and tenets which are applicable to classroom learning.

Transferable knowledge is a key element of deeper learning, and in this section we will briefly outline key concepts and findings from current research on transfer which have greatly contributed to our understandings and informed our pedagogical approach to deeper learning.

First, we argue that the classical definition of transfer is too narrow in scope and why an expanded view of transfer is essential – one which focusses more on real-life situations and highlights the importance of *interpretive* and prior knowledge learners use to 'transfer in' to new learning experiences. Such a revised understanding of transfer will enable us to distinguish two different key aspects of deeper learning: *innovation* and *efficiency*.

Second, we will have a closer look at problem-solving and describe how it is related to deeper learning in order to show what teachers can do to help learners develop further their problem-solving skills. This involves increasing engagement, focussing on deep understanding and helping learners see the deeper structures of a problem through careful analysis of its surface features.

Third, we highlight the importance of the social context of learning and report how a more holistic view of classroom contexts and different ways of framing them can facilitate transfer for individual learners. Finally, we present a number of transfer-facilitating strategies that are recommended in research studies.

4.4.1   Broadening the Scope of Transfer

This section will consider two strong critiques of traditional or classical learning transfer studies: the first by Schwartz and the second by Chi and VanLehn. This is important, since the transfer of learning is a fundamental principle in education, yet – as discussed previously – little attention has been paid to the nature of transfer, especially the impact of surface and deep transfer on learning.

The first critique is captured in the seminal book *Transfer on Trial* (Detterman & Steinberg, 1993). In that book, the authors report that 'most studies fail to find transfer... and those studies claiming transfer can only be said to have found transfer by the most generous of criteria and would not meet the classical definition of transfer' (Detterman & Steinberg, 1993, p. 15). According to the classical definition, transfer refers to 'the degree to which a behaviour will be repeated in a new situation' (Detterman & Steinberg, 1993, p. 4).

Schwartz et al. (2005) criticise this definition for being too narrow in focus because people often do not apply *identical* problem-solving procedures when in a transfer context. This means that if learners apply their own problem-solving mechanisms, which are different from the original ones, such applications do not count as transfer of learning. Schwartz et al. describe learners as typically placed in closed-off ('sequestered') environments, where they have no access to different information sources because these may contaminate the results. The authors argue that in such settings learners are not allowed to learn by trying out an idea and revising it if necessary. Neither do they receive any kind of useful feedback. Schwartz et. al. also report that this seems at odds with studies that demonstrate that when people's abilities to learn new skills are assessed, positive transfer doesn't occur initially but usually requires a number of learning trials. Therefore, Schwartz et al. argue that many lab-based transfer studies are designed to make students 'look dumb' (Schwartz et al., 2005, p. 4). This leads them to propose a different perspective on transfer: rather than conceptualising transfer as something that occurs *after* a particular learning episode, they propagate a view of transfer which includes *preparations for future learning* (PFL) because 'people not only "*transfer out*" of situations to solve problems, they also "*transfer in*" to situations to learn' (see Figure 4.8).

In other words, 'transfer out' is concerned with what may be called direct transfer, where learners apply *directly* what they learned during a learning intervention in order to solve a target problem. 'Transfer in', on the other hand, offers

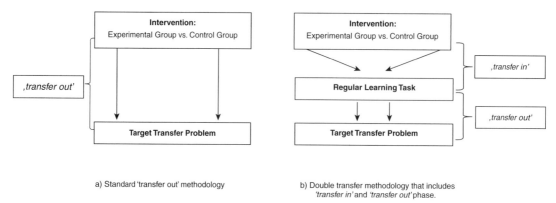

a) Standard 'transfer out' methodology

b) Double transfer methodology that includes 'transfer in' and 'transfer out' phase.

Figure 4.8 'Transfer out' vs. 'transfer in' (adapted from Schwartz et al., 2012)

a different, more indirect perspective, where the learning intervention *prepares* learners for the deeper learning of future content (*regular learning task*), so that they may successfully solve a subsequent target problem at a later stage.

The distinction between 'transferring out' and 'in' emphasises the limitations of traditional ways of assessing transfer. These have mostly focussed on whether or not learners can directly make use of *replicative* (recalling previously learned facts) or *applicative* aspects of knowing (applying knowledge and skills to solve new problems), and neglected a third aspect of knowing which Broudy (1977) calls *interpretive knowing*. We make interpretive use of knowing when we interpret new situations in light of our learning. Interpretive knowledge is hugely helpful because, for many situations, people do not have sufficient memories, schemata or procedures to solve a problem. However, they do have interpretations that shape how they begin to make sense of new situations. Schwartz et. al argue that the way we interpret or frame problems heavily impacts on subsequent thinking and cognitive processing.

An expanded view of transfer which includes the idea of 'transferring in' thus offers new ways of assessing how a specific situation is interpreted by the learner with the aid of prior learning, and how it is interpreted in light of previous learning episodes. Including interpretive knowledge is significant because 'knowing with' (.e. interpretive knowledge) may be as important as 'knowing what' (i.e. replicative knowledge) or 'knowing how' (i.e. applicative knowledge), especially with regards to lifelong learning.

Schwartz et al. argue that providing learners with opportunities to develop interpretive knowledge leads to enhanced learning. Their research seems to indicate that developing students' interpretative knowing 'transfers in' and can lead to better application of knowledge in a 'transfer out' task:

> We assume that innovations relevant to learning arise from useful content knowledge (plus dispositions) that people can transfer in, and therefore PFL (preparations for future learning) assessments of innovation are highly relevant. (Schwartz et al., 2005, p. 48).

If learners are to become familiar with processes and conditions conducive to 'transferring in', educators will need to balance instruction in order to promote two important dimensions of learning that are of profound importance for lifelong learning: *efficiency* and *innovation* (Figure 4.9). 'Instruction that balances efficiency and innovation should also include opportunities to experiment with ideas and, in the process, experience the need to change them.' (Schwartz et al., 2005, p. 50).

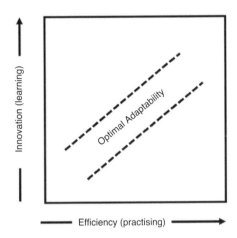

Figure 4.9 Corridor of optimal adaptability
(adapted from Schwartz et al., 2012)

Efficiency is important in all domains and relates to the ability to rapidly retrieve and accurately apply appropriate knowledge and skills to solve a problem or understand an explanation. However, as Schwartz et al. point out, efficiency-oriented practice is often about 'problem elimination' and 'not about in-depth, sustained problem solving' (Schwartz et al., 2005, p. 42). An overemphasis on efficiency may produce routine experts who excel at solving a set of standardised problems but who may show no interest in continuing to develop new approaches to emergent problems throughout their lives. That is why efficiency should be balanced with innovation and adaptability. In the case of mathematics, for instance, such instruction would include:

> opportunities to learn with understanding and develop their own mathematical
> conjectures as well as become efficient at computation. Instruction that balances
> efficiency and innovation should also include opportunities to experiment with ideas
> and, in the process, experience the need to change them.' (Schwartz et al., 2005, p. 50)

This idea is very similar to the ones we presented in the previous section on practice, especially the idea of balancing complex and challenging learning tasks (usually known as communicative practice), controlled practice activities and activities for students to provide feedback and to reflect on their learning. Learning new concepts and how they relate to prior knowledge will increase understanding (in terms of conceptual depth and breadth) and thus provide the groundwork for innovation (when students are asked to use their newly gained knowledge to find new ways to solve new problems) and transfer, whereas deep practice will increase efficiency and performance.

A second critique for different reasons than those by Schwartz et. al will now be considered.

4.4.2 Deep Structures vs. Surface Features: Re-examining Conditions for Transfer

A second critique of learning transfer studies comes from Chi and VanLehn (2012). They argue that earlier studies on secondary problem solving did not control for deep understanding of the first problem, resulting in misleading reports about a failure to transfer. When learners are not able to recognise or abstract that a second problem has the same underlying deep structure as the first, transfer cannot take place. In terms of problem solving, surface features can often be found in the so-called cover-story of a problem (i.e. the literal objects, concepts or entities explicitly described in a problem statement or situation).

The question as to what exactly constitutes 'deep structure' is more complex yet considered fundamental if problem-solving activities are to be successfully achieved. A useful example from Chi and VanLehn illustrates a conundrum: observing students solve a problem successfully may not necessarily be a true indicator for deep understanding, because the correct solution might arise from copying an example solution or retrieving a similar situation. *In other words, learners' knowing the procedure to solve a problem does not guarantee their understanding of the deep structure of the problem.* Moreover, being able to 'see' the deep structure of a problem is what distinguishes novice problem solvers from experts. To illustrate this point, the authors describe a study in which experts and novices were asked to solve problems that looked similar at the surface level but required different principles for solutions. Both problems began with:

> A man of mass M1 lowers himself to the ground from a height X by holding onto a rope passed over a massless frictionless pulley and attached to another block of mass M2. The mass of the man is greater than the mass of the block. (Chi and VanLehn, 2012, p. 184)

The first problem asked students to find the *tension of the rope* (turning it into a force problem) whereas the second asked students to find the *speed* at which the man hit the ground (turning it into an energy problem). The authors wanted to find out how experts and novices look at problems and what cues they would derive from analysing their surface features. They report that novice learners would predominantly focus on individual items (such as 'frictionless', 'tension' or 'pulley') whereas experts would generally focus on processes and dynamic interactions between these items (such as 'before-and-after situation' or 'inelastic collision').

One reason why this study is so important beyond the context of physics is that it reminds us that *we as teachers may think we are on the same page as our students when, in fact, we are not.* The example above suggests that *in order to help our students to really understand, we have to ensure that as teachers we understand how our learners see tasks or problems before we can teach them to 'see' like experts do.* This means that, in order to teach problem solving, teachers have to point out the 'dynamics' of a problem that their learners need to focus on in order to find a solution. In other words, learners need to know how to identify first-order interactions with the help of second-order relationships. This is complex and requires careful attention analysis and planning by teachers. For example, using the previous illustration: in order to find the tension in the rope, experts connect the 'surface cue' with the other interacting features in this scenario. They consider: the interaction of 'tension' in the rope (i.e. the surface cue) with the block and the man (i.e. gravitational force on the block); the mass of the block; the acceleration of the block and its interaction with the gravitational force on the man; the mass of the man; and the acceleration of the man. Simply put, in order to understand the deep structure of a problem, learners must first be taught how to detect relevant *surface cues* or first-order interactions – in this case, the tension of the rope.

This is then followed by learning how to notice the *deeper structure* or second-order relationships in the same problem-solving activity. This demands an understanding of the deeper structures of the problem, involving the block and the man (taking into account gravitational force, mass and acceleration). These deeper structures need to be recognised in order to discover similarities across situations or problems so that transfer of learning can occur and the problem to be solved. This observation leads the authors to formulate a new hypothesis about the way the deep structure of a problem can be seen:

> [T]o understand some principles or solve some problems successfully, students must consider the interactions among some literal features. Thus, the hypothesis we propose here is that experts can 'see' the underlying principle or deep structure of a problem because they can derive the higher order cues based on the interactions of the surface features, in which the surface features can be directly perceived. (Chi & VanLehn, 2012, p. 183)

According to Engle et al. (2012), the 'seeing' or noticing of the interrelationship between surface and deeper structures is especially successful when the transfer mechanisms are activated. These transfer mechanisms seek to increase learner awareness in comparing multiple examples and non-examples of potentially transferable ideas or concepts. A top-down approach involving teaching a principle first then expecting learners to successfully apply that knowledge to solve problems often does not work. Instead, a bottom-up approach supports learners to transfer their knowledge. This can be summarised as follows.

> - *Provide learners with opportunities to notice second-order as well as first-order cues – drawing attention to simple relationships (e.g. equal to, greater-than, less-than).*
> - *Involve learners in comparing good and non-good examples of transferable ideas and concepts, before encouraging them to make their own generalisations.*
> - *Engage learners in mapping between examples and generalisations, and between examples and reasoning.*
> - *Guide learners towards an understanding of inductive reasoning for transfer, to eventually arrive at successful understanding of problems.*

Naturally, most approaches to transfer of learning focus on the learners themselves. Engle et al. (2012) follow a different route by emphasising the social context of learning and its impact on transfer. They argue that learning and transfer contexts are socially framed in different ways. They define framing as 'the meta-communicative act of characterizing what is happening in a given context and how different people are participating in it' (Engle et al., 2012, p. 217). For instance, a teacher can frame a lesson as an isolated experience (bounded framing) or emphasise the importance of the content for future learning (expansive framing). According to Engle et. al., the way that learning contexts are framed is of paramount importance to transfer because content knowledge is inextricably tied with its context of use. They suggest that *connecting settings* is especially conducive to transfer both *during learning* (when students believe that what they are learning is relevant and will be needed later) and *during potential transfer contexts* (when students conclude that what they learned previously is of ongoing relevance). They also advocate *promoting student authorship*, where learners regularly practise being 'authors' of their own learning so that eventually they see themselves as being able to address unfamiliar situations and to generate a response by adapting their existing knowledge.

4.4.3   Summing Up

When talking about transfer of learning, it is important to keep in mind that different forms of knowledge (conceptual knowledge, procedural knowledge and dispositions) transfer in different ways (diSessa & Wagner, 2009). It is also important to acknowledge that the transfer of concepts is different from the transfer of skills. As Schwartz et al. (2005) have shown, there is more to transfer than 'transferring out' of a learning experience. What learners bring into new situations will affect how they transfer out of these experiences. This is why educators need to focus on the replicative, applicative and interpretive aspects of knowing to achieve the desired outcomes. Balancing effectiveness and innovation may be an effective way of preparing students for lifelong learning.

Teachers have a significant role to play when it comes to the facilitation of transfer through expansive framing, positioning students as authors of their own learning or helping them 'see' the deep structures of problems. Most fundamentally, for content to be transferred successfully, it has to be learned in a sufficiently deep, strong and lasting way. Chi et al. (2012) demonstrate that teachers can increase student engagement with content to promote deeper understanding by designing tasks that foster interactive or constructive – rather than passive – engagement. In other words, the design of learning tasks is of fundamental importance. Yet, traditionally, the repertoire of teaching tasks is rarely critically evaluated in terms of the interconnecting task-type and learning-type outcomes. The design of tasks will be revisited in Chapter 8.1.

Having reviewed the transfer literature, Engle et al. (2012) recommend the use of analogies to promote transfer of learning in the classroom. More specifically, they identify the following three mechanisms as especially conducive to transfer to learning:

1. constructing appropriate generalisations;
2. forming useful mappings between examples and generalisations; and
3. constructing mappings between examples as part of analogical reasoning.

4.5   Trajectories for Deeper Learning

In the previous sections, we have suggested how pluriliteracies might promote deeper learning and the development of transferable knowledge by focussing on the key processes of *internalisation* and *automatisation*. This not only begs the question as to how subject-specific literacies can be taught but, more specifically, how progression in literacies development and deeper learning can be conceptualised and mapped. In this section we will discuss the notion of learning progressions and propose ways to map and design literacies trajectories that stem from the core constructs or big ideas of their related disciplines. It should be noted that we refer to learning progressions in the plural because learners will progress in different subject disciplines in different ways. Using the plural form emphasises the nature of deeper learning and the need to pay attention to the specificities of different disciplines and areas of learning. This resonates with a similar move from the use of 'literacy' to 'literacies' (see Chapter 3.1).

Whilst progressions in learning are seen as dependent on 'powerful tools that have the potential to connect research on student thinking to development of curriculum, curriculum materials, large-scale summative assessment, classroom-scale formative assessments, and classroom teaching' (Gunckel et al., 2009, p. 1), opinions as to what actually constitutes learning progression vary considerably. According to the NRC Report *Taking Science to School*, learning progressions are:

> 'descriptions of *successively more sophisticated ways* of thinking about a topic that can follow one another as children learn about and investigate a topic over a broad span of time' (NRC, 2007, p. 219, our emphasis)

Typically, learning progressions evolve around big ideas in a discipline which offer 'explanatory power that link experiences with phenomena, laws, principles, theories and models into a coherent structure' (Gunckel et al., 2009, p. 2). Goldman et al. (2016) have recently identified the five so-called higher-order categories that – taken together – constitute disciplinary literacy:

TABLE 1
Core Construct Categories and Definitions

Core Construct Category	General Definition
Epistemology	Beliefs about the nature of knowledge and the nature of knowing. What counts as Knowledge? How do we know what we know?
Inquiry Practices, reasoning strategies	Ways in which claims and evidence are established, related, and validated
Overarching concepts, principles, themes, and frameworks	The core ideas and principles that serve as a basis for warranting or connecting claims and evidence
Forms of information representation/types of texts	Types of texts and media (e.g. traditional print, oral, video, digital) in which information is represented and expressed.
Discourse and language Structures	The oral and written language forms that express information.

Figure 4.10 Core constructs and definitions for disciplinary literacies (Goldman et al., 2016, p. 6)

Disciplinary core constructs delineate how individual disciplines differ in their approaches to collecting, analysing, evaluating and communicating information. We therefore suggest that when discussing learning progressions into disciplines and contemplating how to conceptualise and map them, those core constructs can be used to inform and guide the development of pedagogic approaches relevant to developing subject-specific literacies.

4.5.1   Mapping Knowledge Pathways into Disciplines

The Historical Thinking Project aims to promote critical historical literacy and represents an excellent case in point to demonstrate how disciplinary core constructs can be used to tie disciplinary inquiry practices, reasoning strategies and overarching concepts to competencies in disciplinary literacy. Seixas argues that in order to think historically, learners need to be able to:

1. establish historical relevance;
2. use primary source evidence;
3. identify continuity and change;
4. analyse cause and consequence;
5. take historical perspectives; and
6. understand the ethical dimension of historical interpretations (Seixas, n.d., para. 1).

According to Seixas, historically literate citizens will be able to detect the uses and abuses of history, assess the legitimacy of claims and have thoughtful ways of debating such issues. However, Seixas also emphasises the notion that such critical thinking only 'becomes possible in relation to substantive content' (Seixas, n.d., para. 5). This resonates with Hilton & Pellegrino's claim that transferable knowledge is tied to disciplinary ways of conceptualising and communicating knowledge. This is why we argue that critical literacy should not be conceived as a separate literacy but must be conceptualised as being part of the overarching concept of disciplinary literacy.

In her book *Mathematical Mindsets*, Jo Boaler quotes a TED Talk by Conrad Wolfram to propose four central aspects of mathematical literacy (Boaler, 2016, p. 26):

1. posing a question;
2. going from real world to a mathematical model;
3. performing a calculation; and
4. going from the model back to the real world, to see if the original question was answered.

According to Wolfram, 80% of school mathematics time is spent on calculating. However, as Boaler points out, employers don't need workers to calculate because this operation can easily be done digitally. What employers need instead, is 'people who can ask good questions, set up models, analyse results, and interpret mathematical answers. [...] What they need is people to think and reason' (Boaler, 2016, p. 27).

The idea that disciplinary thinking can significantly impact people's lives is also prominent in the way that disciplinary literacy is framed in geography. Geographic literacy or geo-literacy focusses on preparing citizens to help them make geographic decisions in their daily lives, such as:

> where to live and work, how to transport themselves, what to buy and how to dispose of it, how to prepare for natural disasters, whether to go to war abroad, where to locate a store or factory, or how to market goods abroad. (Edelson, 2009)

In order to make these decisions, people need to be able to use geographic thinking, such as tracing causes forwards or backwards across space or analysing spatial relationships to predict or explain certain spatial developments (Edelson, 2009).

Geographic literacy evolves from 'doing geography', which includes geographic inquiry, geographic fieldwork and presenting findings in a geographic report (Harte & Reitano, 2016):

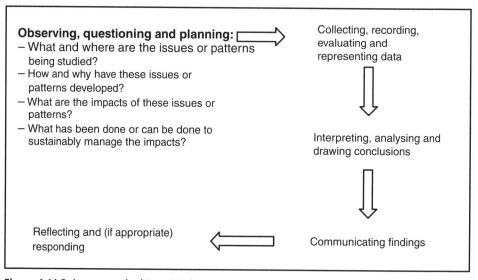

Figure 4.11 Doing geography (Harte & Reitano, 2016, p. 235)

Harte and Reitano's assertion that 'pivotal to geographic inquiry is developing students' procedural knowledge and conceptual understanding of geography' (2016, p. 233) brings us back full circle to our discussion of the core mechanics of deeper learning: in Section 4.2 we argued that conceptual understanding won't evolve without appropriate academic language use. Similarly, Scardamalia and Bereiter assert not only that 'progress of knowledge... is the progress of knowledge building discourse', but also that 'there is no advance of community knowledge apart from the discourse' (2006, p. 112).

We therefore propose that learning progressions in a subject or discipline should explicitly include and map the growing command of disciplinary discourse. In other words, progression in this sense will require an increasing capacity by learners to demonstrate their understanding, emerging from engaging in discipline-specific practices of inquiry – what Polias (2016) refers to as *doing* – and reflection. Yet in order to engage in those specific practices of inquiry, learners need to know how to draw on a developing and increasingly appropriate linguistic repertoire. The question of how subject-specific literacy learning can be promoted in school has been addressed by several scholars, including Veel (1997), Martin and White (2005), Coffin (2006a, 2006b), Halliday and Matthiessen (2004), Martin and Rose (2008) and Llinares et al. (2012). We find Polias's (2016) work, which he developed for science, very helpful. He suggests there are four major activity domains. These are as follows:

1. 'doing science';
2. 'organising science;
3. 'explaining science'; and
4. 'arguing/challenging science'.

Each of these activity domains has a number of corresponding text types, or genres, which students need to master in order to become literate in science. Polias defines genre as a:

> culturally determined way of getting things done, with patterns that can be predicted, to varying degrees, by members of a particular culture. It is a social activity that has a purpose, is enacted trough stages and is realised through language. In terms of the school subjects, the genres are the 'practices' (actions combined with visual and verbal texts) that the teachers and students engage in. It is because these practices have predictable patterns that they can be learned in everyday life and taught in the classroom (Polias, 2006, p. 49).

Table 4.2 (Polias, 2016) demonstrates how those genres and their purposes relate to the scientific processes of constructing knowledge and meaning-making. Mapped out in this way, processes, genres and purposes provide accessible and meaningful guidance for educators, which can also be constructed for any subject discipline.

As shown above, when the subject-specific activities (processes) in which learners engage are tied to specific genres which define the *purpose* of those activities, then it could be argued that genres permeate all subjects of schooling (see Figure 4.12). Since mastering those genres is fundamental for learners to advance their understanding, we propose that genres should be used as one central guiding principle to map subject-specific literacies progressions. Learners demonstrate their learning through their mastery of genres and the learning outcomes they produce in the

Table 4.2 Scientific processes, genres and purposes (based on Polias, 2016)

Scientific processes	Genres	Purposes
Doing things scientifically	Experiments & protocols Laboratory reports Investigations	Instruct someone how to do things Provide a recount of the method, as well as the results, discussions and conclusions. Set out the design and decisions behind students' attempts to behave scientifically
Describing & organising the world scientifically	Descriptions Comparisons Compositions Classifications	Describe multiple aspects/features of a natural or physical phenomenon Compare features two or more physical phenomena Present (describe and/or define) Present different types/classes of a phenomenon
Explaining phenomena scientifically	Temporal explanations (e.g. sequential explanations) Non-temporal explanations (e.g. factorial/consequential explanations, theoretical explanations)	Explain physical phenomena by presenting the events producing the phenomena in chronological order Explain the multiple factors/consequences that contribute to a particular event or phenomenon Define and illustrate a theoretical principle
Arguing scientifically	Arguments Discussions	Persuade to agree with a particular point of view on an issue and sometimes exhort the reader/listener to take action Present the case for more than one point of view

course of complex tasks. Enabling and encouraging learners to explore and master the various genres and genre moves of a subject is fundamental therefore to learning progression. The implications are far reaching: each subject discipline has to prioritise which genres will be the focus of specific tasks and activities to enable learners to become better at engaging, informing and evaluating subject-specific content. Moreover, what is meant by tasks also needs unravelling. In this sense, we use 'tasks' not as exercises typical of published textbooks and worksheets, but as complex learning activities which often require learners to produce subject-specific text types or genres. Tasks may also consist of a series of genre moves which are the building blocks of individual genres. Research suggests, however, that making genres explicit through task design rarely features in current practice (Llinares et al., 2012).

4.5.2 Mastering the Language of Schooling: More than 'Just' Genres

Learning the language of a subject is not 'merely' a question of mastering subject-specific skills/procedures and ways of inquiry. Nor is it only broadening a learner's repertoire of a growing number of genres to reflect and language

Figure 4.12 Taxonomy of major genres learners need to control for success in secondary school (Rose & Martin, 2012)

growing understanding. According to Martin (1992), such progress needs to be accompanied by a shift in the knowledge path from the 'grammar of speaking' to the 'grammar of writing'. This idea is expanded by the concept of a *mode continuum*, which features 'language as action' or 'causal conversation' at one end of the language continuum and 'language as reflection' or 'planned written monologue' at the other.

Janet Freeman shows how this idea can be put into practice by documenting how some of her students moved along the mode continuum in the course of a complex learning task about pendulum swings (Freeman, 2012):

1. **Unplanned reflection**

Craig: We got the… made the… pendulum thing… that had a bit of a… on… a… just of bit of string and a bit of plasticine… and to tie that on and sort of… then we made a…

Jackie: …stuck it to the desk…

Craig: ...to the desk and then we had to put it up higher because it was too long and it would've hit the ground so we put the books under the desk and then we had trouble... um... because it wouldn't work properly and we kept making the string longer and we... um... we got about fifty-eight centimetres... no... fifty-eight seconds... and sixty things... but we never got it exact... the right amount.

2. **Planned oral presentation**

Paula: We had to make a pendulum that would swing sixty times in a minute. First we got a string, some plasticine and a stopwatch... and a ruler. There were two ways we tried to measure the pendulum – first by changing the length of the string and secondly by changing the amount of plasticine... the weight. When the string was seventy-five centimetres long it took fifty-seven seconds to get sixty swings. Then we kept repeating the experiment and changing the length and the weight, but we couldn't get the velocity exact. We think that the longer the string is the longer time it takes.

3. **Written explanation**

'Our conclusion...'

A pendulum consists of a weight suspended on a string, rod or wire. When the weight is moved and let go, the pendulum will swing back and forth in a regular motion. The frequency of the pendulum swing depends on the length of the string or wire. The shorter the wire, the greater the frequency or how fast it goes back and forth. If you know the length of the pendulum, you can work out its frequency.

This example shows that learners can only advance in a subject if there is a dual focus on the processes involved in knowledge construction and knowledge communication. Learners' increase in skills and understanding must be accompanied by a growing ability to reflect on their learning and to express their understanding adequately (with regard to purpose and audience) in both colloquial and increasingly academic language. To do that, learners need to understand and actively navigate the difference between colloquial and academic language in terms of how information is packed and presented, and how interpersonal and textual meaning is established (see Table 4.3):

Table 4.3   The four meaning dimensions and their linguistic features (adapted from Persson et al., 2016)

Colloquial language	Meaning dimension	Scientific language
◀		▶
Loose	**Packing** How densely is content information packed into a text?	*Dense* - Use of nouns, nominalisations and long words
Low - *Use of everyday, high frequency words*	**Precision** Degree of precision in the utterance	*High* - Use of 'precifiers': modifiers (adjectives, adverbs and participles) and amounts - Technical/academic language
Personal, subjective - Use of pronouns (especially first person 'I') and personal names	**Personification** Level of personification/objectiveness in the text	*Abstract, objective* - Use of abstractions
Plain - Paratactical structure - Active voice	**Presentation** How is the information presented and structured?	*Complex* - Use of subordinate clauses and passives, connectives

Progress along the knowledge pathway must therefore be mirrored in the quality of the learners' use and control of the language of schooling. As has already been discussed, progress is manifested through genre moves manifest in the:

1. breadth of obligatory and optional genre moves (building blocks/components of genres);
2. depth of content information ('conceptual complexity') provided in each of these genre moves; and
3. quality of language use at the discourse, sentence and lexico-grammatical level in line with genre conventions (based on Byrnes, H. 2002 as cited in Mohan et al., 2010, p. 222).

Solomon (1983) proposed that an efficient way to boost subject literacy is to empower learners to 'move' back and forth along the continuum, switching from scientific to colloquial language and vice versa, thus moving from embedded to disembedded modes of thinking to deepen their understanding.

The deepest levels of understanding are achieved neither in the abstract heights of 'pure' science, nor by a struggle to eliminate the inexact structures of social communication, but by the fluency and discrimination with which we learn to move between these two contrasting domains of knowledge (Solomon, 1983, p. 58).

However, as Blown and Bryce (2017) point out, this switching between different registers or repertoires does not have to be symmetrical:

> Crossing back and forwards between everyday and scientific language (a 'switching' of different repertoires) is not symmetrical. Teachers, for example, may well challenge pupils orally using ordinary language or set out science questions in familiar contexts, thereby encouraging pupils to resort to their familiar ways of thinking. Crossing back to the symbolic world can be very challenging, as observant teachers know. Nevertheless, with greater confidence, learners can consolidate their use of scientific expressions and endeavour to use them in increasingly less familiar contexts. van Oers (1998) has argued that we do not simply learn to 'dis-embed' ideas, we actually learn to recontextualize our past notions and this is a progressive, iterative process. (Blown & Bryce, 2017, p. 623).

As mentioned before, subject-specific discourses are multimodal, with knowledge representations not being confined to written texts but including non-verbal, visual and audio material, graphic or symbolic representations, and actions (Leisen, 2005; Martin & Rose, 2008; Unsworth, 2004). That is why Hallet (2012) considers developing skills for demonstrating meaning within and across languages – what he terms semiotisation – fundamental to the acquisition of subject-specific literacies:

> Literacy learning in the content classroom is therefore connected with the integration of subject-specific semiotisations into the learner's everyday knowledge, into their active use in subject-specific discourses and in their subject-related everyday discourse.
>
> In the case of CLIL, 'literacy' also entails the capacity to describe and explain symbolic representations and forms (like, e.g. a curve diagram or a map) in a second or a foreign language, in the main language of instruction and/or in one's native language. The latter elements of subject-specific literacies obviously also require mediational competences, or skills that allow learners to translate content matter from and between all the different languages that are involved in literacy learning in a content subject. (Hallet, 2012, p. 196)

Therefore, semiotic 'translation', or conversion, is a key principle of PTDL tasks or deeper learning episodes (see Chapter 8). This is because such tasks provide learners with opportunities to communicate knowledge across registers, modes, languages and cultures, thus helping them become pluriliterate. The figure below presents a visual model of an expanded mode continuum, which plots plurimodal and pluriliterate moves from concrete communication and actions along to more abstract reflexive ones (Figure 4.13).

By extension, such tasks could be 'linguistically upgraded' or redesigned to invite and include the use of learners' home languages. For example, learners could

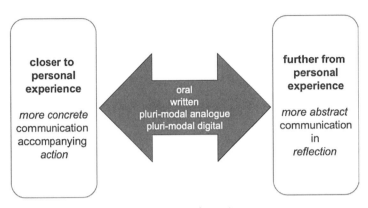

Figure 4.13 Towards a more inclusive mode continuum

be asked to report how specific events are discussed in their countries of origin by summarising (mediating) newspaper articles, podcasts, diagrams, maps and so on in the language of schooling. This would offer several advantages:

1. The use of home languages would allow learners to tap into their L1 conceptual knowledge base.
2. It offers a practical way of advertising and utilising linguistic diversity by way of serving a healthy linguistic diet (Bak & Mehmedbegovic, 2017) in our classrooms.
3. It could inform a principled approach to meaningfully using the concept of translanguaging in subject teaching and learning. From a pluriliteracies perspective, translanguaging might be reconceptualised as a discipline-based, plurimodal activity to *language subject understanding* adequately across the full linguistic and cultural repertoire of learners.

4.5.3   Summing Up

Disciplinary literacies evolve around the big ideas or core constructs of a given discipline. Progress is not linear but multi-dimensional and multi-directional. It involves disciplinary thinking, discipline-specific ways of inquiry, typical forms of representing information and specific text types or genres as ways to adequately share information. This is neatly captured in Polias' notion of the four activity domains of 'doing, organising, explaining and arguing' in school subjects, coupled with the idea that these activity domains have corresponding genres used to communicate the results of those subject-specific activities. We argue that it is this combination of conceptualising as communicating reflected action that informs disciplinary meaning making.

   In the next section, we will introduce the Pluriliteracies Model of Deeper Learning to show how we conceptualise learning progressions in the disciplines through developing learner meaning-making potential along knowledge pathways into disciplines.

4.6   Visualising Deeper Learning

Now that the key underlying principles of the model have been presented, we can start the process of building the Pluriliteracies Teaching for Deeper Learning model in its entirety. To begin with, we will focus on two key dimensions of meaning making: knowledge construction and knowledge communication. Visualising the interconnectivity of these two dimensions involves not only listing the key components of successful knowledge construction and knowledge sharing but also envisioning a pedagogic space where meaning making can occur – visually represented below as two continua:

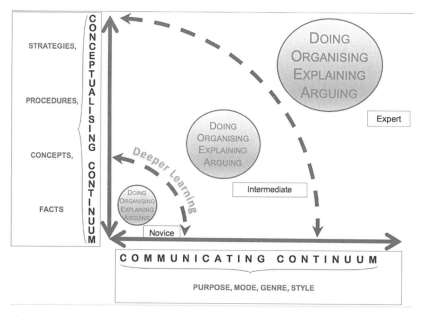

Figure 4.14 Connecting two axes of the PTDL model (Graz Group, 2015)

The PTDL model details how meaning-making potential can be systematically built and increased within that pedagogic space to help learners advance from literacies novices to literacies experts. Accordingly, progress in pluriliteracies encompasses an increase in conceptual understanding of content knowledge as well as a growing command of subject-specific procedures, skills and strategies. These two continua, represented as two axes in the visual above, are required to develop deeper conceptual understanding of the specific contents of a subject as a result of engaging in the specific major activity domains integral to that subject (doing, organising, explaining & arguing).

Since learning cannot be separated from language, progress manifests itself in the learner's ability to communicate knowledge and demonstrate understanding purposefully. This understanding becomes visible in:

1. the growing command of subject-specific text types and genres; and
2. the ability to critically evaluate and extract information from increasingly complex texts in all relevant modes.

In line with what we established in the first section of this chapter, progression in pluriliteracies development manifests itself in the quality of language used by individuals at a number of levels (discourse, sentence, lexico-grammatical) aligned with the genre conventions of specific subjects. It shows in the breadth of obligatory and optional genre moves and the depth of conceptual understanding expressed in those moves.

However, as referred to previously, the issue of linearity and progression remains. It is very important to take into account that progression does not mean that students move from colloquial language to academic language *in a linear way*. Our research does not support the understanding of a dichotomous relationship between colloquial or academic language, or BICS and CALP. We believe the relationship between everyday language and the language of schooling (consisting of subject-specific and generic academic elements) to be far more dynamic and complex than we previously thought.

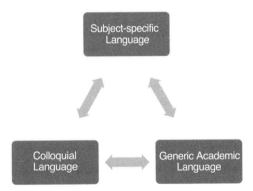

Figure 4.15 Components of language of schooling

This complexity is outlined below:

- We conceptualise academic language or language of schooling as consisting of *both* subject-specific and generic language elements.
- Academic language offers learners ways to abstract complex ideas, whereas the use of colloquial language is ideal for expressing content and negotiating meaning in highly accessible and more concrete ways.

- Progression includes growing command of subject-specific modes (charts, maps, tables, formulas, drawings, etc.) in both analogue and digital as well as hybrid or plurimodal forms.
- Pluriliteracies progression involves a growing awareness of disciplinary cultures that are a prerequisite to successfully communicating knowledge across subjects, cultures and languages.
- Learner progression entails the learner's growing ability to critically reflect and thus self-direct his/her own learning process.

Before we discuss ways of designing learning environments for pluriliteracies progressions, we will explore the inner workings of meaning making – more specifically, the interface of knowledge construction and knowledge communication.

4.7   Cognitive Discourse Functions: Keys to Deeper Learning

As Figure 4.14 demonstrates, there is a curved line linking the two continua of communication and conceptualisation, labelled 'deeper learning'. Throughout the previous section, there has been in-depth discussion about the nature and mechanics of deeper learning. Meaning making is fundamental to that process. Inside the 'engine room' of meaning making lie essential building blocks of cognitive structure and concept formation. These are called cognitive discourse functions (CDFs), and in the following section we will exemplify in greater detail what exactly they are. CDFs have a dual role in meaning making which is highly conducive to promoting deeper understanding and command of subject-specific discourse/language of schooling.

We suggest that CDFs play an essential role in deeper learning for a number of reasons, which are outlined below and discussed in depth throughout this section.

- CDFs are essential tools for integrating the conceptual and communicative dimensions of learning.
- CDFs enable teachers to design lessons which are more output-oriented and which focus on making learning visible.
- Crucially, CDFs function as building blocks for larger text types or genres. Understanding how CDFs can be adapted to verbalise cognitive patterns of varying conceptual complexity guides teachers in differentiating subject-specific instruction for deeper learning by aligning disciplinary demands with learners' strengths and needs.

4.7.1   Understanding Cognitive Discourse Functions

Operating at the interface between thinking and language, CDFs serve as linguistic representations of cognitive learning goals. They have been defined as patterns which develop through specific contextual demands for the purposes of communicating in recurrent ways (Dalton-Puffer, 2007, p. 202). Dalton-Puffer later details those patterns as follows:

> [T]hey are patterns which have arisen from the demand that participants within the institution school orient towards explicit or implicit learning goals and the fact that they have the repeated need for communicating about ways of handling and acting upon curricular content, concepts, and facts (cf. cognitive process dimension of Anderson et al., 2001). It is their very nature to provide speakers with schemata (discoursal, lexical and grammatical) for coping with standard situations in dealing with the task of building knowledge and making it intersubjectively accessible. (Dalton Puffer, 2014, p. 231)

Dalton-Puffer's construct of CDFs consists of seven elements which can each be conceived as a category comprising several 'members' that differ both in size and scope (Table 4.4).

Table 4.4 A construct of CDF types, intentions and members (based on Dalton-Puffer, 2013)

CDF Type	Label	Communicative Intention	Members
1	*Classify*	I tell you how we can cut up the world according to certain ideas.	Classify, compare, contrast, match, structure, categorise, subsume
2	*Define*	I tell you about the extension of this object of specialist knowledge.	Define, identify, characterise
3	*Describe*	I tell you details of what can be seen (including metaphorically).	Describe, label, identify, name, specify
4	*Evaluate*	I tell you what my position is vis a vis X.	Evaluate, judge, argue, justify, take a stance, critique, recommend, comment, reflect, appreciate
5	*Explain*	I give you a reason for and tell you the cause of X.	Explain, reason, express cause/effect, draw conclusions, deduce
6	*Explore*	I tell you something that is potential.	Explore, hypothesise, speculate, predict, guess, estimate, simulate, take other perspectives
7	*Report*	I tell you about something external to our immediate context on which I have a legitimate knowledge claim.	Report, inform, recount, narrate, present, summarise, relate

CDFs, therefore, are an indispensable tool for designing tasks for deeper learning because they offer ways of *integrating both the conceptual as well as the communicative dimension of learning*. CDFs can be used to specify the cognitive operations which learners have to perform in order to understand content through the process of languaging – for instance:

> *Define the term 'subprime mortgage'.*
> *Name the causes that led to the financial crisis of 2008.*
> *Explain its effects on the global economy.*
> *Evaluate different approaches to mitigate these effects.*

Being able to properly define a term such as 'subprime mortgage', for example, clearly requires an understanding of the concept as well as the ability to express that understanding adequately. Naming and explaining invites learners to find *and* connect the dots whilst 'evaluating' requests for a critical review of the strategies and measures employed to curb the effects of the financial crisis. It could, of course, be argued that this is what already happens in classrooms, where learners are often asked to describe, explain, define or evaluate by teachers who have been working with Bloom's taxonomy for decades. So, what is different here?

First, in most classrooms we observed, more emphasis is placed on the teachers using these CDFs in their instructions than on the learners' actual use and mastery of them. But deeper learning cannot be achieved without *learners*' appropriate use of CDFs. Our learners need to perform those cognitive-linguistic operations in order to build and internalise conceptual knowledge (see Section 4.2). That is why teachers' use of CDFs is of secondary importance. Ensuring learners can master the use of CDFs (in increasing complexity) is dependent on teachers providing scaffolding and practice activities to promote understanding (via the process of internalisation) and skill development (through the process of automatisation). This will reap dividends because teachers will be presented with valuable opportunities to formatively assess the level of understanding of their students. Closely listening to the extent to which students are able to language their understanding makes learning visible and reveals their level of understanding (in terms of conceptual breadth and depth). This is why an explicit focus on CDFs is an essential step in moving from an input- to a more output-oriented curriculum.

Second, we argue that there is a subject-specific dimension to CDFs. Arguing history is different from arguing geography or math. Raising learners' awareness of these specificities is key to becoming pluriliterate. Third, contrary to common thinking and practice, we believe it is misleading and not very helpful to think of one CDF being more 'difficult' than another. Whilst 'evaluating' might theoretically be a more cognitively complex operation than 'explaining' or 'describing', we find it more useful to think of these individual operations as co-dependent and interrelated: if the process of gathering information (doing) is partial or inaccurate it will negatively affect how that information will be 'organised' (describing, label-ling, categorising). This in turn will distort our learners' explanations and, conse-quently, their ability to argue their understanding. This is why in a deeper learning classroom, equal emphasis should be placed on the command of any CDF. The concepts presented in the following sections will offer a dynamic view of CDFs and a novel way of conceptualising their relationship.

4.7.2   Cognitive Discourse Functions and How They Relate to Genres

According to Coffin & Donohue, genres vary in size. A complex text type like a lab report can be thought of as a macro-genre, because it consists of several small building blocks or micro-genres such as *hypothesis*, *explanation* and *definition*. In that sense, CDFs function as 'micro genres', which can stand alone or can be com-bined into the larger genres typically used in the various disciplines. The process that turns 'stand-alone' micro-genres into parts of larger genres is called 'embed-ding' (Coffin & Donohue, 2014, p. 53).

Practical example

*In a chemistry unit, learners might initially focus on **describing** the setup of an experiment and **hypothesise** about the outcome of their experiment, which will be conducted in the course of the next few lessons. After planning and conducting the actual experiment, they might move on to focus on **reporting** and **explaining** their findings before subsequently using their data to formu-late a **definition** and embed those micro-genres into a larger one by writing a lab-report.*

This example illustrates how the principles of *deep practice* (see Section 4.2) can be implemented in real-life classroom situations: larger text types or macro genres can be broken down into smaller parts or micro-genres, which can then then be 'chunked up' and practised over the course of time before being put together again to form the whole genre.

4.7.3   CDFs as Keys for Differentiated Learning: Up- and Downscaling Cognitive-Linguistic Complexity

Conceptualising CDFs as both internal building blocks of cognitive structures as well as functional building blocks of subject-specific genres enables teachers to match the conceptual complexity of their subject content with the individual needs and strengths of their learners. This is because such a dual view of CDFs allows us to adjust both the cognitive structure of the content as well as the language used to express and demonstrate understanding. Since this is such a fundamental concept, we would like to further elaborate by demonstrating how this idea can be used to up- or downscale the CDF 'explain' to better match the needs of individual learners. Polias (2016) distinguishes three basic types of explanations:

1. **Temporal Explanations:** Sequential explanations do not have a causal structure. Instead they merely represent the temporal sequence of certain events.

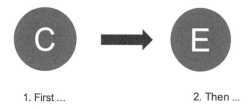

1. First ...   2. Then ...

Figure 4.16 Structure of a temporal explanation

2. **Causal Explanations:** Explanations that are oriented to the causes or factors responsible for a phenomenon are called *factorial explanations*, whilst texts oriented to the effects or consequences of a phenomenon are called *consequential explanations*. Both types of explanations can be mono- or multi-causal:

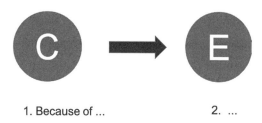

1. Because of ...   2. ...

Figure 4.17 Structure of a mono-causal explanation

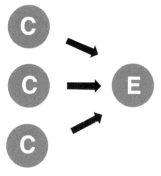

Figure 4.18 Structure of a multi-causal explanation

3. **Theoretical Explanations:** According to Polias, *theoretical explanations* are similar in structure to factorial and consequential explanations, but their purpose is to illustrate a theoretical law or principle. (Polias, 2016, pp. 33–42)

This typology has greatly influenced and expanded our understanding of cognitive discourse functions. Rather than seeing CDFs as static and one-dimensional constructs, we can now conceptualise them as dynamic and multi-dimensional constructs. This way, it becomes possible for teachers to adapt the conceptual complexity of a topic by up- or downscaling the cognitive pattern used to explain the underlying phenomena. For example, in a lesson for younger learners, teachers can resort to simple temporal or mono-causal patterns to explain a certain phenomenon. In fact, for novice learners, it may be enough to understand the main cause leading to the eruption of a volcano or the outbreak of a war. Advanced learners, however, may need to develop a more sophisticated understanding of the world and come to terms with the fact that very often phenomena are multi- rather than mono-causal or -consequential. In that case, teachers can revert to a more complex pattern.

Highlighting the underlying cognitive pattern allows teachers and learners to visualise the causal structure of a phenomenon (i.e. simple causal or multi-causal). This is an important first step in helping learners understand a new phenomenon. Next, learners could be shown how to language the way that different causes and their effects are linked in order to generate and formulate their own explanations. They may start using colloquial language. In that case, teachers might ask their students to move along the mode continuum and convert their colloquial explanations into scientific ones by deliberately changing the way that information is packed and presented to make it more precise and less personal:

1. First, the air is getting warmer, then it rises. Clouds will form and, eventually, rain will fall.
2. In the tropics, air rises in the atmosphere because the warm sunlight makes it expand and causes it to lose pressure. The air then rises and cools off, clouds form and it starts to rain.
3. The intensity of solar radiation causes equatorial air masses to warm and rise. Condensation causes cloud formation and brings about precipitation.

This example illustrates the benefits of applying a functional view of language in the subject classroom: teaching learners how to language cause-effect relations will not only help learners become better at explaining, but first and foremost it will teach them to understand the underlying structure of a given phenomenon. Increased meaning making potential results from deeper understanding *and* the ability to express that understanding adequately. Working on the language *of* and *for* learning is essential to knowledge construction. Developing appropriate and increasingly more nuanced use of CDFs according to challenging tasks demands, and languaging this learning, is language *through* learning (see the Language Triptych in Chapter 2).

Research data shows that such an explicit focus on explanations has significant effects on both the development of academic language and the conceptual understanding of learners (Connolly, 2019; Berg, 2020), all of which promote deeper learning. These data support our claim that the idea of up- or downscaling applies to all seven types of CDFs (see Table 4.4).

Combining this idea with the concept of 'embedding' (see p. 96) allows us to transfer the idea of up- or downscaling from CDFs or micro-genres to more complex text types or macro-genres: in our Lego model (Figure 4.19), which we have developed for teacher professional learning courses to visualise these very abstract notions, this idea is analogous to moving from Duplo to Lego to Technic, or vice versa:

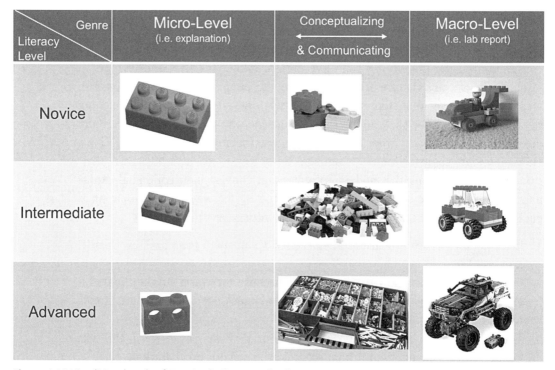

Figure 4.19 Visualising the role of CDFs in pluriliteracies development

Practical examples

Chemistry: *In the chemistry unit outlined previously, the teacher can employ this idea to upscale or downscale the conceptual complexity of the new phenomenon (i.e. redox reactions) and thus increase or decrease the level of difficulty, by:*

- *decreasing or increasing the complexity or difficulty of the experiment;*
- *providing simpler or more sophisticated patterns for the CDFs that make up the lab report;*

- teaching learners simpler or increasingly sophisticated ways of languaging those patterns or enabling them to move from a simple pattern to a sophisticated one;
- raising or lowering the stylistic demands of the genre (i.e. in terms of the use of key terminology, nominalisations, use of the passive voice, linking of paragraphs etc.); and
- decreasing or increasing the difficulty of summative assessment tasks that require the transfer of knowledge.

History: A teacher can deepen a learner's understanding of the causes of World War II by helping the learner move from a sequential explanation pattern to a simple causal pattern, or from a simple causal pattern to a complex causal one, while providing the linguistic scaffolding (chunks in forms of phrases, speaking/writing frames etc.) to express that understanding appropriately.

4.7.4   Summing Up

Cognitive Discourse Functions are fundamental building blocks of deeper learning because they lie at the interface between knowledge construction and knowledge communication. Depending on context, they can stand alone (as micro-genres) or be embedded in larger text types, or macro-genres. A dynamic and multi-dimensional view of CDFs allows teachers to design highly individualised learning experiences by way of adjusting both the cognitive pattern underlying the phenomenon as well as the language used by the students to express content understanding.

This chapter has traced the development of deeper learning and emphasised the mechanics of deeper learning, its cognitive demands and the inherent trajectories for learning progressions. Now it is appropriate to analyse the roles of those who make learning happen – the learners and teachers, those who matter and who validate any model of learning. The next two chapters, therefore, will take a hard look at how the *drivers* of deeper learning impact on learners and the nature of mentoring learning required to activate those drivers within an ecological framework.

5 | Drivers of Deeper Learning

Whilst the theoretical underpinning and rationale for deeper learning presented and discussed in Chapter 4 is based on current thinking and research by academics and educators, its interpretation, application and actual implementation is challenging. Understanding the *mechanisms of deeper learning* is one thing. Generating and sustaining learner commitment and achievement is another.

It is therefore fundamental and timely to consider the impact of the so-called non-cognitive factors (Dweck et al., 2014) on long-term learning and achievement, and how to harness them. In this chapter, we will introduce the *drivers of deeper learning*, arguing that deeper learning will occur only if students embrace a deeper learning mindset, which in turn will help them develop academic tenacity, including the ability to work consistently and persistently over a sustained period of time, to engage in and complete challenging tasks, to successfully interact with their peers and to increasingly self-regulate their learning.

This is, of course, also the case for educators: adopting a pluriliteracies pedagogic approach to enhance deeper learning means that we will have to develop the mindset and skills that will allow us to turn classrooms into deeper learning ecologies, where mentors and mentees form 'learning partnerships'. Learning partnerships are built on ways of transparently enabling learners and teachers to engage in the process of constructing and communicating knowledge 'that go beyond the information given and shape unique episodes of knowledge productive interaction' (Tillema et al., 2015, p. 16) and personal growth.

This leads us to introduce the revised Pluriliteracies Teaching for Deeper Learning (PTDL) model, which postulates that deeper learning rests on three pillars:

- **The mechanics of deeper learning:** Building knowledge and refining skills for demonstrating understanding via the cognitive processes of internalisation and automatisation.
- **Trajectories for deeper learning:** Pluriliteracies development through knowledge pathways.
- **The drivers of deeper learning:** Generating and sustaining commitment and achievement and mentoring learning and personal growth that create an environment conducive to deeper learning.

The model stresses that pluriliteracies development will only take off and can only be sustained when all of the four dimensions of the model are continuously integrated and active (Figure 5.1). This is, in essence, our approach to embracing a holistic view of teaching and learning.

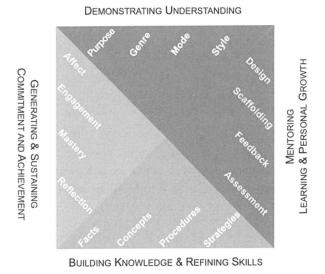

DEMONSTRATING UNDERSTANDING

BUILDING KNOWLEDGE & REFINING SKILLS

Figure 5.1 The revised Pluriliteracies Model for Deeper Learning

Our revised model captures the intricate, complex and dynamic relationships between the mechanics and the drivers that together successfully guide learners through the knowledge pathways when all four dimensions are working together. The model shows that we need to move away from a linear analysis of teaching as a unidirectional, intentional act by teachers to learners. Instead, we promote the genuine co-construction of knowledge and the joint negotiation of learning goals and processes in learning partnerships. We acknowledge the impact that this might have on the way learning and teaching evolves in classrooms, and explore not only how the drivers for deeper learning develop but also the impact this has on designing classroom learning.

Throughout the volume, we have referred to using an ecological lens through which deeper learning is conceptualised and developed. Indeed, the concept of dynamic learning communities which are often described as adopting an 'ecological approach' is commonplace in educational literature. Yet there is little in terms of what learning ecologies actually represent in reality – the construct is multi-faceted and open to wide interpretation. Van Lier (2004, p. 93) positions learning ecologies as 'the ability to adapt to one's environment in increasingly effective and successful ways'. This aligns with Jackson's (2019) definition that an individual's learning ecology comprises:

themselves, their environment, their interactions with their environment and the learning, development and achievement that emerges from these interactions. It includes the spaces they create for themselves, their processes and activities and practices, their relationships, networks, tools and other mediating artefacts and the technologies they use, and it provides them with affordances, information, knowledge and other resources for learning, developing and achieving something that they value. (Jackson, 2019, p. 72)

Van Lier argues that at classroom level, learning ecologies can awaken in learners (and educators) a 'spirit of inquiry and reflection, and a philosophy of seeing and hearing for yourself, thinking for yourself, speaking with your own voice, and acting jointly within your community' Van Lier (2011, p. 99). We argue, therefore, that learning ecologies lie at the core of co-constructing values-driven, inclusive and socially just, dynamic classroom spaces which support individuals to feel valued and have a sense of achievement in what they do. Whilst for many educators such ideals are familiar, ways in which these might be practised in transparent and tangible ways remain challenging in the daily business of classroom learning.

This is why the PTDL approach had to explore how individual learners can be better encouraged to accept responsibility for their own learning through being supported, encouraged, curious and challenged. The design of the model is predicated on designing deeper learning episodes (see Chapter 8) within deeper learning ecologies where mentors and mentees are engaged in the processes of constructing and communicating knowledges. By adding a mentoring dimension, which counterbalances the affective dimension, we sought to arrive at a genuinely integrated model of teaching and learning.

This chapter is about the learner. Given the dimension described in the model as 'learner commitment and achievement', we focus on unravelling learner mindset and affective factors for generating and sustaining commitment and achievement. As indicated on the PTDL model, we emphasise four key areas: affect (well-being, learner mindset, motivation and commitment, and teacher mindset); student engagement and strategies to boost engagement; mastery; and reflection. These key areas will now be analysed.

5.1   Affect

Learning and teaching objectives at the classroom level often focus on defined learning outcomes (i.e. factual and conceptual understanding, skills and strategies), without necessarily making transparent affective goals, such as those for learner beliefs and mindsets, self-efficacy, motivation and well-being. Yet, as is emphasised by Pellegrino and Hilton, affective outcomes are increasingly pertinent for deeper learning since 'intellectual openness, work ethic and conscientiousness, and positive core self-evaluation' (National Resource Council, 2012, p. 4) impact individual learning. Whilst it is generally accepted and understood how affective or non-cognitive factors affect learning, we argue that unless the affective domain is directly and transparently linked to knowledge progression by cultivating appropriate conditions for learning within an integrated model of teaching and learning, its full impact will not be realised.

In other words, for deeper learning to be successful, it needs to be situated within learning ecologies – classroom environments – which connect desired learning outcomes and literacy development with the individual needs, strengths and interests of an increasingly heterogeneous student body 'to support a safe, engaging learning climate where students can take risks, make mistakes and drive their own learning' (Parsi, 2015).

5.1.1 Well-Being

As has been repeated throughout these chapters, learning is not only a matter of cognitive development but also of shared social practices. The effect of the learning environment on learner achievement is well documented, with increasing emphasis placed on actively 'igniting' physical behavioural, emotional and cognitive engagement (Ning & Downing, 2012).

Student well-being is a multi-faceted construct that is larger than academic achievement alone. It is composed of physical, affective, cognitive, economic and social domains and can be defined as 'a student's perception of their quality of life, success, and life satisfaction' (Nelson et. al., 2015, p. 21).

There is growing evidence that school-related well-being impacts students' learning and health (Konu & Lintonen, 2006; Suhrcke & de Paz Nieves, 2011, OECD/PISA 2015, 2017). The effect of well-being on cognitive performance is also supported by Morcom (2015), who holds that caring relationships are a prerequisite for working effectively and that a teacher's role is to create shared affective spaces where such relationships can grow. Renshaw (2013) speaks of the affective dimension as an 'enabling condition' for scaffolding to be effective. He argues that learning with and from others is as much about building relationships as it is about mastering a specific skill.

These arguments lead to sensitive issues, which are less prevalent in the integrated curriculum literature and challenge the realities of an inclusive classroom ethos. They concern the impact of an increasingly mobile demographic of classroom learners and the range of languages, cultures and creeds which emerges. They also concern the impact of individual differences in the classroom in terms of wealth, background and perceived abilities, which challenges 'bell-curved thinking' (Fender & Muzaffar, 2008).

Whilst these challenges, issues and dilemmas were discussed in Chapter 1, the point we make here is that there is a gap between acknowledging the 'new normal' and conflicting challenges of social justice, equality and fairness, and successfully transforming them into more inclusive classroom practices – especially given that in current pluriliteracies thinking and integrated learning contexts, the pedagogic discourse is limited. Research literature and professional advice on the 'multilingual turn', inclusion, differentiation and transformative teaching is significant and plentiful, but it has not been transparently incorporated into and widely disseminated within the CLIL community. According to Florian (2015, p. 16), inclusivity assumes that 'individual differences between learners do not have to be construed as problems inherent within learners'. She takes the view that knowledge develops through shared activity on the understanding that 'every learner is different'. Building on Florian's Inclusive Pedagogical Approach in Action (IPAA) Framework (Florian, 2014) and Scotland's National Framework for Languages: Plurilingualism and Pluriliteracies (Coyle et al., 2018), one way forward has evolved from extensive work in understanding how learning ecologies can address some of the inherent challenges. Rethinking learning partnerships constantly emerges as offering a tangible space for exploring ways of developing inclusive and emotionally safe practices. However, it must be emphasised that learning partnerships are not a 'solution' but rather dynamic opportunities for further thinking. Learning partnerships permeate the PTDL model. In sum, the fundamental importance of student well-being and emotional engagement and their relationship to deeper learning has not received much attention within the CLIL community. Consequently, methodology has primarily focused on knowledge construction and on developing cognitive, metacognitive and linguistic skills in learners. In constructing the PTDL approach we set out to specifically include the impact of the interrelationship between learners and teachers by focusing on two dimensions of the four-sided model, bringing them together in significant inclusive learning partnerships.

> Deep learning, enabled by technology, is an increasingly common phenomenon taking place inside and outside the classroom. In the new world, individuals have the freedom to learn any topic that interests them, at any time of the day. This changes the role of schools and creates opportunities to focus learning on projects and topics that inspire students. (Fullan & Langworthy, 2014)

5.1.2   Learner Mindset

Research by Carol Dweck and her colleagues makes evident how learner beliefs (i.e. learner mindset) influence behaviours that in turn impact academic achievement. Numerous studies indicate that learners do significantly better if they believe that their intellectual abilities and talents are not limited. This indicates what has become known as a *growth mindset*, as opposed to a fixed mindset, which is characterised by learners' beliefs that their abilities and talents cannot be changed (Dweck, 2006; Paunesku et al., 2015). A recent large-scale study conducted in

Chile reports that the relationship between mindset and academic performance holds true at every level of society on a national scale (see Figure 5.2). The data show that students with a growth mindset consistently outperform those with a fixed mindset (Claro et al., 2016) and establishes a causal link between mindset and academic achievement.

The study also documents a relationship between mindset and economic disadvantage, since learners from low-income families were far more likely to endorse a fixed mindset. These results stress the necessity to address the affective dimension of learning and suggest that helping students change their beliefs and mindsets about learning may be an effective way to combat academic underachievement and socioeconomic inequalities, and thus be an integral part of inclusive literacy programmes.

5.1.3   Mindset and Motivation

According to Self-Determination Theory (Deci & Ryan, 2000), students' willingness to invest in their own learning is driven by learner motivation and the degree to which the three basic, innate psychological needs are satisfied: the need to belong or feel connected, the need to feel competent, and the need for autonomy or self-determination.

In 2009, Pink added 'mastery' and 'purpose' as two additional dimensions of intrinsic motivation (Pink, 2009). Mastery is described as the pleasure learners derive from being engaged in exciting and challenging tasks. The sense of purpose, which has been identified as a notable feature of resilience, relates to commitment, meaning and the belief that one's activities are of benefit to others (Brooks et al., 2012).

According to Goldstein and Brooks (2007) there are five major characteristics of the mindset of motivated students:

1. Perceiving the teacher as supportive adult.
2. To believe that whether they learn as students is based in great part on their own motivation, perseverance and effort.
3. To recognize that making mistakes and not immediately comprehending certain concepts or material are expected features of the learning process.
4. To have a clear understanding of their learning strengths and learning vulnerabilities.
5. To treat classmates with respect and realizing that maintaining a caring, respectful classroom and school is the responsibility of each member of that classroom and school.

(Goldstein and Brooks, 2007 as cited in Brooks et al., 2012)

Again, such 'lists' are familiar to educators. However, what we are proposing is that unless all of these factors and their role in learning are made transparent for learners and integrated in learning environments, learners will not be made aware

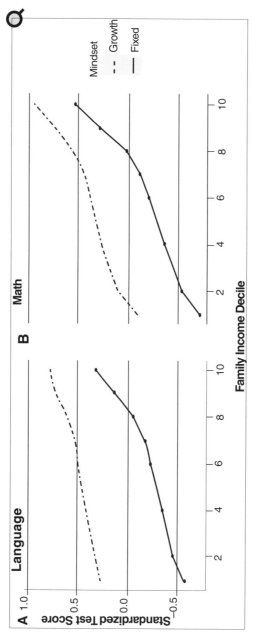

Figure 5.2 The correlation between family income and standardised test score in students with growth and fixed mindset

of how to take responsibility for their own learning or understand the importance of so doing. Without this, deeper learning as a holistic sustainable phenomenon will not happen. Claxton (2013) goes as far as to suggest that teaching which 'over-helps' students to 'get the grades they need but deprives them of opportunities to learn how to struggle productively on their own and with peers' (2013, p. 7) is likely to engender a lack of resilience and resourcefulness in students. We therefore turn to considering the teacher's role.

5.1.4　Teacher Mindsets

Student and teacher mindsets are closely linked: according to Brooks et al. (2012), the mindsets of teachers will shape their expectations, teaching, practices and relationships with students. Therefore, the more aware teachers are of these assumptions, the more they can change those beliefs that may work against a positive classroom environment.

> It is our belief that educators can nurture mindsets associated with increased motivation, engagement and resilience as a natural part of their classroom teaching practices. It is important to note that reinforcing social-emotional skills should not be perceived as an 'extra curriculum' that ciphers already limited time from teaching academic subject matter. In fact, our position is that the more secure and engaged students are, the more motivated they will be to meet academic requirements. (Brooks et al., 2012, p. 544)

Goldstein and Brooks identified teacher assumptions and beliefs that are most likely to motivation, engagement and resilience:

1. To appreciate that they have a lifelong impact on students, including on their sense of hope and resilience.
2. To believe that the level of motivation and learning that occurs in the classroom and the behaviour exhibited by students has as much, if not more, to do with the influence of teachers than what students might bring into the situation.
3. To believe that all students yearn to be successful, and if a student is not learning, educators must ask how they can adapt their teaching style and instructional material to meet student needs.
4. To believe that attending to the social-emotional needs of students is not an 'extra-curricular' option that draws time away from teaching academic subjects, but rather a significant feature of effective teaching that enriches learning.
5. To recognize that if educators are to relate effectively to students, they must be empathic, always attempting to perceive the world through the eyes of the student and considering the ways in which students view them.
6. To appreciate that the foundation for successful learning and a safe and secure classroom climate is the relationship that teachers forge with students.

7. To recognize that students will be more motivated to learn and more engaged in the classroom when they feel a sense of ownership or autonomy for their own education.
8. To understand that one of the main functions of an educator is to be a disciplinarian in the true sense of the word, namely, to perceive discipline as a teaching process rather than as a process of intimidation and humiliation. Disciplinary practices should reinforce self-discipline, which is a critical behaviour associated with resilience.
9. To realize that one of the greatest obstacles to learning is the fear of making mistakes and feeling embarrassed or humiliated and to take active steps to minimize this fear.
10. To subscribe to a strength-based model, which includes identifying and reinforcing each student's 'islands of competence.'
11. To develop and maintain positive, respectful relationships with colleagues and parents.

(Goldstein & Brooks 2007, as cited in Brooks et al., 2012, p. 550)

Of course, whilst such familiar lists provide 'all-encompassing' reminders, it is also easy to dismiss them as a given – yet they are rarely conceptualised in terms of being drivers for genuinely and transparently co-constructing deeper learning. Indeed, each one of the points above require in-depth analysis, discussion and perseverance by educators to translate them from being abstract goals to tangible contributors to ethos building for task design. These are in essence the foundations for learning partnerships. In other words, each of these in turn could become a single focus and, to be useful, would need to be transformed into inclusive practices.

5.2   Student Engagement

Why and how students become engaged in their learning is dependent on many dynamic factors. Significant literature on student motivation suggests it can be understood as the direction and intensity of one's energy, leading to certain behaviours. Student engagement, however, is not synonymous with motivation. Student engagement is a complex construct consisting of multiple dimensions, which together contribute to successful learning. Described as 'energy in action' and relating to the connection between a person and an activity, engagement reflects the degree of active involvement in a task or activity.

Wang et al. (2016) emphasise behavioural, social, affective and cognitive dimensions which are dynamically interrelated and lead to the development of specific habits and attitudes towards learning. Cognitive engagement refers to the amount and types of cognitive strategies that learners employ to process content. The strategies they choose directly impact the quality of the learning process (Lam et al., 2012; Sani & Hashim, 2016): *deeper learning rests on deep engagement*, which results from the use of strategies for deeper processing, which is associated with cognitive elaboration of content; shallow processing involves 'rote memorization, basic rehearsal, and other types of superficial engagement with the new material' (Lam et al., 2012, p. 405). Engagement involves student investment in their own learning, demonstrating perseverance and using positive approaches towards successful task completion, classrooms and schooling, as well as relationships with peers and teachers (Ulmanen et al., 2016).

Research on student engagement indicates that emotional engagement, which becomes apparent in the quality of the dynamic relationships or learning partnerships of learners with teachers and peers, impacts on cognitive engagement. Sustaining cognitive engagement, in turn, further increases behavioural engagement and may therefore lead to improved task performance (Pietarinen et al., 2014) and academic achievement. Emotional and cognitive engagement are both socially embedded. Engagement is thus highly dependent on the quality of interaction manifested in the daily pedagogic practices adopted by teachers.

Some research emphasises that the extent to which individuals are engaged in their learning depends on their understanding and effective use of instructional strategies (Shernoff et al., 2016; Ulmanen et al., 2016). Following this argument further elevates the fundamental role of strategy instruction by the teachers – it is thereby seen as critical, underlining its importance in professional development for teachers (see Chapter 4.1). For others, engagement is demonstrated by classroom behaviours and beyond-school educational or academic activities, such as following personal goals or making career choices (Wang & Degol, 2014; Wang et al., 2016).

5.2.1   Strategies to Boost Student Engagement

It's hard to over-emphasise the effect of student engagement on deeper learning. This is why it is crucial for teachers to specifically adopt strategies to generate and sustain engagement in their learners. The reason why we briefly introduced Self-Determination Theory previously is that it emphasises the role of various dimensions of the social context in enhancing or diminishing student engagement, and thus provides a useful framework to help teachers design learning environments that boost student engagement. A more recent 'multi-variant' study by Hospel and Galand (2016) further emphasises the significance of the relationship between the learning environment and learner engagement by focussing on two dimensions referred to as 'autonomy support and structure'. Whilst there is a vast literature on learner autonomy and learner strategies (Chamot & Harris, 2019; Plonsky, 2019), the crucial point re-emphasised by Hospel and Galand is the need to make transparent the interrelationship between environment and engagement (i.e. when the teacher provides structure to classroom learning it is positively associated with self-regulated learning and the encouragement of emotional engagement). They summarise *structure* as the amount and clarity of information given to students about *how* to meet expectations and achieve desired educational outcomes. The study evidences how the degree of structure impacts on learner behavioural engagement, cognitive engagement (self-regulated learning) and emotional engagement (positive attitudes and emotions). Teachers provide structure by communicating expectations and by providing guidance, optimal challenges and feedback. Hospel and Galand suggest that *autonomy support* is dependent on and integral to emotional engagement, defined by the degree of psychological freedom and choice teachers provide for students when determining their own behaviours. The pluriliteracies approach, however, makes a very clear distinction between teacher feedback and pedagogic discourse shared with learners, and individual learner encouragement. It is fundamental that teachers themselves make a clear distinction between mentoring learners and *mentoring learning.* As is well documented (see Little, n.d.; Prichard & Moore, 2016), teachers can support student autonomy by offering choice and rationales for mandatory activities, highlighting meaningful learning goals, presenting interesting activities, adopting students' perspectives and avoiding use of control (Hospel & Galand, 2016). However, the point we wish to reiterate is that, as educators, unless we find ways of bringing together both familiar and less familiar dimensions of learning, their impact on deeper learning will not realise its ultimate potential.

In Chapter 2, the importance and implications of 'curriculum making' by learners was discussed in detail, alongside Hood and Tobutt's (2016) emphasis on the need for learners to 'make learning their *own*' – that is, making learning personally relevant and meaningful. An interesting recent study (Priniski et al., 2018) introduced the concept of the *Relevance Continuum.* This framework is especially helpful in our context because it identifies the factors and variables that can help learners develop a sustained personal interest, which is an essential component for lifelong learning. Relevance is defined as a 'personally meaningful connection to the individual' (Priniski et al., 2018, p. 12). The authors describe the continuum as consisting of three types of relevance, as Figure 5.3 demonstrates.

Relevance Continuum

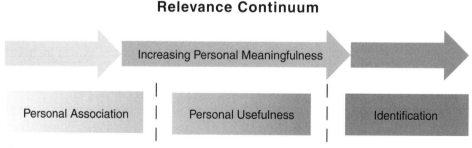

Figure 5.3 Relevance Continuum (adapted from Priniski et al., 2018)

Personal association is considered to be the least personally meaningful type of relevance. This is because the content is not perceived to be directly relevant, although the learner can associate it to a personal object or memory. *Personal usefulness* describes the perception that the content could be useful in fulfilling an important personal goal. *Identification* is the most personally meaningful type of relevance because at that stage the content is perceived to be part of the learner's identity.

Moreover, the Relevance Continuum reminds us again of the need to make transparent to learners the underlying nature of what they are learning and how this can be developed further according to their own individual interests, goals and identities. This is mentoring learning. Such 'learning conversations' enable both teachers and learners to develop strategies to maximise perceived relevance to enable learners to discover and explore connections to the content- 'the more personal meaning the students perceive, the more they will be motivated to engage with the content' (Priniski et al., 2018, p. 13).

Increasing relevance may also be the key to help learners move from a 'momentary increase in attention and affect' (Priniski et al., 2018, p. 13), *towards individual interest*, which is described as 'a predisposition to re-engage with a particular activity or topic over time'. Whereas situational interest does not require relevance and can also be triggered by novelty, surprise or other attention-capturing factors, 'development of individual interest requires increasing stores of value and knowledge and increasing identification' (Priniski et al., 2018, p. 14). Therefore, increasing task relevance may be an effective strategy to get learners to re-engage with a topic and arrive at a more complex understanding of the content. The more learners are encouraged to articulate and pursue their own learning goals, to make appropriate choices and to develop a meta-awareness of their own learning, the more likely they are then to feel in control. This not only provides learners with a sense of self-value and purpose, it also encourages a passion for learning and self-determination. It is interesting to note that it was only relatively recently that discussions about developing a love of learning, resilience, habits of mind and growth mindsets etc. became part of commonplace educational discourse, and even more recently that 'struggling', making errors, extreme challenge and 'mastery' became seen as potentially positive drivers for learning (Claxton, 2013). In sum, the Learning Futures programme led by the Paul Hamlyn Foundation & Innovation Unit (2012) reported:

> Approaches are effective in stimulating deep engagement when they are implemented in such a way as to enable students' sense of agency and identity, and a learning experience which feels authentic and meaningful whilst progressively handing over responsibility for learning to students. Paul Hamlyn Foundation & Innovation Unit (2012, p. 16)

5.3   Mastery

According to Anderson & Krathwohl, mastery of knowledge and skills lies at the heart of all teaching and learning. Mastery describes an individual's ability to activate (mental) operations in order to solve problems (Anderson & Krathwohl, 2001; Dalton-Puffer, 2013). To develop mastery, it is critical that learners experience tasks that enable them not only to document their own progress but also to understand the processes involved in successful task completion. In other words, learners not only need to develop the knowledge to perform successfully, they also need to develop a strong belief that they are capable of completing such tasks successfully.

When learners believe they can solve problems and complete tasks successfully, they will develop the will to persevere when faced with difficulties (Bandura, 1997). In other words, 'mastery experiences' increase learners' sense of self-efficacy. Moreover, teachers can use feedback to help learners develop self-efficacy as a 'key personal resource in self-development, successful adaptation, and change' (Bandura, 2006, p. 4). Self-efficacy encourages positive self-evaluation and is a precursor to sustained learner engagement. According to Hsieh et al., having high self-efficacy may lead to more positive learning habits such as 'deeper cognitive engagement, persistence in the face of difficulties, initiation of challenging tasks and use of self-regulatory strategies' (2007, pp. 457–8).

Learners with high self-efficacy tend to adopt what can be termed *mastery goal orientation*, which 'activates a focus on developing competence through an emphasis on improvement, learning, and deepening understanding' (O'Keefe et al., 2013, p. 51). O'Keefe further reports that there is fairly strong evidence linking the perceived goal structure of the classroom to personal goal endorsement, as well as achievement-related behaviour and beliefs. In other words, teachers' mindsets and goal orientation and the way these beliefs are implemented in the classroom have a huge impact on learner mindsets and goal orientation. The OECD (2017) reiterates that high performance standards correlate positively with academic achievement and that in schools where teachers have lower expectations of their learners these low expectations correlate with poor academic performance.

Long-term goals seem to be especially efficient in promoting long-term engagement and tenacity when those purposes go beyond the individual. Dweck's research (2014) indicates that when high school students are motivated by a desire to contribute to society, they adopt a growth mindset. Interestingly, similar patterns were not found when these students were motivated by more self-oriented desires, like making money or gaining social status. It must also be emphasised that mastery brings with it a sense of achievement and success. The challenge for educators is to ensure that all learners experience achievement and success whatever their level, abilities or capacities. This is fundamental if we are to 'live' social justice in the classroom and grow an ecological perspective on ensuring that all individuals belong to a learning community.

5.4   Reflection

Self-reflection is a core construct of self-regulation and as such constitutes both a means of learning as well as a goal itself (Boekaerts, 1999; Zimmerman, 2000). According to Heemsoth and Heinze (2016), self-regulated learners knowingly set appropriate learning goals and plan their own learning episodes. They select strategies which enable them to monitor their own progress and which guide them when they meet difficulties so that they can adapt their own learning behaviours accordingly. However, learners do need explicit support and guidance in how to develop these processes. In terms of examples, the 5 Rs (Huang, 2017) might provide useful guidance in encouraging learners to understand themselves as learners better. These are: *recalling* (e.g. recalling an episode/event); *recapturing* (e.g. capturing the emotions, accomplishments, and challenges); *relating* (e.g. relating what was recalled to previous personal experiences); *rationalising* (e.g. understanding the patterns or learning from experiences to create meaning from past events); and *redirecting* (e.g. engaging in purposeful thinking directed towards future actions). Indeed, carefully planned tasks which encourage reflective learning and which do not seem as 'add-ons' at the end of units of work, but are ongoing and embedded into processes of regular learning, are essential.

> [M]y students' audio recordings of individual or pair/triadic spoken reflections, video recordings of individual or pair/triadic spoken reflections, and video-stimulated individual or pair reflections (i.e., videotaping an activity and then replaying the recording as a stimulus to elicit thoughts regarding the task performance) have led to some of the most moving, memorable, and insightful personal discoveries. (Huang, 2017)

According to Costa and Kallick (2008), in the reflective classroom, teachers encourage learners to make meaning from their learning, to compare intended with actual outcomes, to evaluate their metacognitive strategies, to analyse and draw causal relationships, and to synthesise meanings and apply their learnings to new and novel situations. Crucially, Costa and Kallick maintain that 'students know they will not "fail" or make a "mistake," as those terms are generally defined. Instead, reflective students know they can produce personal insight and learn from *all* their experiences' (2008, p. 222).

Furthermore, educational policies and curriculum guidelines promote the use of self-reflection as a means of encouraging and growing positive attitudes and support towards learning beyond schooling – that is, lifelong learning (European

Commission, 2001). Whilst there is a paucity of research in the relationship between school experiences and willingness to engage in lifelong learning, self-reflection is a predicator for continued interest and motivation for learning, according to Lüftenegger (2017). As Rogers (2001) once said: 'Perhaps no other concept offers… as much potential for engendering lasting and effective change in the lives of students as that of reflection' (2001, p. 55).

5.5   Interdependence of Growth Areas

Thus far, we have described aspects of personal growth in learning and teaching in a linear manner, which is certainly misleading. Two aspects need to be taken into account. First, personal growth in all aspects occurs both in the learner and in the teacher. Developing affect, engagement, mastery and reflection are ongoing challenges for all who are involved in the process of teaching and learning. Second, the aspects of personal growth are mutually interdependent and interact in a complex pattern. In search of sources and effects of teacher self-efficacy, Zee and Koomen (2016, p. 7) present a model in which teacher self-efficacy impacts the quality of classroom processes that are critical for student achievement, which in turn supports teacher self-efficacy. The complexity of the relationships between well-being, motivation, achievement and teacher self-efficacy requires all aspects or elements to be considered and balanced carefully. Two assumptions can be made: if any one aspect is neglected, it is likely to negatively affect the entire system (e.g. if there is a lack of emotional support in the classroom, teacher and student well-being will suffer, potentially impacting poorer academic achievement and resulting in low self-efficacy in both the teacher and the student). If, on the other hand, an aspect is strengthened or boosted (e.g. when teachers gain self-efficacy as a result of personal development and supervision), this will impact other aspects, such as student motivation or academic achievement. Fullan and Langworthy (2014, p. 11) suggest that when teachers and students are together engaged in a meaningful partnering for learning:

> teachers not only become learners themselves, but also begin to see learning through the eyes of their students. This 'visibility' is essential if teachers are to continuously challenge students to reach for the next step, and if they are to clearly see whether teaching and learning strategies are achieving their intended goals. (Fullan & Langworthy, 2014, p. 11)

This aligns with Tough (2013), who suggests that we are 'rediscovering' the power of strong, supportive relationships between teachers and students.

In this chapter, we have explored the drivers for deeper learning, essentially from the learners' perspective but increasingly indicating that the roles of learners and teachers are inextricably intertwined. Whilst the implications of the interrelationship between teachers and learners are far-reaching, the drivers for deeper learning provide some guidance. They provide insight into the nature and the fundamental importance of the affective dimension of learning by showing how selected affective factors interact with the cognitive dimension of learning. Therefore, an understanding of the drivers of deeper learning and the way they interact with the mechanics of deeper learning will enable teachers to design learning trajectories and to purposefully mentor deeper learning and personal growth within deeper learning partnerships which may require a fundamental rethink of current practices. The implications for mentoring learning from an ecological and pluri-literacies perspective will be discussed in Chapter 6, where the role of the teacher will be critically explored.

6 Mentoring Deeper Learning

Chapter 5 outlined the need to bring student affect and growth required for deeper learning into the frame. At the same time, the role of the teacher – in terms of facilitating growth by creating the most conducive conditions for learning and progression – is embedded in ecological processes which stimulate and refine effective meaning making and knowledge construction. Supporting learners to 'own' learning goals and engage in subject development through a commitment to the successful achievement of those goals, however, is dependent on complementary actions and ways of being by the teacher.

This complementarity, predicated on using and developing an understanding of pedagogic principles conducive to growth mindsets, requires teachers to orchestrate the other three dimensions of the PTDL model: *generating and sustaining achievement and commitment, constructing knowledge and refining skills* and *demonstrating and communicating understanding*. This bringing together and facilitation for deeper learning constitutes the fourth dimension, which defines the teacher as instrumental in *mentoring learning progression and personal growth*. The nurturing of growth mindsets is based on key principles for designing and evaluating learning, scaffolding and supporting learners, and feedback. This orchestration is fundamental in terms of building on what our current, yet dynamic, knowledge and understanding of classroom learning and teaching is. Educators know a great deal about each of the four dimensions and how they might interrelate, but deeper learning requires all dimensions to work together as an integrated whole dependent on specific ways of designing and evaluating learning. This section will explore these further.

6.1 Designing Learning

For some time, the UNESCO's four pillars of learning (International Commission on Education for the Twenty-first Century, 1996) have been used extensively to capture dynamic processes which interconnect in learning-rich classrooms. The ways in which teachers enact their *knowing, doing, being* and *enabling* is fundamental to developing shared classroom practices which promote deeper learning. There is significant research into teacher knowledge and understanding (e.g. Shulman & Shulman, 2004; Verloop et al., 2001; Bernstein, 2000; Banks et al., 1999). However, the case for teachers themselves 'owning' and understanding their own distinctive pedagogic principles, as in Shulman's (2005) 'signature pedagogies', is promoted by the work of Van Lier (1996). As discussed in Chapter 2, he argues that it is only when teachers articulate their own pedagogic principles or Theory of Practice that significant shifts happen in designing different 'patterns of actions, activities and interactions' (Schatzki et al., 2001) for different classes and different learners. The principles of PTDL require both a holistic and dynamic sense of understanding ways in which cognitive and metacognitive development connects with self-efficacy, affect and teacher guidance. In this way, a steer for designing and evaluating classroom learning comes to the fore. Fullan and Langworthy usefully summarise this position as leading to 'sophisticated pedagogic capacities, which require expertise across a repertoire of different teaching strategies and continuous evaluation of where students are in their learning progressions' (2014, p. 8).

The previously mentioned UNESCO Report (2018) foregrounds teachers as designers of learning environments. It signals the need for a significant shift in the ways teachers conceptualise learning (we also refer back to Chapter 2, where learners are seen as 'curriculum makers') and literacies – in the broadest sense – which permeate their classrooms, encompassing the physical, social and cognitive spaces therein. From an ecological perspective, the physical space – its organisation and co-ownership – impacts on learning in ways which suggest that spatial literacies, identities and agency are critical for deeper learning. This point will be discussed in more detail in Part III. There has been a significant shift in rhetoric over the past few decades towards student-led approaches to learning, where the teacher's role is often defined as a 'guide on the side' and a facilitator of learning. We propose a fundamental shift in conceptualising the role of the teacher and the subsequent implications for designing teaching and learning. We propose that the teacher's role encapsulates ways of doing, knowing, enabling and being through integrated, inclusive processes of *mentoring learning.* This is significantly different from mentoring the learner. It involves a highly proactive role based on interacting with learners to enable thinking and learning to be more visible, where dialogic learning conversations are the norm. Hattie & Yates (2013) suggest the teacher's role is both facilitator and activator of learning, prioritising the latter as more powerful in terms of enabling learners to achieve their goals. Yet within an ecological paradigm, the emphasis has to be on ways in which learners and teachers work together to stimulate growth and achieve shared goals, as discussed above. This is *mentoring learning*, a term coined by Tillema et al. (2015), which draws on a wide range of teaching approaches and uses a repertoire of strategies, from teacher-led input to project and inquiry-based learning. According to Fullan and Langworthy:

> Teachers who play dynamic, interactive roles with students – pushing students to
> clearly define their own learning goals, helping them gain the learning muscle to

effectively pursue those goals, and supporting them in monitoring how they are doing in achieving those goals – have extremely strong impacts on their students' learning. Such teachers do not 'let the students learn on their own' but instead help them master the difficult and demanding process of learning. (Fullan & Langworthy, 2014, p. 20)

Building on 'dynamic, interactive roles with students' is fundamental to mentoring learning, which nurtures partnerships between teachers and learners. These partnerships are based on mutually negotiated learning pathways and the design of challenging tasks that enable learners 'to learn about themselves as learners and continuously assess and reflect upon their own progress' (Fullan and Langworthy 2014, ii). This connectedness, emphasised by Stoll and Louis (2007), also promotes teacher reflexivity on their own practices in transparently enacting the notion of *everyone a teacher, everyone a learner*. Mentoring deeper learning shapes unique 'episodes of knowledge productive interaction', which require the teacher to design and evaluate dynamic processes inherent in meaning making. The centrality of meaning making in mentoring learning emphasises informed participation and scaffolded learning through appropriate feedback, assessment and personal growth.

6.2   Pathways for Learning

One of the greatest challenges facing teachers is finding ways of ensuring that dynamic learning pathways are appropriate for individuals as well as groups of learners. The need for a repertoire of strategies to be built up over a period of time involves experimenting and, to an extent, some risk taking. Finding the 'best' way to provide the 'best' learning opportunities is dependent on how the four dimensions interact, not on ready-made formulae and quick-fix solutions. This position resonates with Marzano's (2017) 'high yield' strategies, which emphasise the need to adapt lesson design, teaching routines and interaction patterns according to the overall purpose and learning goals of the lesson and beyond – that is, its role/function within a larger unit (e.g. presenting new content, practising and deepening lessons, knowledge application lessons, reflecting learning).

The pathways that emerge from the interconnectedness of learner growth and mentoring learning also draw together the dimension of *demonstrating and communicating understanding* with that of *constructing knowledge and refining skills*. In order to navigate these pathways appropriately, learners need to develop confidence and experience a sense of achievement through feedback and assessments affirming conceptual *and* linguistic progression. Learners require support through scaffolded learning to define and redefine goals, and teachers need to be prepared to design, redesign and re-sequence tasks, so that learning is increasingly visible to an individual learner, other learners and the teacher. The challenge of successful problem solving and knowing how to transfer learning impacts learner aspirations. Marton and Saljo (1976) emphasise the transformation from surface learning to deeper learning facilitated by 'collaborative enterprise' (Stoll & Louis, 2007) between learners and teachers and the co-development of physical and virtual tools.

In other words, whilst much more is expected and demanded of learners (e.g. to build their confidence through personal feedback and encouragement, with the overall aim to unleash, indeed create, their awareness of their own potential), teachers have to retain an active role in defining students' learning goals (Fullan & Langworthy, 2014). The challenge of this endeavour cannot be over-emphasised, especially given the diversity of learners, in terms of their social, cultural and linguistic experiences. The need is paramount for ongoing dialogue towards a shared understanding of what 'successful' learning looks like for all learners, building on individual differences not as barriers requiring differentiated learning outcomes but as pathways along which individuals feel valued and have a sense of achievement. It is at this very point that enabling learners to understand mastery and develop perseverance and determination goes hand in hand with teachers transparently mentoring learning and scaffolding strategic understanding, which leads to personal growth for each individual. Much has been written about changing classroom demographics impacting social, cultural, linguistic and cognitive diversity (May, 2014; Deppeler et al., 2015). However, the need to ensure that all learners are valued through inclusive pedagogic approaches is at the core of our pluriliteracies approach – since personal growth and learner progression is inherently embedded in the concept of *mentoring learning*. This is not to simplify or pay lip service to the challenges of meeting individual learner needs, but to reiterate that all learners are individuals and all individuals have specific and general learning needs – these are addressed and nurtured through learning partnerships underpinned by mentoring learning. This message permeates the chapters of this book.

A visualisation using Lego (Figure 4.19) demonstrates how as learners progress through different levels they require different strategies to support their learning. Teacher understanding of these levels is critical for learner growth, which is built on connecting all four dimensions. Marzano (2017) details a range of fundamental teacher strategies which focus on engaging learners, building positive learning relationships and crucially communicating high teacher expectations for all learners, including 'reluctant' individuals. Similarly, Universal Design for Learning principles (CAST, 2011) identify teacher strategies which provide 'multiple means of engagement' that offer options for recruiting interest, learner choice for sustaining effort and persistence, clear guidance for developing skills and confidence building for self-regulation.

In short and to reiterate, the Pluriliteracies Teaching for Deeper Learning position is clear: when all four dimensions together form a transparent base for designing and mapping learning pathways operationalised through a wide range of design strategies, the resulting tasks and sequences have the potential to promote learner confidence and learner agency. PTDL is ecological and focusses on designing and 'growing' a learning environment which is flexible and responsive to learners so as to foster commitment and resilience, nurture progression and growth and encourage choice and confidence in navigating learning pathways. This, we propose, will provide learners with the tools and experiences needed for personal growth and lifelong learning.

6.3 Scaffolding Revisited: Mentoring Learning and Personal Growth

Terms such as 'scaffolding' and 'Zone of Proximal Development' (ZPD) have been widely used in recent years and have become an integral part of CLIL learning and teaching methodology. However, for most people scaffolding infers providing students with enough supporting materials and strategies to help them complete a given task where the ZPD focusses on ensuring learners are working alongside 'more knowledgeable others'. In *Sociocultural Theory and the Pedagogical Imperative in L2 Education*, Lantolf and Poehner offer a critical interpretation of Vygotsky's sociocultural theory. They argue that the often quoted ZPD may very well be the most well-known but least understood contribution to psychology and education. Quoting Miller (2011), they claim that Vygotsky has become a 'mythical figure serving as a kind of totem around which to gather various clans of like-minded believers' (Lantolf & Poehner, 2014, p. 147). They further report that as early as 1984, Wertsch worried that the ZPD had become so widely used in research and applied to such varied learning and pedagogical interactions that the concept was in danger of losing all explanatory power and meaning.

According to Lantolf and Poehner, the main reason why the ZPD construct is often misinterpreted, and reduced to particular task-related problems that a learner is able to perform with the help of a teacher or in collaboration with peers, is that readers often seem to overlook that Vygotsky distinguished learning from development. They maintain that the great practical significance of the ZPD to education is that it offers a way for orienting instruction not towards the products of past development, as evidenced in learner independent performance, but *towards emerging abilities* that are manifest in learner participation in joint activity with others.

We argue that the notion of mentoring learning and personal growth challenges us to focus our teaching not only on products of past development but also on emerging abilities that may become manifest in learner participation in joint activity with others: 'what a learner can do today in a cooperative activity, s/he can do tomorrow independently' (Lantolf & Poehner, 2014, p. 149).

Therefore, we propose a revised understanding of scaffolding as mentoring learning and personal growth in *dynamic* and *multi-dimensional* ways. Scaffolding interpreted as mentoring learning is *dynamic* in that it spans every episode/instance of learning and teaching (Figure 6.1). It is both proactive and responsive, differentiated and individualised; it ranges from short-term lesson planning to mapping long-term learning trajectories.

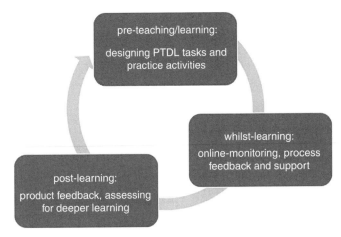

Figure 6.1 Dynamic scaffolding for mentoring learning and personal growth

Scaffolding interpreted as mentoring learning is *multi-dimensional* because it targets every domain of learning – that is, the affective, cognitive/meta-cognitive, sensorimotor and social domains needed to develop a wide range of competences (Dettmer, 2005):

Table 6.1 Multi-dimensional scaffolding for mentoring learning and personal growth (adapted from Dettmer, 2005)

Domain	Process	Content	Purpose	Goal
Cognitive	Thinking	Intellectual	Expand thinking	Gain knowledge
Affective	Feeling	Emotional	Enhance feeling	Develop self-understanding
Sensorimotor	Sensing & moving	Physical	Cultivate senses & movement	Nurture expression
Social	Interacting	Sociocultural	Enrich relationships	Cultivate socialisation
Unified	Doing	Holistic	Optimise potential	Realise self-fulfilment

Although we acknowledge that much more work needs to be done in this field, we realise that when scaffolding is interpreted as mentoring learning and personal growth, it requires us to critically reflect on educational and pedagogic objectives. These goals have been described abundantly in the literature. In 2018 the Council of Europe (2018) coined the phrase 'democratic culture', which resonates with the underlying values of PTDL. Democratic culture is used to describe competence which draws collectively on learner values, attitudes, skills and understanding:

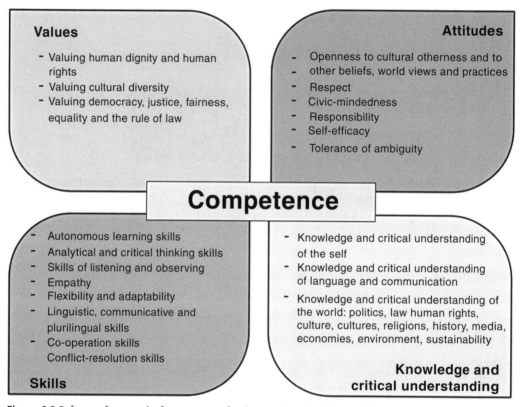

Values

- Valuing human dignity and human rights
- Valuing cultural diversity
- Valuing democracy, justice, fairness, equality and the rule of law

Attitudes

- Openness to cultural otherness and to other beliefs, world views and practices
- Respect
- Civic-mindedness
- Responsibility
- Self-efficacy
- Tolerance of ambiguity

Competence

- Autonomous learning skills
- Analytical and critical thinking skills
- Skills of listening and observing
- Empathy
- Flexibility and adaptability
- Linguistic, communicative and plurilingual skills
- Co-operation skills
  Conflict-resolution skills

Skills

- Knowledge and critical understanding of the self
- Knowledge and critical understanding of language and communication
- Knowledge and critical understanding of the world: politics, law human rights, culture, cultures, religions, history, media, economies, environment, sustainability

Knowledge and critical understanding

Figure 6.2 Reference framework of competences for democratic culture (Council of Europe, 2018, Vol. 1, p. 38)

Recently, the PLATO programme coined the phrase 'positive learning' to describe the overarching goals of education in the Age of Information. Positive learning empowers learners not only to become critical, highly informed and reflective citizens with the ability to evaluate situations and take informed decisions, but more importantly to act responsibly and ethically for the good of our planet and its population (cf. Zlatkin-Troitschanskaia et al., 2017).

As we have argued before (Meyer et al., 2017), PTDL as a pedagogical approach to deeper learning could form the nexus of and the vehicle for positive learning, since the ability to critically evaluate situations and reach informed decisions necessitates deeper understanding, using a wide range of transferable knowledge and problem-solving skills (Figure 6.3).

Clearly, there are significant ethical dimensions to positive learning which need to be addressed in order to discuss and map potential trajectories for responsible and moral behaviour of young learners. In 2015, seventeen Sustainable Development Goals (SDGs), along with 169 associated targets, were agreed upon by all member states at the United Nations. We believe that the notion of sustainable development could provide an ethos for education and prepare learners to confidently face global, social and environmental challenges.

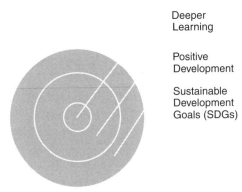

Deeper
Learning

Positive
Development

Sustainable
Development
Goals (SDGs)

Figure 6.3 Deeper learning, positive development
and sustainable development goals

Making sure that disciplinary learning objectives align with the SDGs, along with periodic assessment as to how short- and medium-term learning goals pertain to the overarching goals/notion of positive learning, might offer a way to harmonise/counterbalance scaffolding learning *and* personal growth. These are considerations which traditionally lie outside the remit of the daily work of the classroom teacher. We are suggesting, however, that it is inside the classroom that outside realities, ideals and values impact on how we scaffold meaning making and how mentoring learning is enacted.

6.4   Feedback for Assessing Learning

Feedback can impact our beliefs about our work and our judgements about quality, and can have other costs. The art is turning these costs into benefits in terms of deeper, worthwhile and valuable learning (Hattie and Clarke, 2019).

Much has been written about the role of feedback for learning over the last few decades, consistently foregrounding the importance of formative processes such as those promoted by Assessment For Learning (The Assessment Reform Group,

1999). In a pluriliteracies approach, the nature of feedback and the mutual under-standing adopted by teachers and learners towards its integration into the learning process is not only fundamental to that growth and progression, but positioned as being at the 'critical nexus' between learning goals, tasks and learning outcomes for deeper learning, on the one hand, and student engagement, task performance and the development of a growth mindset on the other.

After a review of existing research, Hattie and colleagues have developed a model of feedback for enhanced learning.

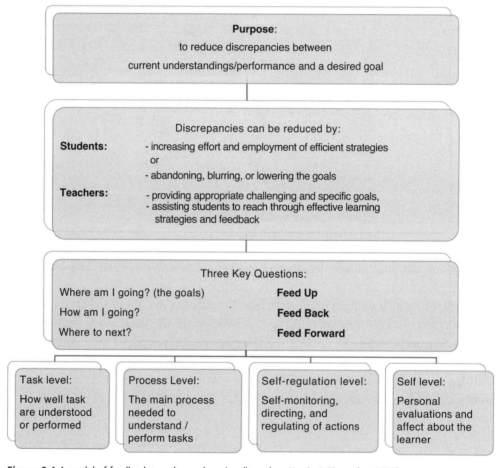

Figure 6.4 A model of feedback to enhance learning (based on Hattie & Timperley, 2007)

Accordingly, feedback can be defined as 'information provided by an agent (e.g. teacher, peer, book, parent, self, experience) regarding aspects of one's perfor-mance or understanding' (Hattie & Timperley, 2007, p. 81).

Meta-analyses have helped identify key aspects of efficient feedback: feedback should offer clear and specific learning goals; offer helpful information on the current state of the learning process; and inform about ways to improve task performance (Wollenschläger et al., 2016). These elements have been incorporated in Hattie and Timperley's model (see Figure 6.4) in the form of three key feedback questions:

1. 'Where am I going' (referring to transparency of learning goals, a.k.a. *feed-up*);
2. 'How am I going' (referring to information on current task performance, a.k.a. *feed-back*); and
3. 'Where to next?' (referring to individual cues on how to reach desired performance level, a.k.a. *feed-forward*). This aspect is usually considered to be the most important one.

Hattie and Clarke (2019, p. 5) maintain that effective teaching includes both the provision of constructive tasks, environments and learning, and the assessment and evaluation of students' understanding of this information. That learners are taught *how* to receive, interpret and make use of feedback is considered to be of higher importance than how much feedback is offered by teachers, since 'feedback given but not heard is of little use'.

In the feedback model, there are four levels of feedback:

1. the task level;
2. the process level;
3. the self-regulation level; and
4. the self level.

The level at which the feedback is directed impacts its effectiveness. Hattie and Timperley hold that whilst feedback about self is the least effective, feedback about regulation and process are powerful in terms of deep processing and mastery of tasks. Moreover, feedback aimed to move students *from task to processing to self-regulation* is considered to be the most effective. The authors also report a link between feedback at the process level and the enhancement of deeper learning.

In addition, Wollenschläger et al. have examined the potential of rubric feedback. Their research study identifies individual performance improvement information as the most effective type of feedback on the learning process. According to the authors, teacher-given rubric feedback, especially when it includes *feed-up*, *feed-back* and *feed-forward* information, leads to more accurate self-evaluative performance judgements in learners and may increase performance (2016).

Based on this research, we recommend the joint construction of rubrics which make transparent defined goals, processes and task outcomes by involving learners in processes which define, refine and advance new knowledge and lead to successful task completion and improvement (see Chapter 9 for practical examples). Given the emphasis on ecological growth, the active involvement of peers to support both collaborative and iterative self-assessment lies at the core of formative feedback and is critical for raising learner awareness and confidence in a 'how to do it better' mindset and in creating a constructive feedback culture. Feedback is a key driver for progression within the PTDL model, built on carefully designed and transparently agreed principles. In essence, the PTDL conceptualisation of feedback encapsulates mentoring learning.

Regarding personal growth and personal development, it is difficult to exaggerate the impact of teacher feedback on learner mindsets. In 1998, Mueller and Dweck conducted a study where students were either praised for their *intelligence* ('You must be really smart at these problems') or their *effort* ('You must have worked hard at these problems') after successful task completion (1998, see also Cimpian et al., 2007; Dweck, 2007; Kamins & Dweck, 1999). They reported that praise for intelligence tended to put learners in a fixed mindset, whereas praise for effort tended to put learners in a growth mindset. When learners were given the chance to work on another task, one that was either more challenging (i.e. one that they could learn from) or a less challenging one that basically guaranteed error-free performance, learners who had received praise for intelligence tended to choose the easy task, whilst learners who had received praise for effort chose the more challenging task and the opportunity to learn. After that, learners were confronted with more challenging problems. The study reports that those learners who had received intelligence praise started to lose confidence and enjoyment when they began to struggle with the problems, whilst students of the other group remained confident. According to Mueller & Dweck, these findings suggest that intelligence praise does not boost motivation and resilience but instead could lead to learners developing a fixed mindset.

Such research findings[1] support our view of how teacher beliefs and actions are intertwined with learner development and academic achievement. It is important for us to move from a dualistic view of teaching and learning to an understanding of learning partnerships that are more organic and symbiotic in nature.

Dweck's research has led to the development of the Growth Mindset Feedback Tool.[2] This offers language frames for teachers to provide principled and informed feedback for six prototypical classroom scenarios. We highly recommend teachers observe their own their own feedback routines and explore the feedback tool, since it can be used to adapt Hattie's feedback model, especially at the process and self-regulation level.

---

[1] For more recent case studies, see www.mindsetworks.com/science/Case-Studies.

[2] Available at https://s3-us-west-1.amazonaws.com/mindset-net-site/FileCenter/
MM3J5l0126930FPPC4TD.pdf.

1. *When learners struggle despite strong effort*
   a. Ok, so you didn't do as well as you wanted to. Let's look at this as an opportunity to learn.
   b. What learning strategies are you using? How about trying some different ones?
   c. You are not there, yet. *Or,* When you think you can't do it, remind yourself that you can't do it yet.
   d. I expect you to make some mistakes, since we're learning new things. If we examine what led to our mistakes we can learn how to improve.
2. *When learners are lacking specific skills needed for improvement*
   a. Let me add new information to help you solve this.
   b. Here are some strategies to figure this out.
   c. Describe your process for completing this task.
   d. Let's practise this so we can move it from our short-term memory to our long-term memory.
   e. Give it a try – we can always fix mistakes once I see where you are getting held up.
3. *When learners are making progress*
   a. Hey, do you realise how much progress you've made?
   b. That's a tough problem/task/concept that you've been working on for a while. What strategies are you using? They are really working for you.
   c. I can see a difference in this work compared to your earlier work. You have really grown with _____.
   d. I see you using your strategies/tools/notes/etc. Keep it up!
4. *When learners succeed with strong effort*
   a. I am so proud of the effort you put forth.
   b. I am very proud of you for not giving up, and look what you have to show for it!
   c. Congratulations – you really used great strategies for studying, managing your time, controlling your behaviour, etc.
   d. I want you to remember for a moment how challenging this was when you began. Look at how far you have come!
5. *When learners succeed easily without effort*
   a. It's great that you have that down. Now we need to find something a bit more challenging so you can grow. That's what we all come to school to do.
   b. It looks like your skills weren't really challenged by this assignment. Sorry for wasting your time!
   c. I don't want you to be bored because you're not challenging yourself.

> d. We need to raise the bar for you now. You're ready for something more difficult.
> e. What skill would you like to work on next?
> 6. *When learners don't put in much effort and then don't succeed*
>   a. I understand that it may seem daunting at first. How can we break this down into smaller tasks so it's not so overwhelming?
>   b. What are your goals for this assignment/class/year? How can you make a plan to achieve those goals? What effort will be required?
>   c. It looks like you're not putting forth much effort. Is this the way you see it? If not, what is it that you are doing, and how can I help you with some new strategies?
>   d. What are the barriers to your success? How can I help you overcome them?
>   e. Remember when you worked really hard for _____ and were successful? Maybe you could try those strategies again.

6.4.1   Feedback for Deeper Learning

Throughout this volume, we have argued that deeper learning rests on three pillars: deeper understanding, deep practice and the development of a growth mindset. Also, we have repeatedly stated that deeper learning and the development of transferable knowledge and skills are tied to domain- or discipline-specific ways of constructing and communicating knowledge. Therefore, we posit that feedback for deeper learning should prioritise those three key aspects of deeper learning by providing *feed-back*, *feed-up* and *feed-forward* on:

a) learners' understanding of disciplinary content (conceptual and factual knowledge);
b) learners' command of subject-specific ways of constructing and communicating understanding (skills and strategies); and
c) learners' mindset – that is, self-regulation with regard to improving a) and b).

All three of these aspects become manifest when learners actively demonstrate their understanding. It is therefore of paramount importance for learners to receive opportunities to make their learning visible, to be provided with specific feedback and – most importantly – to revise their work to demonstrate improved understanding. These considerations made us rethink and critically re-evaluate the task model at the heart of task-based learning and propose an alternative, which we have called Deeper Learning Episodes and which we will present in Part III.

6.5   Conclusions

Earlier iterations of the Pluriliteracies Teaching for Deeper Learning model emerged from educators and academics needing to address some fundamental conceptual shortcomings in current CLIL methodologies (Meyer et al., 2015; Coyle et al., 2017). The innovative structure and processes inherent in our project for the European Centre for Modern Languages[3] have enabled us to adopt an ecological, inclusive growth cycle connecting researchers, curriculum planners and practitioners from different fields, subjects and cultures. This dynamic cycle, consisting of five inter-related processes – *problematising, theorising, growing by diffusion, practising* and *realising* – is detailed in Coyle et al. (2017). This cycle continues to support the evolution of the model far beyond its original purpose and intent.

In moving away from visualisations which are two-dimensional and fit onto the page, we began to conceptualise how the dynamics of learning that are continual-ly interacting and in flux could be represented.

Figure 6.5 Fully animated 3D model of deeper learning environments

The dimensions outlined in the 3D model form the basis for learning partnerships. As teachers and learners interact within and across these dimensions, they extend the space and create a dynamic momentum which fosters growth, thus evolving the basis into a three-dimensional space. This space must be designed to maximise

---

[3] Pluriliteracies Teaching for Learning, available at www.pluriliteracies.ecml.at.

interactivity between the dimensions in order to grow deeper learning ecologies. In other words, all dimensions must be activated and integrated for deeper learning to occur. Since deeper learning is dependent on disciplinary cultures, adopting a pluriliteracies approach provides learning pathways into the subjects of schooling.

These four dimensions also provide teachers with feedback and understanding. They guide learning trajectories by mentoring individual learning through those different domains. (Co)constructing tasks and activities with increasing sophistication and abstraction – as illustrated in the Lego images (Figure 4.19) – are what constitute individual learning progressions. This reveals that deeper learning is not only a matter of constructing and communicating or demonstrating knowledge. Indeed, for deeper learning to occur, the affective conditions which impact on learners need to be factored into the equation, activated and supported by teacher mentoring for learning. Conducive conditions for learning depend on teacher self-efficacy and affective classroom processes and carry through to learner achievement and well-being (Zee & Koomen 2016).

In turn, research suggests that the creation of positive growth conditions for learners impacts the teacher's own sense of well-being and self-efficacy (Lomas et al., 2017). Teacher emotions, such as enjoyment during teaching, have also been shown to correlate with clarity and variety of instruction, and caring and support for students (Frenzel et al., 2016). Frenzel concludes that teacher awareness of their own role in constructing conditions which foster student learning and adjustment is likely to reinforce teacher enjoyment.

Our revised Pluriliteracies Teaching for Deeper Learning model attempts to capture across four interrelated dimensions the intricate relationships and complexities between *generating and sustaining learner commitment and achievement*; *mentoring learning and personal growth*; *constructing new knowledge and refining skills*; and *demonstrating and communicating understanding*. We have moved away from a linear analysis of teaching as a unidirectional, intentional act by teachers to learners. The empirical evidence we reviewed can be summarised along two lines:

- Teaching efficiency is all about addressing individual learning needs – for example, by using appropriate communication, scaffolding and feedback strategies based on the teachers' diagnostic expertise and teaching repertoire.
- Multiple dynamic factors involved in teaching and learning determine mutually reinforced 'lived-through' processes defined by teacher-learner relationships.

We have tried to demonstrate in this chapter that whilst teaching and learning encompass a wide range of dynamic dimensions, elements and conditions, its complexity is rarely considered in an ecological, unified, inter-relational way. We believe it is a crucial step forwards to present this holistic picture in ways that explain and guide pedagogic thinking, which can then be translated into coherent classroom principles, processes and practices.

PART III
Putting a Pluriliteracies Approach into Practice

· ·

The third part of the volume has two purposes. First, there is a focus on the implications of adopting a pluriliteracies model in the classroom. Second, it has become apparent that the role of language teachers has to shift from merely enabling pluriliteracies across other disciplines, to the position where language teachers as subject experts in their own right are not only brought into the frame but identified as being fundamental to the development of disciplinary literacies. Clearly, this involves detailed, practice-oriented discussions, decisions and exploration working with the demands of diverse contexts – which is outside the remit of this book. However, we seek to provide an overview of the key issues to provide a guide for further development, action research and school-based enquiry to ensure that the interpretations and practices of PTDL are shared and critiqued and contribute to building a dynamic learning community. Part III argues for a paradigm shift which is needed to develop learning ecologies as classroom ways of being, doing, working together and achieving. Chapter 7 considers the digital dimension and the concept of 'learnscapes'. Chapter 8 looks at how an ecological lens provides ways of practising deeper learning. Chapter 9 repositions language teachers as subject experts and explores how they are well placed to make a fundamental contribution to transforming classroom practices. The book closes with 'looking forwards' – not as a future, distant, 'blue skies' reflection but as a call to educators and researchers to rethink, explore and have confidence to bring about change.

7 A Paradigm Shift: From Classrooms to Learning Ecologies

7.1 Integrating the Digital Dimension[1]

> While it is possible to teach for deeper learning without technology, it is hard to imagine how our schools will scale up such instruction without support from digital tools and media.
>
> (Dede, 2014, p. 4)

In this chapter we would like to argue that in line with recent technological and sociocultural imperatives, creating deeper learning environments is increasingly reliant on educational technology. The potential of technology can no longer be denied, due to its capacity to blend traditional and non-traditional face-to-face and authentic learning activities to promote student voice and agency and call for new pedagogies which are:

> more reflective of engagement, proactively support structural steps to both personalize student learning and engage parents and communities in that learning and preparing educators to support a safe, engaging learning climate where students can take risks, make mistakes and drive their own learning (Parsi, 2015, para. 7).

Rapid technological developments are changing the ways we live our lives in terms of work and leisure. Yet in educational settings, the role of technology is lagging behind, especially regarding its impact on the quality of learning. Throughout the last two decades, the potential of technology has shifted from teaching students how to use digital tools to using tools to support the development of cognitive and creative skills, and currently:

> the focus is squarely on learning, not tools... students still need to be proficient in foundational technology skills, but that's not the end. It's the means to an end where the expectation is that students will use technology when appropriate to take charge of their own learning. (International Society for Technology in Education, 2016)

---

[1] This section is based on an article we published in 2018. However, when we wrote that article, the conceptual work on our framework had not been completed. Including some of the most central thoughts of the article here affords us the valuable opportunity to put digital media use in context with all four dimensions of our model.

Dede echoes these thoughts when he states that the focus of educational technology has turned from 'artificial intelligence to amplifying the intelligence of teachers and students' (2014, p. 7). He calls for teaching strategies and principles which are geared towards deeper learning and which integrate the use of information and communications technology (ICT) because 'technology as a catalyst is effective only when used to enable learning with richer content, more powerful pedagogy, more valid assessments, and links between in- and out-of-classroom learning' (Dede, 2014, p. 6).

The web has become more pervasive and interactive, characterised by features such as 'tagging, social networks and user-created taxonomies of content called "folksonomies"' (Borland, 2007). It is clear that Web 3.0 – enabled by the convergence of technology trends such as ubiquitous connectivity, network computing, open technologies, open identity and semantic web technologies (Spivack, 2007) – will further impact formal and informal learning. Given the increasing use of digital tools, however, the question remains as to if and how technology will support deeper learning in the classroom.

The 2016 edition of the International Society for Technology in Education Standards lists seven key areas of digital literacies, along with indicators and age bands to guide the development of skills and competencies needed to engage and thrive in a connected, digital world. These are listed below, since we believe that developing digital literacies is fundamental to becoming a pluriliterate citizen and goes far beyond the narrow interpretation of 'using computers in the classroom'.

1. Empowered Learner: Students leverage technology to take an active role in choosing, achieving and demonstrating competency in their learning goals, informed by the learning sciences.
2. Digital Citizen: Students recognize the rights, responsibilities and opportunities of living, learning and working in an interconnected digital world, and they act and model in ways that are safe, legal and ethical.
3. Knowledge Constructor: Students critically curate a variety of resources using digital tools to construct knowledge, produce creative artefacts and make meaningful learning experiences for themselves and others.
4. Innovative Designer: Students use a variety of technologies within a design process to identify and solve problems by creating new, useful or imaginative solutions.
5. Computational Thinker: Students develop and employ strategies for understanding and solving problems in ways that leverage the power of technological methods to develop and test solutions.
6. Creative Communicator: Students communicate clearly and express themselves creatively for a variety of purposes using the platforms, tools, styles, formats and digital media appropriate to their goals.

7. Global Collaborator: Students use digital tools to broaden their perspectives and enrich their learning by collaborating with others and working effectively in teams locally and globally.

(International Society for Technology in Education, 2016)

Educational technology has the potential to provide teachers and learners with an array of tools which – when used appropriately – have the potential to transform learning. Transforming learning and building on the principles discussed in previous chapters involves personalising the learning experience, promoting joint knowledge construction through collaborative learning tools, broadening access to learning through online environments and learning management systems, and providing tools that support learners as creators. Dede (2014) goes further in suggesting the need to explore virtual worlds and gaming (simulations and augmented reality) to enhance students' motivation and engagement by providing learning opportunities familiar to their out-of-school world.

Ultimately, the transformative potential of digital tools lies in their ability to establish connections between what Brown and Thomas (2014) refer to as: 'learning about', which describes the more traditional sense of school-based learning; 'learning to do', which is often realised through problem-based and project-based pedagogies; and 'learning to be' or 'becoming', which is currently centred in informal learning. 'Learning to be' is 'fundamentally about identity formation, and generative for deep engagement as well as the formation of intrapersonal and interpersonal skills'. (Brown & Thomas as cited in Dede, 2014, p. 4). For example, Eerikainen's study (2015) used 'notebooking' as a means for younger learners with limited L2 as the language of schooling to progress their science. Tablets provided the locus of learning in two ways. First, they provide a learning log to document progression and self-monitoring and assessment, through reviewing different iterations of text, collating feedback and accessing reflective triggers and becoming more aware of the process of deeper learning. Second, tablets provide a tool for writing, discussing and co-creating representations of new learning involving visual cues such as videos, graphs and diagrams. Using the Book Creator application, learners captured images of their work in progress and became increasingly self-directed in drafting, critiquing, peer reviewing and so on. Eerikainen reports significant development over a six-month period in the learners' engagement in increasingly complex self-directed tasks and the language used therein, together with ease in activating 'during-task' discussions, for learners with initially limited L2 language capacity. In this instance, the digital tool not only acted as an instruction tool but evolved into a strategic learning space, which enabled both learners and teachers to co-create dynamic learning partnerships. This position leads to a more integrated and holistic view of learning and focusses attention on optimising spaces so that using appropriate digital tools is normalised and digital literacies are core. In the

Pluriliteracies Teaching for Deeper Learning model, digital literacies form a sub-category of subject-specific literacies. Digital literacies develop as learners apply subject-specific skills and strategies to critically decode or encode digital text or work through digital channels (i.e. they use digital modes to build and share knowledge).

In the next section we will argue that framing PTDL within a deeper learning paradigm offers a trajectory for the integration of digital media because it provides practitioners with theory-based criteria to discern the specific added value of its use or application. As Higgins, Xiao and Katsipataki emphasise, it is the 'pedagogy of the application of technology in the classroom which is important: the how rather than the what.' (Higgins, Xiao & Katsipataki, 2012, p. 3) This is the crucial lesson emerging from the research.

Given some of the radical re-thinking required to transform classroom practices that support the growth of PTDL, creating appropriate conditions for learning and understanding the underlying principles upon which PTDL is built is challenging and complex. It cannot easily be translated into a series of 'quick-fix' plans, since a more 'organic' understanding of learning is emphasised to encourage learners – with support from their teachers – to develop the knowledge, skills, attitudes and confidence needed to become increasingly pluriliterate. Creating optimal conditions for learning is at the core of the model, and modes of learning involving digital technologies (starting with those technologies which are by no means 'new' but are poorly understood as learning tools) are integral to deeper learning. In essence, the notion of creating safe 'integrated learning spaces' is fundamental to developing and sustaining a pluriliteracies approach to learning. In this way our understanding of 'integration' as 'learning spaces', which is contentious and unresolved in CLIL developments (Nikula et al., 2016a), is at the core of the PTDL model.

7.2   Reconceptualising Integrated Learning Spaces for Deeper Learning

To sum up what we have stated so far, providing students with opportunities to successfully engage in all the dimensions of subject learning necessary for the successful acquisition of pluriliteracies requires learning environments that engage learners on multiple levels by:

- encouraging student buy-in and rewarding long-term commitment;
- providing challenging complex tasks to allow students to (co-)construct and share/communicate knowledge and understanding, as well as promoting the use of subject-specific skills and strategies and adding complementary controlled practice/focus-on-form activities to systematically support the automatisation of those skills; and
- promoting learner agency and creativity.

We have also made the case that digital media and educational technologies must form an integral part of a deeper learning environment because of their potential to significantly increase learner engagement. Strengthening learner engagement involves establishing deeper connections between learners and their learning environment through processes of customisation and individualisation. Web 3.0 and its associated technologies make it possible to customise elements considered to be highly indicative of successful subject and language learning (Becker et al., 2016; Dede, 2014; Hallet, 2012; Hattie & Yates, 2013; Kapp 2014; Lantolf & Poehner, 2014; Lyster, 2007; Meyer, 2010; Ortega, 2008; Ritchhart et al., 2011) and thus respond to the different needs of individual learners. Table 7.1 is by no means exhaustive but exemplifies the added value that the use of educational technology promises. It indicates the kind of deliberate and evidence-based modifications needed if learning environments are to succeed as spaces for making learning deeper, more engaging, highly individualised and transparent.

Table 7.1 Added value of educational technologies

Elements of learning environment	Added value of ICT	Sample application
(Co-)constructing knowledge	Making input/content more immersive	Google Street View, HP Reveal, Earth AR, Star Walk, Power of Minus Ten, Book Creator, book widgets
	Matching language level of input/content material and skill level of learner	newsela.com, newsinlevels.com, listenwise.com, News-O-Matic,
	Providing tools to make thinking/conceptual development visible	CmapTools, Ideament, Explain Everything
Online support	Online dictionaries etc.	visual.merriam-webster.com, macmillandictionary.com, visuwords.com, ozdic.com, wikipedia.org
Practice	Personalised/joint practice of lexical elements	vocabulary.com, vocapp.com, flashcardstash.com, Quizlet
Sharing knowledge	Enabling and managing learner collaboration beyond the classroom	schoolastic.com, edmodo.com, etc., mindmeister.com, padlet.com
	Increasing authenticity of learning outcomes/products	Blogs, wikis, BoomWriter,
Promoting autonomy	Using e-portfolios for student work	Moodle, Seesaw, eBackpack,
Motivating students	Gamifying the classroom	Classcraft
Feedback & reflection	Creating back channels and using exit tickets	Socratic, Quizlet, Kahoot, Poll Everywhere, SurveyMonkey

Clearly, the integration of digital tools will not only require a new technological infrastructure but will also have to empower teachers to make better use of instructional strategies, especially if the goal is 'to help all students, not just an elite few to reach mastery of ambitious standards' (Dede, 2014, p. 1).

Educational technology blogger Gerstein argues that the evolution from Web 1.0 to Web 3.0 could be used as a metaphor to demonstrate how education should be evolving to accommodate rapid change in technology, related learning outcomes, student needs and community expectations. The implications for formal teaching and learning contexts are exceedingly challenging, as set out in Table 7.2.

Table 7.2   From Education 1.0 to Education 3.0 (adapted from Gerstein, 2013)

	Education 1.0	Education 2.0	Education 3.0
Meaning is…	dictated	socially constructed	socially constructed and contextually reinvented
Technology is…	confiscated at the classroom door (digital refugees)	cautiously adopted (digital immigrants)	everywhere (ambient, digital universe)
Teaching is done…	teacher to student	teacher to student and student to student	teacher to student, student to student student to teacher, people-technology-people (co-constructivism)
Learning is taking place…	in a building (brick)	in a building or online (brick and click)	everywhere
Hardware and software in schools are…	purchased at great cost and ignored	open source and available at lower cost	available at low cost and used purposively

The following scenario showcases how some of the above-mentioned digital platforms, applications and tools can be used to create ecologies for deeper learning by promoting pluriliteracies development within an Education 3.0 paradigm.

1. **Doing:** Learners are tasked to do research on a current topic (e.g. political developments in the USA, Brexit, COVID-19, global warming) using newsela.com. This multi-language news platform offers learners the ability to adjust the difficulty of the chosen text to their specific reading level. In-built comprehension quizzes provide instant feedback to the learners and

inform teachers on their learners' reading skills development. By clicking a word they don't understand, learners will be provided with a definition, explanation, image and audio recording of the actual word by the dictionaries in their mobile devices. Throughout, learners are encouraged to record words/phrases/collocations that they may not understand or find noteworthy and use them to create interactive flashcards on Quizlet, which not only offers different kinds of gamified practice/learning activities and games but also allows them to share their flashcards with their teachers and peers. The learners may then move on to do further research using perspecsnews. com. This app curates news articles from a variety of resources to offer three different perspectives (pro, neutral, con) on every topic presented. In multilingual settings, students may analyse how the topic is reported in different countries. This not only provides authentic opportunities for translanguaging activities; such comparisons also provide an intercultural perspective on the issue/topic.

2. **Organising/Explaining:** To deepen their understanding and make their own learning visual, learners might then continue to create a digital concept map on the topic of their research using cMapTools. In contrast to mind-mapping, concept maps require users to label the connections between individual facts or keys terms and thus support the formation and internalisation of conceptual knowledge. Sharing and comparing their digital concept maps with other learners not only serves to visualise their understanding but also offers an incentive to language their understanding and to correct conceptual misunderstandings/misrepresentations.

3. **Arguing:** Next, students will be asked to communicate and demonstrate their understanding of the topic by turning their concept maps into a 'text' of a specific a genre and mode (e.g. oral or written) of their choosing, using an app that best suits their text/product and needs. The first draft of their learning outcome/product (i.e. the video, the cartoon, the blogpost, etc.) will be uploaded to their password-protected learning management system platform, such as Edmodo or Scholastic, and reviewed by their peers using lexis and collocation tools such as ozdic.com or words-to-use.com. The corrected drafts will then be uploaded and sent to their teachers before they will be published in their personal digital portfolio, on a classroom blog, website or Padlet.

Situating PTDL within an Education 3.0 paradigm requires rethinking the way we traditionally conceive formal learning and learning spaces in order to bridge the gap between formal and informal learning. As has been constantly reiterated throughout this volume, deeper learning rests in great part on student engagement.

Engagement is fluid yet dynamic, societally driven yet highly individual. It cannot be promoted or sustained by traditional one-size-fits-all approaches to teaching and learning.

Instead, we propose further investigation into the potential of integrated, hybrid spaces where educational technologies are used along with traditional and transformative teaching methods to personalise learning experiences and to bridge formal and informal learning. We suggest that this will increase student engagement (cognitive, emotional and behavioural) and promote learner agency. To make the ecological underpinning of the new paradigm transparent we will refer to these integrated learning spaces as *learnscapes*.

8 | Learnscaping: Designing Ecosystems for PTDL

This chapter explores further the implications for extending Deeper Learning Episodes and provides some initial guiding questions which position educators as designers of learnscapes.

The design, guidance and supervision of learnscapes requires alternative approaches to teaching and learning which call on a wide range of competences. Learnscaping requires reconceptualising how we grow shared, safe, plurilingual learning spaces. These spaces normalise digital learning. They seek to provide engaging opportunities for promoting learning based on increasingly challenging subject understanding, enabled by individual language progression – that is, all the components brought together into a learning ecology. Many educators, however, are ill equipped for the challenges of teaching and mentoring digital age learning. The International Society for Technology in Education lists five key competence areas for teachers and corresponding performance indicators:

1. Facilitate and inspire student learning and creativity.
2. Design and develop digital age learning experiences and assessments.
3. Model digital age work and learning.
4. Promote and model digital citizenship and responsibility.
5. Engage in professional growth and leadership.

(International Society for Technology in Education, 2008, 2016)

Yet, in identifying the five competences, it is clear that development and progression in each is dependent on the growth of the others, which requires both holistic and detailed planning, mentoring and consideration of the interweaving strands (conceptualised as an ecosystem). Acknowledging the spatial dimension of learnscapes allows us to highlight and address elements that have been neglected in pedagogic discourse: despite their hybridity, such spaces follow certain architectural principles regarding layout and interaction that may prove detrimental or conducive to deeper learning and the way knowledge is constructed and shared.

> Technology needs to be understood as spatially configured and entangled with the material world. When people are using digital tools and resources in activities that lead to learning, place and the material qualities of things matter (Flynn et al., 2018).

For example, in our master seminars, pre-service teachers are required to design and create learnscapes in the form of digital textbooks as part of their workload.

This has taught us that the way we present information, how we conceptualise and implement interaction with the digital content or how we facilitate individual learning pathways in those next-generation textbooks, may be as important to the learning experience and engagement as the selection of materials and revised understanding of task design that we present in the next section. This again stresses the need for a more holistic approach to teaching and learning, and challenges us to incorporate aspects into the design of learning episodes which we have previously neglected. Another example consists of co-created learning spaces where researchers, pre-service and in-service teachers and their learners co-conceptualise 'shared learning spaces' (Coyle & Al Bishawi, 2016). These shared spaces seek to develop awareness in terms of physical, social and cognitive spaces which impact on learning ecologies and lead to emergent learnscapes for deeper learning. There is growing literature on the development of learnscapes across a broad range of contexts, including environmental and sustainable agendas, confirming a need to extend our thinking across a broader range of contexts (e.g. Mulcahy et al., 2015 or Flynn et al., 2018).

The next section turns to the design of the tasks within learnscapes. The need to explore the nature of designing tasks for deeper learning whilst aligning those tasks with the dimensions of the model is evolving.

8.1   Designing Deeper Learning Episodes

In the context of schooling, it goes without saying that lesson planning is a fundamental activity for teachers and teaching. The concept of a lesson is temporally bounded. A great deal of time is spent on planning and detailing tasks and activities according to appropriate learning intentions related to an agreed curriculum within a specific time frame. An emphasis throughout this book, however, has been on design principles for learning. These focus on aligning tasks and activities to create Deeper Learning Episodes and subsequently extend them into coherent, intentional and purposeful learning milestones transparently connected to a curriculum. To clarify what we mean by learning episodes, we will offer an explanation and subsequently explores the implications of such a modus operandi, taking into account that 'classrooms are amongst the most complex, unpredictable, fast-moving work environments that exist' (Dudley, 2019, p. 21). We seek to outline guidance on design principles, task design and sequencing. We acknowledge that over time these will be even further refined and revised by practitioners, but for the moment they provide initial reminders and navigation tools for embarking on new ways of designing learning.

A learning episode is not limited to specific timetabled lessons. Design principles encourage planning (or designing) which focusses on episodes rather than individual lessons. An episode can be short but it is more likely to progress over a series of lessons, depending on intentions, purposes and outcomes (sometimes referred to as 'products'). An experimental study in New Zealand (Hipkins et al., 2010) focussed on what participants called 'extended learning episodes'. In one particular school, teachers developed and enacted their own design principles in order to maximise the learning value of three-day learning episodes, and to understand:

> the challenges posed by the design principles, at both planning and enacting stages. Just as learning can emerge in the spaces between students, so it can also emerge in the spaces that the teacher, with the help of the students and all the relevant resources they can collectively marshal, intentionally engineer (Hipkins et al., 2010, p. 59).

According to the research findings, the three-day episodes became consolidated in the overall structure of the school's learning programme due to the apparent benefits to student and teacher learning. This illustration serves to indicate the non-temporal nature of deeper learning episodes. It emphasises how extending episodes in very different ways according to pedagogic contextual opportunities draws on design principles developed through phases for designing Deeper Learning Episodes.

As stated previously, deeper learning develops within deeper learning ecologies or *learnscapes*. These three-dimensional spaces are non-linear and sequential and come into being when all four dimensions of the PTDL model are active at the same time. Teachers can transform traditional classrooms into deeper learning ecologies by designing (through planning) and sustaining (through dynamic and interactive scaffolding) tasks and activities which focus on deep understanding and deep practice. Deep practice and deep understanding require a growth mindset in both learners and teachers:

> When teachers were *teaching for understanding* and giving kids *feedback in a way that grew their understanding* and were giving them *a chance to revise their work* in order *to demonstrate their improved understanding*. That's when they were passing on their growth mindsets. (Carol Dweck, Education Week, 2016, emphasis added)

We take the following stance: deeper learning ecologies are dependent on the formation of learning partnerships between learners and teachers. Learners need to actively engage in deeper learning processes with teachers who generate and sustain the conditions for learner engagement, achievement and the development of a growth mindset as mentors for personal growth.

8.1.1 Task Design for Deeper Learning

As discussed in previous chapters, deeper learning and the development of transferable knowledge and skills are tied to domain-specific processes, tasks and activities which foster deep understanding. In order to enable students to engage in deep practice in a school context, they need to be aligned with the five core constructs of disciplinary literacies (Chapter 4.5), the four prototypical activity domains of the subjects of schooling (Chapter 4.5.1) and, most importantly with learner strengths, needs and interests:

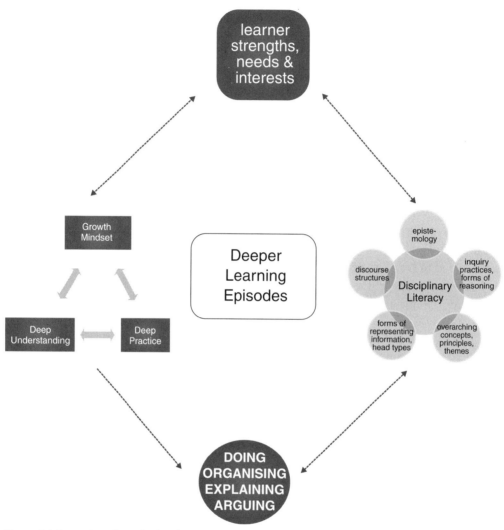

Figure 8.1 Deeper Learning Episodes alignment

This *alignment* constitutes a unique and indispensable feature of deeper learning tasks and activities. It comprises aligning disciplinary core constructs, knowledge activity domains of schooling and the mechanics of deeper learning with learner strengths, needs and interests. It is this alignment that distinguishes tasks for deeper learning from traditional tasks and activities. Moreover, to emphasise that crucial difference we have coined the term Deeper Learning Episodes for tasks and supporting activities which promote pluriliteracies development.

Deeper Learning Episodes are significant because they transparently align different elements of deeper learning and span 'traditional' lessons as units of time in order to ensure that different phases of learning can evolve, and in so doing focus on individual and collective needs of learners. The multi-dimensional nature of deeper learning requiring the design of episodes can be summarised as follows:

- The design process, as set out in Figure 8.1, requires the alignment of:
  - the five disciplinary core constructs;
  - the knowledge and activity domains of schooling (i.e. tasks and activities which are built according to the curricular demands of subject disciplines and actively involve learners in doing, organising, explaining and arguing their learning);
  - the appropriate discourse functions and their corresponding genres and modes;
  - the mechanics of deeper learning, involving deeper understanding and deep practice; and
  - individual learner strengths, needs and interests.
- The design span typically consists of several lessons forming a complex unit. Quality learning takes time and deeper learning episodes fully acknowledge temporal as well as pedagogic demands – an issue often overlooked in professional guidance.
- Deeper Learning Episodes combine and compound phases of surface learning, consolidation and transfer of learning, along with matching practice activities.
- Deeper Learning Episodes provide a range of opportunities for learners to demonstrate understanding, reflect on their learning progress, revise their work and demonstrate improved understanding.

Critical to designing Deeper Learning Episodes are the notions of *task fidelity* and *sequencing*, which we will now explore.

8.1.2 Task Fidelity

To help educators assess the quality of Deeper Learning Episodes, we would like to introduce the construct of '*task fidelity*' to evaluate the degree to which Deeper Learning Episodes promote deeper learning through design principles. *Task fidelity* is fundamental to designing deeper learning ecologies or learnscapes. It provides learners with opportunities for deeper learning through experiencing:

- *Relevance* (personal and practical);
- *Practical knowledge building and knowledge using*, with the *doing* or *application* (inquiry, problem-solving, etc.) according to subject-specific practices;
- Development of *subject-specific literacies* discourses and practices (literacies);
- *Languaging* and *demonstrating* learning across subjects and languages;

- Co-construction of transparent *transfer* pathways (abstraction, contextualisation, relational transfer and schema building);
- *Mentoring* learning and personal growth (dynamic scaffolding, feedback and assessment);
- *Increasing awareness, engagement and progression* across all four activity domains;
- *Critical reflection, revision* and *self-improvement through deep practice;*
- *Assessment for deeper learning* cycles and praxis; and
- *Partnership* working in a collaborative learnscape.

The ten elements listed above constitute the key principles of task fidelity for deeper learning. However, we are aware of their complexity and all-encompassing nature when designing episodes. Through conversations and workshops with colleagues, teachers, teachers in training, teacher educators and curriculum designers, we have collaboratively designed and refined a prototypical yet flexible structure for Deeper Learning Episodes. These provide a means of accommodating the principles and requirements described above (Figure 8.2).

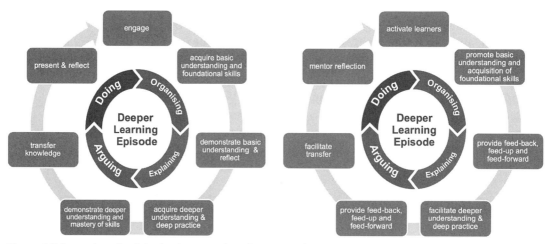

Figure 8.2 Deeper Learning Episodes: learner and teacher perspective

8.1.3   Sequencing

As shown above, Deeper Learning Episodes consist of a number of interconnected phases where teachers and learners jointly engage in complementary activities to incite and sustain deeper learning processes. These four phases are described below.

- Each Deeper Learning Episode begins with an *activation phase.* The activation phase seeks to generate learner engagement, activate prior knowledge, establish relevance and set the ground for transfer learning through expansive framing. Its focus is on facilitating learning by setting clear goals – for example, by using advanced organisers.

- During the *surface phase* learners explore new ideas, facts, concepts and skills to acquire a basic understanding of the content, which they demonstrate through a first learning product. The teacher provides *feed-back*, *feed-up* and *feed-forward* at different levels (e.g. task, process, individual and collective), as appropriate, to help learners reflect on their learning experience, to open pathways for further learning and to sustain their engagement.
- The *consolidation phase* focusses on creating opportunities for learners to deepen their understanding (internalisation of conceptual knowledge) and to deep-practice specific skill sets (to support automatisation). As before, learners demonstrate improved understanding and a growing mastery of skills through a learning product or products which reflect their progress. Individual or joint reflection, along with specific feedback and subsequent revision activities, pave the way for deeper learning.
- During the *transfer phase*, learners are challenged to apply their knowledge to different contexts and situations. Such application involves utilising their knowledge and skills through investigating, experimenting, problem solving or decision making. As before, demonstration of understanding, reflection, feedback and revision are indispensable parts of this phase.

The four phases presented above provide a design sequence for deeper learning. Ideally, one episode will organically flow into the next one, triggering spiral learning processes and pluriliteracies development the way we envision it in our three-dimensional model. This reconceptualisation enables greater coherence between the four phases outlined above and the design principles for *task fidelity*. We are not suggesting that each task must embrace simultaneously all aspects of task fidelity, but that over time these are monitored, and tasks are purposely designed to assure the ten principles are transparent in any co-constructed learnscape. We suggest therefore that unravelling the implications of task design for deeper learning, guided by principles of *alignment*, *task fidelity* and *sequencing*, may provide a useful starting point for discussion and reflection in the ongoing constant analysis of what works in classrooms and why.

8.2 Guiding Questions for Designing Deeper Learning Episodes

In this section, we introduce a set of guiding questions to help teachers design, mentor and evaluate Deeper Learning Episodes. Building on the concept of *task fidelity* and its design principles, these questions address all four dimensions of the PTDL model. They can be used as a practical tool to align the mechanics of deeper learning, disciplinary core constructs, school knowledge domains and activities with learner strengths, needs and interests. As outlined in the previous section, this alignment is a fundamental requirement for Deeper Learning Episodes. It is key to personalising the learning experience in such a way that standard-based teaching objectives translate into highly personalised learner goals, which we like to refer to as '*learner subjectives*'. The concept of learner 'subjectives' resonates with Biesta's (2015) notion of subjectivisation in education, which underlines the importance of encouraging young people to 'exist as subjects of initiative and responsibility rather than as objects of the actions of others' (Biesta, 2015, p. 77). For Biesta, subjectivisation relates to the same fundamental principles of PTDL – 'learner autonomy, independence, responsibility, criticality and the capacity for judgment' (2015, p. 85).

First, we introduce the PTDL questions and offer additional comments to explain the importance and relevance of each question. In setting up these questions, we have followed and reframed the basic principles of *backward planning* originally proposed by Wiggins & McTighe in *Understanding by Design* (2005).

> Deliberate and focused instructional design requires us as teachers and curriculum writers to make an important shift in our thinking about the nature of our job. The shift involves thinking a great deal, first, about the specific learnings sought, and the evidence of such learnings, before thinking about what we, as the teacher, will do or provide in teaching and learning activities. (Wiggins & McTighe, 2005, p. 14)

We fully agree with the authors that without clarifying the desired results of our teaching and understanding of how those goals translate into learner activities and achievements, we won't be able to distinguish interesting learning from effective learning. However, our understanding of the nature of deeper learning has led us to adapt and expand the original three-step method (*identify desired results, determine acceptable evidence* and *plan learning and instruction*) into a set of four interrelated questions. We wish to reiterate at this point that any such questions are dynamic and evolve according to learning contexts and increased theoretical and professional understanding. It should also be emphasised that across all four questions, transparently identifying the teaching and learning strategies that facilitate deeper learning is critical to translating principles into practices. We return here to the importance for educators constructing their own Theory of Practice as outlined in Chapter 2 (Van Lier, 1996). This process is based on principles built on shared theoretical and practice-based understanding. Selecting from and adding to the questions below is encouraged, since 'owning' these principles is integral to the dynamic processes involved in constructing a Theory of Practice. In order to begin this dynamic and iterative process, the four guiding questions of PTDL are:

1. What do I want my learners to know or be able to do?
2. How will my learners demonstrate increasingly deeper understanding at the surface, consolidation and transfer level?

3. What is the best way for my learners to actively co-construct knowledge?
4. How can I support my learners *every* step of the way?

The shift to four questions offers several advantages. First, it accommodates the four phases of deeper learning (*activation, surface learning, consolidation* and *transfer*) and it acknowledges the need for reflection and revision. It matches the structure of Deeper Learning Episodes. Second, it reflects our understanding of learning partnerships, which assigns mentors and mentees different roles but shared responsibilities in the process of deeper learning. Third, it also embraces principled ways of encouraging learners to be driven and inspired to learn and to sustain that learning over time, thereby developing their own understanding of the value of that learning on many different levels – not least for personal fulfilment.

Because each question is directly connected to one dimension of our model, it might be useful to have another look at those four dimensions:

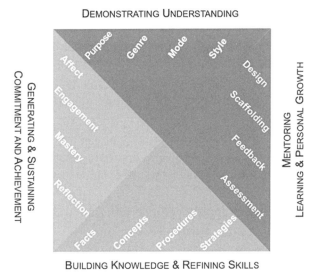

Figure 8.3 The PTDL model

The questions are now explored further.

8.2.1   Knowledge Building and Refining Skills: What Do I Want my Learners to Know/Do?

We believe that this is *the* most important question for teachers to ask when preparing/designing extended Deeper Learning Episodes. Starting with this question will immediately shift the focus away from more teacher- or curriculum-centred approaches (e.g. What do I have to teach tomorrow? What does the curriculum require me to do?) and instead put the learner – their strengths, needs and interests – front and centre. This question refers to the knowledge (factual, conceptual, procedural and strategic/metacognitive) that we want our students to acquire in the course of an extended Deeper Learning Episode, and will help define the learning outcomes. The follow-up questions are meant to further support teachers in the process of aligning the knowledge dimension with the disciplinary core constructs to promote the development of subject-specific literacies:

a. Inquiry practices and forms of reasoning:
   - What subject-specific procedures and strategies will my students use to construct knowledge?
   - Is inquiry deductive or inductive?
   - What problems can be posed and solved?
   - What factual and conceptual questions need to be asked and answered?
   - Where can I provide opportunities for critical thinking?
b. Overarching concepts, principles and themes:
   - What subject-specific conceptual lens do I want my students to use in order to understand the content (big ideas, key concepts)?
   - What connections can be drawn between new and familiar concepts?
c. Epistemology:
   - How do I interpret 'epistemic fluency' in my specific curriculum area/s and across other areas of the curriculum? Epistemic fluency is 'a deep understanding of how knowledge works, the capacity to participate in the creation of actionable knowledge and a sense of how to reconfigure the world in order to see what matters more clearly and enable oneself, and others, to act more knowledgably'. (Markauskaite & Goodyear, 2016, p. 20)
   - How do I enable my students to understand the ways in which knowledge is constructed and interpreted in my discipline?
   - How do I enable my students to distinguish between justified beliefs and opinions?

8.2.2 Demonstrating Understanding: How Will I Know They Know?

Following up with the second question is crucial because the only way for teachers to determine whether their teaching and student learning has been successful is by reading, listening to or closely observing evidence of learners demonstrating their understanding. This typically involves the demonstration of specific skills or the presentation of a learning product as a result of investigating and responding to an authentic, challenging and complex problem or task. Questions A to C are intended to align learning outcomes with disciplinary ways of communicating knowledge and school-related knowledge and activity domains:

a. What are the specific products I wish my learners to develop and evaluate?

   - How do I ensure that individual learners have a shared understanding of the goals of their own learning outcomes, the tasks and the ways of 'validating' the outcomes? How will learners begin to use (initially with guidance) the following questions to guide their own learning:

      ○ What is the purpose of the communication? Who is the audience?

      ○ What mode is possible/adequate/ideal/best suited for our purposes?

      ○ What are the characteristics of the respective text type?

      ○ What are the language demands of the respective text type?

      ○ Which specific strategies encourage my learners to understand, practice and compose text?

b. Discourse structures:

   - What discourse functions do the students need in order to produce the desired text type? At what level?

   - What style/register is adequate for the communicative purpose?

   - What specific language patterns/features are required?

8.2.3 What is the Best Way for my Learners to Co-construct Knowledge?

This question aims at aligning subject-specific ways of knowledge construction and knowledge communication with learner strengths, needs and interests. Indeed, we have already underlined the importance of aligning both the mechanics and drivers of deeper learning in order to generate and sustain learner commitment and achievement.

a. Which process of knowledge construction will inform task design: inquiry-based learning, problem-based learning, experimenting or inquiry-based learning, etc.?

b. Which of these processes is best suited (i) for surface learning, (ii) to consolidate learning and (iii) for transfer leading to deeper learning? (iv) Which type of materials will students use in the process?

c. What kind of social interaction patterns can I use to support co-construction of knowledge and learning partnerships (e.g. solo-, pair-, groupwork; jigsaw activities, think-pair-share)?

d. Where do I position student voice and choice with regard to Questions A to C, so that it is visible and acted upon?

e. How can I use digital media to support these processes?

8.2.4   How Can I Support Learners Every Single Step of the Way?

This question is all about providing support and making sure that we as teachers help learners achieve a level of mastery and experience their investment in the learning process paying off, which in turn will nurture a growth mindset.

a. How can I trigger, increase and sustain student engagement?
    - How can I make topics relevant and meaningful?
    - How can I offer choice in terms of process and product, and support autonomy and agency?
    - How can I support learners' use creative and alternative ways of problem solving?
    - How can I incorporate opportunities which draw on my students' past experiences, prior knowledge and cultural identities?
    - How can I personalise the learning experience?
b. How can I help learners reach the next level?
    - How can I support and guide their learning in terms of process and product?
    - How do I provide ample time, space and opportunity for deep practice?
    - How do I promote/assess transfer of learning?
        ◦ How can I help my learners notice the deeper structure of a problem?
        ◦ How can I support analogy learning? Consider these questions:
            • Which generalisations can be constructed from the content of my lesson?
            • How can I help my learners see how examples and generalisations are related?
            • Which examples should be compared to support analogical reasoning?
        ◦ What do efficiency and innovation mean in my context and how do I balance them?
    - How do I encourage my students to reflect meaningfully on their own learning?
    - How do I facilitate constructive peer feedback?
    - Is my assessment based on clear and hard criteria for deeper learning?
c. How can I support personal growth?
    - How do nurture well-being and I provide a safe and inclusive environment?
    - How do I engender resilience, grit and curiosity?
d. How can I use digital media to support us all?

It is clear that such a complex set of questions may be interpreted as a list of impossible demands made on increasingly busy professionals. We are aware of this. However, it is important to reiterate that these guiding tools are suggested as a means for triggering shared teacher learning through discussion with colleagues and classroom exploration with learners and other educators and researchers. It is at this point that such guidance may serve to ask difficult questions, to disrupt the status quo (see Chapter 2) and, above all, provide educators with the *confidence* to select from the panoply, agree a focus and rethink what might start to make a difference. There is a long way to go – but we need to encourage learning communities to take ownership of key ideas and underlying principles and apply these to their own contexts.

Repositioning the Language Classroom in Pluriliteracies Contexts

As was noted in Chapter 2, few studies have focussed on the role of *language teachers* rather than the role of language in bilingual settings and their collaboration with subject specialists (Dale et al., 2018a). In this chapter we challenge the assumption that the language teacher's principle contribution to CLIL contexts is expertise in language teaching and learning to support subject disciplines. This is not to minimise the importance of subject and language teacher collaboration – in some contexts this is extremely successful and pedagogically beneficial. However, we suggest an alternative which positions the language teacher as a subject specialist with a significant contribution to make in developing the pluriliteracies landscape. We explore ways in which the modern-, foreign- or second-language teacher (referred to where appropriate throughout this chapter as 'language teacher') can reframe their 'subject' as one which has increasing importance and value in our 'post-truth' world, not only in bilingual classrooms but also in monolingual contexts where the timetabled 'language lesson' provides an inclusive space for developing a critical understanding of languages, cultures and literatures.

9.1 The Role of the Language Teacher in CLIL Contexts

From its earliest inception, CLIL has been interpreted as integrating in some way practices embedded in subject teaching and language teaching. The complexities of what this means from both a theoretical and practical perspective have continued to challenge educators and researchers ever since. It was readily recognised that neither subject teachers nor language teachers had a repertoire to easily transform their regular teaching into classroom learning that led to learners' disciplinary and linguistic development being able to satisfy national curricula in the two areas – that is, in the subject discipline and in the foreign or other language. With the exception of some nations, where university degrees encouraged two majors, thus enabling some teachers to enter the profession with an advanced level of understanding of a subject discipline and another language, the emphasis throughout the last two decades has mainly been on professional development and classroom exploration of enabling subject teachers to work through the medium of another language in diverse contexts with very different demands.

CLIL quickly became associated with English – the hegemony of which as a medium of instruction on a global scale is well documented. Experts in English Language Teaching (ELT) and Teaching English as a Second Language (TESOL) were quick to respond by emphasising how language-oriented thematic content resonated with communicative language teaching approaches in English lessons. Some time ago, Darn (2006) summarised this position from a language point of view, suggesting that CLIL guides language processing and supports language production in the same way as ELT by teaching strategies for reading and listening, and structures and lexis for spoken or written language.

> A CLIL 'approach' is not far removed from humanistic, communicative and lexical approaches in ELT, and aims to guide language processing and supports language production in the same way that an ELT course would by teaching techniques for exploiting reading or listening texts and structures for supporting spoken or written language (Darn, 2006, p. 2).

However, Darn also identified the need to rethink language education both politically and socially, since:

> at the extreme, it could be argued that CLIL materials are the subject matter of other disciplines, that CLIL teachers are well versed in both language instruction and a content subject, that learning a language and learning through a language are concurrent processes, and that the traditional concepts of the language classroom and the language teacher are without a future since they do not fit the CLIL model. (Darn, 2006, p. 5)

The suggestion that the 'traditional concepts of the language classroom' were no longer relevant to the range of pedagogic approaches demanded by CLIL led to sensitivities around the status and role of language teachers. Language lessons were under-represented in CLIL research (Dale et al., 2018a). In some instances, a strong renewal of interest emerged in ensuring that the *content* of language lessons was motivating for learners, acknowledging the importance of real-world issues and drawing on well-established approaches such as project-based or content-based language learning. In a similar vein, Deller noted the need for language teachers to make their content interesting:

> because there is no real content… We therefore have to spend a lot of time thinking up topics that work and engage our students. This is a great advantage of CLIL. Our content is ready made (Deller, 2005, p. 29).

Debates around the nature of content to be learned in the foreign or second language classroom, diverse approaches to language learning and teaching which CLIL learners require in subject-oriented lessons, the status of subject teachers and language teachers in different CLIL contexts, the nature of integration and collaboration between teachers of subject disciplines and language teachers – have spawned different 'solutions' over many years. Different CLIL models, pedagogic approaches and resources emerged, promoting a range of orientations, reflected in the different developmental stages of CLIL outlined in Chapter 1. It must be pointed out that in this chapter we are not 'judging' those developments – all of these have been made, and continue to be so, by educators wanting the very best for their learners to live their lives as multilingual global citizens. What we are seeking to understand better is what this means for the language teacher, as the role of the subject teacher is already constantly analysed. We address Dale's concern that:

> Excluding the language teacher from CLIL practices renders the language teacher invisible and underplays the changing position of the language teacher in bilingual education. (Dale, 2020, p. 13)

From a language teacher's perspective, several issues emerge depending on the context and the interpretation of CLIL or bilingual classroom learning. The list is not exhaustive but representative of recent developments according to the professional and academic literature:

- What is 'content' in language learning and how much importance is this given in a language curriculum?
- How can language teachers realistically access the depth of subject knowledge required to teach increasingly difficult concepts relative to a subject curriculum in the language chosen?
- How is curriculum time distributed between language learning and subject learning?
- What is the goal of language teaching and learning as a curriculum subject? How is this assessed?
- Does CLIL suggest that subject teachers decide on content and delivery while language teachers take on the role of language 'assistants'?
- What is the role of languages other than English in a CLIL context saturated by English?
- What happens in countries where language teachers lead the CLIL movement?
- What do we mean by language teacher and in which contexts are they referred to as such?

Questions such as these are familiar, depending on a myriad of contextual variables which impact in different regions and countries according to education policies and curricular thinking (Bower et al., 2020). None of them is straightforward – for example, Banegas argues that in bilingual education such as CLIL, 'content should also include language as a system of subsystems, as an object of study positioned in systemic functional linguistics' (Banegas 2012, p. 115). However, these questions reflect issues of great significance to the professionalism, identities and self-esteem of individual teachers, which often lie beneath the surface (Borg, 2018). As referred to in Chapter 2, the study of Dale et al. (2018a) identified different 'lineages' of language teachers (foreign-language teachers, first-language teachers and second-language teachers), and demonstrated how teacher identities underpin the choices they make, the principles they enact and the beliefs that propel their classroom practices. Their study, which led to a framework for *language teachers* in bilingual education, was built on a literature survey which revealed a 'plethora of understandings in the inquiry areas of language, content, pedagogical and collaborative practices' as well as some 'thorny issues' for language teachers in CLIL contexts (Dale et al., 2018a, p. 376). The framework was constructed to enable language teachers to clarify their choices, their identities, their language and content focus, and their positions relative to each other and subject teachers. Dale's doctoral thesis (Dale, 2020) concludes that a shift in perspective in the language teacher's own teaching from focussing only on a foreign language itself to being a subject teacher of language and literature is required, building on a usage-based rather than a structure-based view of language and informed by, for example, cognitive discourse functions (see Chapter 4.7) genre pedagogy (see Section 9.5) and the PTDL model.

However, as we have indicated throughout Parts II and III, there has been a sea change in educational thinking in response to global issues and perceived future needs of our young people. It is recognised that traditional approaches to both subject teaching and language teaching, whether they are integrated or not, are not sufficient to lead to deeper learning for all young people in our schools. That is, *both subject* teaching and learning *and language* teaching and learning need to adapt to societal global demands. Education systems around the world are awash with reforms seeking to achieve a more socially just and multiculturally attuned experience throughout schooling and beyond, including school improvement; raising the level of attainment; closing the gap; skills-based learning; agile leadership; digital literacies and so on. More recent research studies and publications have crucially opened up the dialogue (Nikula et al., 2016a; Dale, 2018b; Dale, 2020; Coyle & Chopey-Paquet, 2020), taking further the points raised in Chapter 2 to provide insights into 'alternative perspectives' on how language classroom practices might provide a 'legitimised contribution' to educating young people. Coyle and Chopey-Paquet's longitudinal study (2020) follow a language teacher's transition over the period of a year from working in a more traditional language classroom to becoming and being a subject expert (i.e. a teacher of creative writing using Gothic literature as the content and literacies as the 'subject'). The teacher reflected:

it's a big, big shift from traditional modern languages teaching! It's not to follow a grammatical spine, but to think of what kind of critical thinking and concepts children have cognitively and why not apply them to the L2 classes (Coyle, D. & Chopey-Paquet, 2020, p. 15).

The ideas, theories and practices discussed in this volume have provided us with a means to reposition CLIL and bilingual education, pushing beyond the boundaries into pluriliteracies-oriented spaces. With this in mind, we now seek to reposition the *language teacher* and *language learning* within the PTDL model. In other words, we seek to pose alternative questions to those listed previously. So far, we have focussed on the role of content subjects in promoting pluriliteracies development in our learners. In this chapter we examine the crucial role we believe language education can play in this regard.

9.2   Language Teaching and the Pluriliteracies Landscape

In this section we return to two of the challenges raised previously. The first builds on Darn's (2006, p. 5) argument that identifies the need to rethink language education as providing learner experiences which include – yet go beyond – the language system and general communication. The second suggests that neither traditional subject teaching nor language teaching is sufficient for responding to the rapidly changing societal demands on our young people in both monolingual and bilingual settings. This is not to criticise teachers, their professional expertise and commitment to young people, but rather to acknowledge that national education systems that define success criteria through measurable outcomes do not easily facilitate significant and timely shifts in pedagogic thinking. It is for these reasons that we focus on classroom practices and explore the potential which enables language teachers to be change agents in their own classrooms. To do this requires a repurposing of ways in which languages are taught and learned. We begin by exploring ways of reframing language teaching and learning as a 'subject discipline'. We seek not only to respond to Dale's suggestion that 'recent developments which place subject-specific literacy at the heart of CLIL risk side-lining language teachers' (2020, p. 168) but also suggest that language teachers can experiment and adapt learning pathways in their classrooms to create their own pluriliteracies environment – which is *not* dependent on other subject disciplines. We intend to promote debate and exploration by offering 'a view of language, and tools for teaching, to help move beyond structure-based views of language' (Dale, 2020, p. 166). However, this 'moving beyond' does not suggest that the structure of language and language forms, the lexis and the grammar of a language are of little value, but rather that their many roles (Llinares et al., 2012) are repositioned as fundamental linguistic tools in the complex meaning making process.

We shall first investigate the role of culture and cultures inherent in language teaching before unravelling how 'literature' and literacies have untapped potential for the language teacher in developing inclusive pluriliteracies practices for deeper learning.

9.2.1   Culture Investment and Language Teaching

The concept of culture is complex to define and is open to extremely wide interpretation. It is not our intention to engage in a detailed analysis of key concepts but instead to challenge thinking and outline possible pathways for ways in which language teachers might promote 'culture' and 'cultures' in ways which are fundamental to pluriliteracies education. According to Landis, 'there have been many definitions of culture. None are adequate, for how can one define that which makes up almost the totality of human experience?' (1972, p. 54). Yet, over centuries there has been an underlying assumption that language teaching is somehow inextricably linked to the 'culture' of the target language country. There are several errors in this assumption: the notion that culture is fixed and factual (e.g. the British eat bacon and eggs for breakfast); that a focus on one major target language country is adequate (e.g. France rather than francophone countries); and that a language community indicates a shared culture (e.g. English as a world language or global Englishes). The diversity of cultural layers that exist within a community and within nations is less visible to learners. As teachers are aware, attempts at representing national cultures promulgated in textbooks, which tend to focus on festivals, foods, clothing and the arts, can lead to stereotypical interpretation. Yet learners often have a curiosity about difference and similarities such that comparison between peoples is perceived as an interesting element of language learning. Therein lies the conundrum, echoed in Stern's (1992, p. 295) view that 'culture is the necessary context for language use'. This will be explored further.

The move to emphasise communication rather than language systems became prominent in the later decades of the twentieth century. An emphasis on communicative language teaching, alongside the development of cultural awareness, 'otherness' and intercultural competence emerged (Buttjes & Byram, 1991; Bateman, 2002; Broady, 2004) and with it a plethora of communicative approaches to learning. With a focus on communicating rather than knowledge building, according to Alptekin:

> learning a foreign language becomes a kind of enculturation, where one acquires
> new cultural frames of reference and a new world view reflecting those of the target
> language culture and its speakers. (Alptekin, 2002, p. 58)

We would argue that what is meant and understood by such enculturation requires careful and sensitive analysis (Savignon & Sysoyev, 2002). Whilst Nault (2006) suggests that culture teaching and language teaching are inseparable, Neuner (1997) emphasises the need to take into account the situated nature of the communication and the role of mediation required for any communication to be truly meaningful. However, this raises a 'thorny' issue: 'culture teaching' cannot be generalised (as for example in grammar teaching) but requires careful 'exploration and description' because, as Kramsch (1993) points out, the rules for creating meaning

are dynamic. Conceptualising 'culture' and 'cultures' as mediating tools fundamental for meaning making (Wertsch, 1998) resonates with the growing demands
of multilingual and multicultural learners in increasingly diverse classrooms. This
position is built on the premise that individuals make meaning through their own
cultural tools, not by applying externally validated cultural 'norms'.

Gay (2010) makes the case for culturally responsive teaching contingent on
raising learner cultural understanding and developing intercultural competence
(Deardorff, 2006). She argues for:

> seeing cultural differences as assets; creating caring learning communities where
> culturally different individuals and heritages are valued; using cultural knowledge of
> ethnically diverse cultures, families, and communities to guide curriculum development,
> classroom climates, instructional strategies, and relationships with students; challenging
> racial and cultural stereotypes, prejudices, racism, and other forms of intolerance,
> injustice, and oppression; being change agents for social justice and academic equity;
> mediating power imbalances in classrooms based on race, culture, ethnicity, and class;
> and accepting cultural responsiveness as endemic to educational effectiveness in all
> areas of learning for students from all ethnic groups. (Gay, 2010, p. 31)

Pratt and Foley suggest that, drawing on the work of Scarino and Liddicoat (2009),
such an approach encourages all learners to:

> value, respect and engage with the identities, languages, histories, geographies,
> ideologies and cultures in their own lives and to interact with others across linguistic
> and cultural borders (Pratt & Foley, 2020, p. 85).

Strong moral imperatives – reflecting those embedded in, for example, the United
Nations Sustainable Development Goals – resonate with what any teacher would
want for their learners. Nonetheless, we argue that language teaching and learning spaces offer transparent ways of enabling individuals – whatever age, stage
or heritage – to develop their own cultural tools to understand, deconstruct and
reconstruct language in use that impacts on an individual's sense of self and
worth. This does not happen unless learners are guided in using and developing
necessary skills. Culturally responsive teaching, therefore, requires an approach to
teaching and learning which identifies the skills and experiences needed to guide
learners in understanding how meaning making happens and their role in those
processes. So, what does all this mean?

The work of the New London Group (Cazden et al., 1996) has had significant
influence on recent thinking in the language learning world. The authors argue
that the multiplicity of communication channels and increasing cultural and linguistic diversity in our current world necessitates a much broader view of literacies
than is portrayed by traditional language-based approaches. Instead they emphasise the importance of multiliteracies which enable learners to become agentic in

deconstructing and reconstructing meaning through tasks that foster fundamental active and critical engagement. In similar vein, the Douglas Fir Group (2016) promotes a trans-disciplinary approach to language learning and using which seeks to expand learners meaning-making resources and identities by fostering:

> [a] profound awareness not only of the cultural, historical and institutional meanings that their language-mediated social actions have, but also... of the dynamic and evolving role their actions play in shaping their own and others' worlds. (Douglas Fir Group, 2016, p. 25)

Both groups emphasise the need for teachers to go beyond encouraging cultural awareness in language-focussed contexts and instead embrace ways of developing what we refer to as *cultural consciousness* in all learners. The term *cultural consciousness*, coined by Jackson in 1975, is used here in contrast to cultural awareness to stress the need for the active involvement of the learner in using cultural tools. This stance is embedded in the critical literacies movement (Street, 1995; Luke, 2000; Janks, 2013; Panos, 2017), where all learners are given opportunities to reflect and understand themselves in relation to other cultures and languages (Pratt & Foley, 2020). In contexts where teachers are responsible for enabling migrant learners or those who do not have the language of schooling to learn in mainstream classrooms, the role of critical literacies has had a significant impact on the development of pedagogic principles (e.g. in EAL (English as an Additional Language) classrooms). According to Pratt and Foley, critical literacies inspired by the genre movement (Halliday & Martin, 1993; Fairclough, 1989; and Street, 1995) enable learners and their teachers 'to understand how one's culture and language shapes the perception of oneself, of the world, and of our relationship with others' (Pratt & Foley, 2020). In this sense, texts (in the broadest sense) are seen as cultural tools which need to be carefully analysed and interpreted to make visible and challenge identities, power relations and social inequalities. Janks et al. (2014) also emphasise ways in which texts construct identity. They foreground how language and discourse can be used in powerful ways to shape identities and inequalities. Similarly, Holland et al. (1998, p. 128) advocate the use of powerful cultural resources or artefacts that resonate with or challenge those of students. This, they suggest, supports the growth of inclusive and self-aware 'safe' spaces which connect meaningfully across language and cultural boundaries. Bennett's Model of Intercultural Sensitivity provides a useful heuristic which monitors how an individual's intercultural communicative competence may shift from ethnocentrism to ethnorelativism through exploration of world views. This model is explored further in Section 9.5.

However, it would appear that such significant changes in thinking have impacted little on how 'foreign' language teachers' work in schools is conceptualised (Bower et al., 2020). There may be several reasons: the work of language teachers is consistently conceptualised across national curricula as focussing on the structures and grammar of the language through speaking, reading, listening and writing tasks whilst claiming to develop communicative competence; ways in which cultural awareness and learning about other cultures is typically formalised in text books do not address the sensitivities of *cultural consciousness* or make visible cultural tools for mediating meaning making, knowledge building and shaping identities; literacies in the foreign language classroom do not explicitly connect with literacy approaches in first or additional language contexts; and the critical literacies movement, involving approaches such as those described previously, is one which has little buy-in from language teachers and indeed may be perceived as irrelevant, especially for younger learners. And yet, the repositioning of cultural elements of language learning which impact on deepening learner understanding, alongside the need to develop critical literacy skills for constructing and using cultural tools, suggests that language teachers may be well placed to develop culturally inclusive and language-rich learning spaces in their classrooms. These issues will be further discussed after briefly considering how 'literature' – long associated with language learning – may also open up new possibilities for pluriliteracies language teaching and learning.

9.3   Literature, Literacies and Language Teaching

Note: In this chapter we use 'text' in its broadest sense referring to language manifestations in all modalities – spoken, written, audio, video, graphic, plurimodal etc.

It is generally accepted that the study of literature provides a lens through which an analysis of language and underlying cultural references, alongside the expression of fundamental human issues, can be interpreted, discussed and evaluated. In many traditional language-learning contexts, the study of literature is often reserved for those who have attained a high level of linguistic competence, especially in upper secondary and tertiary education. In those contexts, literature studies tend to focus on interpreting the literary text through, for example, translation, characterisation and stylistic analysis. Younger learners, on the other hand, have limited access to literature, usually through edited or simplified versions of literary texts (issues around perceived level of language complexity in authentic literary texts remaining unresolved). Instead, greater emphasis is placed, for example, on transactional roleplays, rather than those stimulated by stories or increasingly multimodal texts which have more potential for encouraging creative, spontaneous and culturally aware discourse. Widdowson's observation many decades ago remains valid:

It's not easy to see how learners at any level can get interested in and therefore
motivated by a dialogue about buying stamps at a post office. There is no plot, no

mystery, there is no character; everything proceeds as if communication never created a problem interaction. (Widdowson, 1983, p. 33)

This leads us, therefore, to consider the role and nature of literature in language teaching and learning, which has undergone significant change over recent decades. Koutsompou (2015) notes a recent upsurge of interest in literature and its untapped potential, described by Carter (2007) as 'an explosion in work in literary and cultural theory, a development that has provided a strong basis for exploration of the relationship between literature, language and education'. Carter distinguishes between a *functional interpretation* of literature – providing, for example, opportunities for vocabulary acquisition and developing reading or comprehension strategies – and an *ontological interpretation*, inviting readers into 'a world of fantasy, horror, feelings, visions… put into words' (Murdoch, 1950) which transcend temporal, social and cultural worlds.

Following Brumfit and Carter's (1986) seminal text *Literature and Language Teaching* describing literature as 'an ally of language', Long (1991) outlined three potential approaches for literature teaching (cultural, language and personal growth models) which resonates with Duff and Maley's (1990) promotion of an *integrated* model for using literature in the language classroom. They argue that literature provides learners with authentic text using a range of styles and genres (poetry, short stories, novels); it encourages learners to construct meaning; and it provides learners with opportunities to engage in creative, reflective experiences for developing linguistic and cultural awareness. Agustin Llach (2007, p. 9), drawing on much earlier work, summarises strong arguments to support literature as an integral part of language learning.

> It presents with authentic and varied language material, it provides with contextualized communicative situations, real patterns of social interaction, and use of language (Collie & Slater, 1987, p. 2), it highlights the central role of the learner in the learning process and stirs up interaction in the classroom, it motivates learners by allowing them to relate what is being read to their own experience since it calls on emotional responses (Collie & Slater, 1987, p. 2), and it contributes largely to develop further reading skills like 'deducing the meaning and use of unfamiliar lexical items', 'understanding the communicative value (function) of sentences and utterances', 'recognizing the script of a language', etc. (Grellet, 1981, pp. 4–5). (Llach, 2007, p. 9)

Moreover, recent controversies focussing on dominant cultural representation and social injustice have resulted in the gradual displacement of the 'literary cannon' (the classification of literature into those considered the most important) with 'more pragmatic concerns and the power of more contextualised and relativised theories of language and literature' (Carter, 2007). Thus, emergent moves to reposition literature in the language classroom extend far beyond the study of literature as an 'authentic' canvas for honing language skills. As arguments from the 1980s and 1990s gain renewed momentum, they inform and are open to current adaptation, thereby contributing to the dynamic of emergent thinking within our educational landscape. Building on the notion that literature – in its many forms and modalities – provides 'authentic' text which is open to analysis, critical interpretation and meaning making, thus guiding the learner to discover 'not just what a text means, but also how it comes to mean what it does' (Short, 1996) transforms ways in which literary text can be embedded in any language classroom.

We find Goldman et al.'s (2016) synthesis of the preceding arguments helpful in guiding the repositioning of the role of literature in language teaching. Based on Lee at al.'s argument that 'epistemological orientations to literary interpretation dimensions entails several dimensions' (Lee et al., 2016), Goldman et al. posit that literature can provide 'a window into interrogating the human condition and the world in which we live', alongside texts which open dialogue, 'privileging interrogating presumed authorial intent, valuing communities of readers who dialogue with one another within and across time', all of which crucially provide 'attention to both content and form as they work together to convey meaning' (Goldman et al., 2016, p. 10). These messages have far-reaching implications in terms of how language teachers can reappraise the nature of content to be learned and work with the opportunities inherent in progressing relevant and meaningful linguistic form of the language required. According to Short (1996), however, the teaching of language and the teaching of literature involves 'disconnected pedagogic practices' (Carter & McRae, 1996, p. xxiv). It is our intention now to explore how we can connect those practices by re-visioning language and literature in the contemporary language classroom.

9.3.1   Connecting Pedagogies for New Practices

Two significant points emerge from the discussion thus far. First, if we expand the concept of literature in its many different forms as providing cultural artefacts, then those artefacts or texts – in the broadest sense – have authenticity, cultural value and meaning. To reiterate, the content learned in language lessons, discussed in the previous section, whilst usually conceptualised as 'thematic', lies in the nature of meaning making (concepts, information and ideas) communicated through different types of texts (cultural artefacts) and their relevance to the worlds of the learners, deepening their self-awareness and sense of identity.

When literary texts are considered multiplicitious and studied alongside a broad range of other text types (e.g. advertisements, newspaper reports, magazines, popular song lyrics, blogs, social media and multimodal texts from the 'everyday' to the classical), their pedagogic potential shifts to a 'new reality', fostering 'self-awareness and identity in interaction with a new language and culture' (Carter, 2007, p. 10). Prioritising the fundamental role of text across different modalities is far removed from using a comprehension passage with closed questions created to test understanding. These are often bounded by formal grammatical rules and based on normalised expectations of classroom behaviours and what is considered 'correct'. When text is the currency for critical understanding and *cultural consciousness*; when text communicates ideas and concepts which are relevant, challenging and thought-provoking; when text provides the space for mediated learning and meaning making; when text evidences linguistic progression through learners' increasingly nuanced construction and use of language forms and their interpretation – then, the language classroom affords potential for deeper learning.

The second point, building on the first, suggests that when those pedagogic processes are situated within an academic literacies framework, learners collaboratively and explicitly investigate the range of 'genres, modes, shifts, transformations, representations, meaning-making processes, and identities involved in academic learning within and across academic contexts' (Lea & Street, 2006). Drawing on the work of scholars such as Kramsch (1993), Alderson (2000), Kern (2000), Carter also points out that:

> awareness dawned that literature, since it had continuities with other discourses, could be addressed by the *same pedagogic processes* as those adopted for the treatment of all texts to develop relevant skills sets, especially reading skills, leading in particular to explorations of what it might mean to read a text closely (Carter, 2007, p. 6).

This resonates with Goldman et al., who reinforce the need to enable the learner to engage in tasks which develop their capacity to:

> coordinate diverse—and sometimes contradictory—information and perspectives *from multiple texts*, accounting for authors' intent, evaluating evidence presented in the text, and judging the relevance and usefulness of each text for the task at hand (Goldman et al., 2016, p. 4; our emphasis).

However, this raises the question as to the nature of tasks required to provide language learners with the opportunities to develop the skills and understanding required for complex reading and reasoning (interacting and engagement) with a wide range of text, including literary text, in the language classroom. Goldman et al.'s (2016) study offers a clear steer in this direction, situating literature within a disciplinary literacies framework. Developing a conceptual framework across three disciplines (mathematics, science and literature) and focussing on reasoning and argumentation as fundamental to learning in any discipline, their work explores how using literature (texts) to develop reading and reasoning skills significantly shifts the nature of tasks offered to learners.

> Literary argumentation—like other formal models of argumentation—entails supporting claims with evidence, reasoning to support the evidence, warrants that provide credibility for the reasoning, and the response to actual and anticipated counter claims (Toulmin, 1958).

Their 2016 study repositions the study of literature (literary text) in line with other academic disciplines and opens up ways in which all learners can progress and develop their literacies skills (reading and reasoning) as their level of language develops accordingly. Moreover, we believe that aligning language learning with science and mathematical learning significantly elevates the pedagogic agenda and challenges the notion that language learning is not a 'core' discipline restricted to communicative competence and linguistic understanding. Table 9.1 below indicates common or shared learning goals across disciplines for reading and reasoning. These goals resonate with the pluriliteracies model presented throughout this volume. In accordance with this chapter's focus on the language teacher, Table 9.2 outlines how the common learning goals apply to literary reading, operating on two interrelated levels: the development of skills involved in reading, synthesising, constructing arguments, evaluating and demonstrating understanding (all of which have been analysed in depth in Part II); and the language and discourse required to engage in these processes.

However, in terms of disciplinary content, there is a significant challenge specific to the language teacher. In subjects such as science, argumentation will be embedded in the disciplinary culture of science (Chapter 4.4), where the language of science and the nature of the argumentation are focussed on accepted ways of being and doing science, especially in the earlier years of schooling. However, literary texts offer a much broader canvas – social, political, economic and cultural issues are much more diverse in terms of their conceptual implications, which impact on learners' reading, interacting and reasoning. Moreover, the cultural identities and life experiences that learners bring to working with text suggests that judgements are open to wider contestation than in science contexts, although these are potentially limited by the linguistic means to express them coherently.

Table 9.1   Learning goals for reading and reasoning from multiple sources (Goldman et al., 2016)

1. Engage in close reading of texts as appropriate to the disciplinary task and text.
2. Synthesize within and across aspects of texts important to the disciplinary tasks and texts,
3. Construct written arguments with claims, evidence, and warrants, organized logically and expressed clearly and that reflect disciplinary norms for argument.
4. Establish criteria for judging interpretive claims and arguments that are appropriate to the discipline.
5. Construct arguments explaining the logic of how the claims are supported by evidence using appropriate disciplinary criteria for claims, evidence, and logic.
6. Demonstrate understanding of the nature of knowledge and how that knowledge is constructed as appropriate to the discipline.

Table 9.2   Learning goals for literary reading (Goldman et al., 2016)

1. Engage in close reading of texts and show evidence that the reader has employed literary strategies to notice salient details with regard to plot, characterization, and rhetorical as well as structural choices made by the author.
2. Synthesize within and across literary texts patterns and anomalies in order to construct generalisations about theme, characterization, and the functions of structural and language choices made by authors.
3. Construct written arguments with claims, evidence, and warrants, organized logically and expressed clearly, using appropriate academic language. Arguments address author generalisations and/or structural generalizations (Hillocks & Ludlow, 1984).
4. Establish criteria for judging interpretive claims and arguments that address author generalizations, explaining how the text meets the criteria and justifies the claim (Hillocks, 1986,1995). Justifications may be drawn from the text; from other texts, literary constructs or critical traditions; or from the reader's judgments from experience in the world.
5. Construct arguments addressing structural generalizations (Hillocks & Ludlow, 1984), explaining the logic of how the claims are supported by evidence in the author's choices about use of language (e.g., structure, word choices, rhetorical devices).
6. Demonstrate understanding that texts are open dialogues between readers and texts; literary works embody authors' interpretations of some aspect of the human condition (which the reader may reject); authors make specific choices about language, structure, and use of rhetorical devices upon which the reader may draw in constructing interpretations.

This leads to some interesting questions – might it be that learning to read and reason (argue) using a broad range of text in another language, transforms the language classroom into a disciplinary learning environment? Might it be that if language skills are progressed in line with the literary skills outlined Table 9.2, moving from a single text to a multi-text model, deeper learning in the language classroom can not only be clearly defined but monitored, assessed and evaluated? The challenge remains outlined by Goldman et al. as follows.

> [M]eaning-making repertoires that middle and high school students need to develop in order to enter this problem-solving space require the skill sets and dispositions that are more reflective of what a range of expert readers bring to the enterprise. Without such a repertoire, novice readers, especially in middle and high school, are more likely to reject the value of complex literary texts out of hand rather than being enticed by their complexity. (2016, p. 11)

The implications for enabling learners to work in that 'space' raises an urgent need to explore ways in which the development of meaning making repertoires can be designed, developed and evaluated by language teachers to ensure that texts, including literary texts, are accessible for all learners – that is, conceptualising the progressive stages for deeper learning of literature in the language classroom. We argue that developing such challenging 'meaning making repertoires' enabling novice through to advanced learners access motivation and perceived value in working with text, is fundamental for language teachers – and needs to be explored further.

9.3.2 Towards Conceptualising Deeper Learning through Literature

Diehr and Suhrkamp (2015) propose a useful competencies model of literary development which evolves when three clusters of *interdependent* competencies are promoted:

Figure 9.1 A model of literary competences (Diehr & Suhrkamp, 2015)

As well as linguistic and discursive competencies, they suggest that learners need to develop motivational and attitudinal, aesthetic/cultural and cognitive competencies in order to fully appreciate, analyse, interpret, evaluate and respond to literary texts. They developed descriptors for each cluster which are similar in nature to the ones used in the Common European Framework of Reference for Languages:

Table 9.3 Motivational and attitudinal competencies (adapted from Diehr & Suhrkamp, 2015, translated from German by the author)

Can assume a critical and knowledgeable receptive stance that will enable them to read and understand literary texts in a foreign language, with regards to:
- the selection of texts;
- the motivation to read, listen or view literary 'texts' in a foreign language;
- developing an interest for literary interpretations with regard to content, structure and culture;
- personal approaches to texts;
- confidence in their own reading skills;
- perseverance and frustration tolerance; and
- expectations as readers

Can form associations and develop emotional and creative responses to texts

Can become immersed in literary texts, develop empathy for different perspectives and relate them to their own or other people's perspectives

Can enjoy a creative-playful approach to literary texts and appreciate essential aesthetic features of literary texts

Table 9.4 Aesthetic and cognitive competencies (adapted from Diehr & Suhrkamp, 2015, translated from German by the author)

Can understand literary texts which are age appropriate and commensurate with their language proficiency (with regards to plot, characters, conflicts, motives, themes and figurative language use)

Can use their worldly knowledge to fill gaps in literary texts and to form hypotheses and evaluate them while reading

Can develop mental models of the fictional world to make it come alive

Can analyse and interpret aesthetic means (character constellation, suspense curve, temporal structure) in various literary genres (prose, poetry, drama) (i.e. close reading)

Can use aspects of the historical or cultural context and use them to advance their understanding of the text

Can critically analyse and evaluate interpretations offered by a literary text

Table 9.5 Linguistic and discursive competencies (adapted from Diehr & Suhrkamp, 2015, translated from German by the author)

Can activate their linguistic knowledge and skills while reading literary texts

Can apply relevant strategies according to their intentions as readers (language awareness, language learning awareness)

Can communicate their imaginative, associative and emotional responses in an increasingly differentiated, critical and evaluative way in a wide range of genres and modes

Can recognise and use the linguistic 'diet' offered by a literary text (in terms of lexis, communicative patterns, genre and genre moves) to increase their language proficiency

Can articulate and negotiate their literary interpretations with others while using fundamental terminology

Can personally respond to literary texts by creating their own texts (non-literary, literary, visual or film) while attending to essential genre conventions

Since many of our educational systems prioritise the development of competencies, detailed taxonomies such as those outlined above provide useful foundations for designing classroom learning. Moreover, returning to Goldman et al.'s learning goals (Table 9.2) – especially those outlined in the sixth point – the role of the learner in interpreting text is reinforced. However, Moje et al. usefully remind us that:

> adolescents' ways of knowing, believing, thinking, and acting shape the ways they engage in reading, writing and speaking and listening… just as our own ways of knowing, believing, thinking and acting shape the ways… we teach' (Moje et al., 2000, p. 166).

They warn against ways in which 'we often lump learners into a one-dimensional mould called individual' (2000, p. 166) without taking into account the discourses – what Gee (1996, p. 131) refers to as 'thinking, feeling, believing, valuing and acting'

– that each individual uses to identify and position themselves and others as members of social groups. Earlier in the chapter, we raised the importance of raising learner cultural consciousness by building on what learners bring with them – their identities and belongingness. According to Moje et al. (2000, p. 167) texts 'are more than sites of information or aesthetic expression; they are cultural tools' for establishing ways of knowing and personhood (Street, 1994). This places responsibility on the language teacher in terms of the choice of texts used – not as linguistic artefacts but as socio-cultural tools for curriculum making which are integral to culturally responsive and inclusive language teaching. In other words, selecting text only according to its lexical and grammatical level of difficulty is no longer appropriate. Instead, co-selection of texts with learners according to their interests, identities, creativity and civic responsibilities – alongside the development of skills required to access and interpret texts, gradually leading to greater nuanced and sophisticated discourses – suggest progressive pathways for deeper learning in the language classroom. This will be detailed in a subsequent section. In line with the definition which we offer in Chapter 4, deeper learning results in the development of transferable knowledge and skills. With regards to literature as defined throughout, we propose that deeper learning of literature challenges learners to move beyond the stage of surface learning – where texts are treated as stories – to reach a level of interpretation where texts are treated as complex cultural discourses:

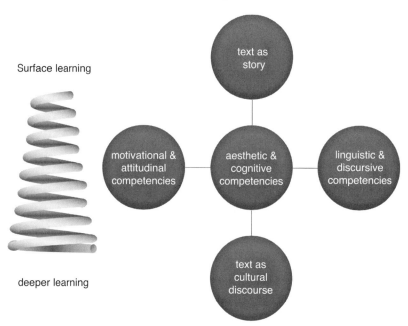

Figure 9.2 Deeper learning literature

As Goldman and others report (2016, p. 4), to fully appreciate texts as discourse, competent readers must reach an *intertext level* of understanding to realise how a given text relates to other texts by coordinating diverse and sometimes contradictory information and perspectives from various texts; accounting for authors' intent; evaluating evidence presented in the text; and judging the relevance and usefulness for the task. It also requires valuing learners' own contexts and identities. This is why we need to expand traditional reading comprehension models in the deeper learning literature classroom and move from single texts to multiple sources of information as learners develop their discourses.

This is the crossroads – we are all familiar with the argument that despite the potential of literary reading in the language classroom, there are insurmountable barriers to meaning making, due to the complex linguistic demands of the text. However, we refute this rationalisation. If learners do not have the necessary literacies-oriented skills and support to work with text, they will not be motivated to do so. It is therefore our collective responsibility to explore alternatives. The following sections of the chapter will explore the classroom implications of the reframing of modern language teaching and learning through a literacies and pluriliteracies lens. As Dale notes: 'Much work remains to be done applying genre pedagogy, cognitive discourse functions and the pluriliteracies model to the teaching of language, literature and culture' (2020, p. 167). In taking up this challenge we endeavour to encourage discussion, cut through contested barriers, and provide triggers for critical reflection and feedback in order bring L2 learners and their social-local worlds to the fore.

9.4   Repositioning the Language Teacher in a Pluriliteracies Context

The following is a summary of arguments presented so far:

1. The question about the content of language learning can be reformulated as follows:

> The content of language learning and teaching in schooling is open to wide interpretation. This can be seen as advantageous. It provides the language teacher with opportunities to select diverse and specific texts (in discussion with learners) which provide pathways for progression by developing ways of using social, cultural and linguistic tools for meaning making across languages. When learners are involved in deeper learning, drawing on the texts used for knowledge-building, analytical competencies and discourses, they will be developing skills which are transferable. These skills in turn will impact on the development of other subject-specific disciplinary skills.

2. Language teachers can provide learners with a wide range of experiences over time, which develop their understanding of how meaning is created through the use of language. In the language classroom, these are not necessarily embedded in subject disciplines but can relate to world issues, learner interests and negotiated themes. Through constant critical reflection and mentoring, and making these processes visible, learners can develop increasing competence in text analysis and text co-construction in line with literacy strategies across languages. This competence in developing critical literacies cannot easily be linked to a grammar-dominant approach. However, this does not mean that grammatical understanding and the functional use of language has no place. On the contrary, the language teacher has the skills to ensure that practising and negotiating linguistic forms is essential to using them for constructing meaning and self-reflection – provided it is visible.

> Among the key insights learners must gain about a language system is its meaning-making resource quality rather than a rule-based quality. Importantly, the resources in question are located in the combined system of lexicogrammar not grammar and lexicon considered separately and are intricately related to the functions to which language is adapted. (Byrnes, 2011, p. 148)

3. Pedagogic approaches which are rooted in social justice and inclusion value a critical literacies approach to language learning and using. Critical literacies guide learner understanding of how analysing language enables interpretations of underlying messages to impact on a dynamic sense of value and identities across linguistic and sociocultural boundaries. It is hardly surprising that critical literacies for language learning – in the sense of learning other or foreign languages – has not influenced language classroom practices. After all, the critical analysis of text has not traditionally been part of the (foreign, modern/other) language classroom repertoire in many countries. However, the case is very different for language teachers who are working in EAL contexts, where learners from different cultures and with a range of first languages are there to learn English as the language of schooling. These teachers have been grappling with ways of working appropriately with critical literacies in the multilingual classroom. If we accept that language plays a critical role in how learners make sense of their worlds and that human action is mediated by language and other symbolic systems embedded in cultural contexts, then language teachers too have a responsibility to explore and make visible different socially and culturally situated practices with their learners. According to Jones:

> Critical literacy is like a pair of eyeglasses that allows one to see beyond the familiar and comfortable: it is an understanding that language practices and texts

are always informed by ideological beliefs and perspectives whether conscious or otherwise. (Jones, 2006, p. 65)

Put simply, by supporting and guiding a deeper, multi-layered understanding of a range of texts, learners become empowered to understand the non-neutrality of the texts they meet. In essence, if language teachers are to foster a sense of social justice through the use of literary texts (in the sense developed throughout this chapter) from which emerge sensitive issues relating to – for example – power, race, class and gender, then all learners will begin to understand 'how we use language to construct and express view and version of ourselves and others' (Shor, 1992, p. 191). Moreover, there is now a sense of urgency. Against the backdrop of fake news, social media and complex multimodal texts, interest in critical literacy is growing globally. It could also be argued that given the global escalation of difference – such as gaps between rich and poor – educators everywhere need to put issues of poverty and social justice high in the classroom agenda, embracing an openness around the (de) colonisation of curriculum, the dominance of western white politics and global urgencies around the planet, energy and technology – all of which have been dismissed for many as being too sensitive or politically oriented for classroom discourses. We believe that language teachers have a critical role to play in shifting these agendas. Shor summarises what critical literacies mean for the language teacher as follows:

> Habits of thought, reading, writing, and speaking which go beneath surface meaning, first impressions, dominant myths, official pronouncements, traditional clichés, received wisdom, and mere opinions, to understand the deep meaning, root causes, social context, ideology, and personal consequences of any action, event, object, process, organisation, experience, text, subject matter, policy, mass media, or discourse. (Shor, 1992, p. 192)

We argue that the need to prioritise these discourses in the language classroom embraces the underpinning values of PTDL and provides pathways for developing critical literacies through textual analysis from the earliest stages. This shift is fundamental and increasingly urgent.

4. Understanding what text means conceptually for the language teacher is crucial to expanding pluriliteracies development. The texts used in class can be plurimodal and pluricultural. They range in style, length and purpose. Texts are interpreted through uncovering their cultural layers of meaning. A text can be a paragraph from a newspaper, a video clip of a TV show, a short story, a song, a novel or a blog by a learner. Texts are dynamic – they take account of our rapidly changing world and societal and political influences in rapid ways which are not possible for some printed resources such as textbooks. Texts

are living cultural tools. In short, a text may be relatively simple to access yet to engage the learner in developing appropriate discourses, enabling critical analysis and cultural consciousness for inter-texting and deeper learning, will require a significant shift in reframing language teaching as a subject discipline within a pluriliteracies paradigm (Figure 9.3). It will also reposition the language teacher as a powerful change agent in our rapidly changing world.

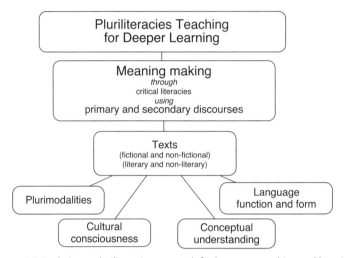

Figure 9.3 Exploring a pluriliteracies approach for language teaching and learning

9.5   Mapping Literacies Development in the Language Classroom

9.5.1   Common Practices

Building on the ideas underpinning a shift in the repurposing of language teaching and learning in schools we will now explore the implications for classroom practices from a literacies perspective. We begin by sharing reflections based on observations from the field which triggered some pertinent questions.

We are often invited by schools to watch and observe innovative and high-quality teaching and learning. Interestingly, many of these lessons share similar patterns. For example, learners may engage in jigsaw activities which are often based on an information gap, where students read, watch or listen to an array of authentic texts. In a next step, learners share their findings in groups. Typically, lessons end with learners presenting their 'product' such as a poster, video, blogpost – to demonstrate their learning. Depending on the schools' infrastructure, these tasks may be supported by digital tools to a higher or lesser degree.

At first glance, such lessons seem to meet all the requirements of task-based language learning: learners process authentic input, negotiate meaning by engaging in co-operative tasks and they jointly produce a learning outcome. They are also likely to receive feedback from their teachers during the so-called 'focus-on form' phase.

At a closer look, however, we often notice that the individual texts learners are given to read, watch or listen to in order to extract information, are only being processed at a surface level both in terms of content (i.e. factual and conceptual understanding) and language (i.e. words, collocations, chunks or useful phrases etc.). Accordingly, the actual demonstration of understanding, the individual or joint presentation of a learning outcome, is usually quite short and, in terms of conceptual breadth or depth, rather shallow. At the same time, the language used to communicate and express understanding is often not task-adequate. In terms of register, the produced texts score high neither on a colloquial nor academic scale.

Teachers report that that due to various curricular constraints, there is little time for individualised and in-depth feedback and that learners rarely have opportunities to deepen their understanding and revise their drafts. Similarly, in seminars on teaching literature in the language classroom, students relate that they find it increasingly difficult to reach an in-depth understanding of a literary text which goes beyond comprehending and analysing the text at the plot level to uncover textual meaning at the discourse level.

From discussions with many classroom teachers from various countries, we believe that such observations, even if they are not empirically grounded, indicate that the competences taught in the foreign language classrooms might not be mastered at a level that will allow learners to transfer their knowledge and skills to other texts – a supposition which was raised in the first section of the chapter.

This raises a set of intriguing questions:

1. What is deeper learning in the language classroom? How do we define and evidence it?
2. (How) is it possible that competency-based language teaching does not seem to promote mastery and transfer in ways which promote deeper learning? In other words, if deeper learning leads to transferable knowledge and mastery of skills, then how can we conceptualise language learning that focuses on deeper understanding, deep practice and the development of a growth mindset?

One explanation for performance shortcomings might be found in Christodoulou's observation that educational thinking and classroom design has fallen prey to a very far-reaching misunderstanding. This misunderstanding is based on the assumption that practising a complex skill or engaging in a complex task means learners automatically become better at it. As we stated in Chapter 4, this assumption is highly problematic because learners depend on 'detailed, knowledge-rich mental models stored in long-term memory' for optimal performance. We also reported in Chapter 4 that these mental models are acquired in what Christodoulou calls *learning tasks*. From this perspective, we hypothesise that language class-rooms currently tend to favour *performance* tasks over *learning* tasks and that this imbalance might be a plausible reason for inadequate task performance and, by extension, language learning. Another possible explanation might be that we misdiagnose classroom activity as learning and that we equate behavioural engagement with cognitive engagement. However, the fact that learners appear to be 'busy' does not necessarily mean that they are engaged in learning which is challenging or which leads to deeper understanding. In Chapter 5.1 we stated that deeper learning rests on deep engagement and the use of strategies for deep processing and cognitive elaboration. Shallow processing, on the other hand, is characterised by rote learning and superficial engagement with new content.

From a second-language acquisition perspective one could argue that a pre-dominant focus on performance tasks does not guarantee sufficient depth of pro-cessing of the input; that providing rich, authentic and multimodal texts does not ensure that learners will pick up new words and phrases and incorporate them into their mental lexicon; that more student collaboration which will increase talking time per learner and thus quantity of learner output might not necessarily mean quality in terms of complexity, adequacy or accuracy; that scaffolding or feedback which teachers provide will not necessarily be noticed and picked up by the learn-ers, and so on. However, given the positioning throughout this chapter, we posit that in order to do well in performance tasks, learners need not only to understand texts but to interact with them and to develop their use of cognitive, cultural and linguistic tools to negotiate meaning – that is, receive opportunities to build cognitive models and schemata and then practise ways that allow them to deepen their awareness and understanding *and* to automatise their communicative skills (discourses) whilst making sure that engagement remains high and deep (compare Chapter 5.2). This of course begs the question as to what exactly subject-specific literacies mean in the context of language learning and how the texts and tasks aligned with these can be conceptualised, mapped out and taught from a more holistic ecological perspective.

9.5.2   The Role of Text, Task Types and Discourses

Given the importance afforded to text as content, text as culture and text as lan-guage, one of the challenges is designing tasks to support the development of pluriliterate language use which empowers learners to successfully communicate knowledge and understanding across cultures and languages. The extent and nature of these competences for knowledge building, analysis and communication neces-sitate specific attention to supporting learner use and evaluation of linguistic tools, to activate cultural consciousness and develop increasing confidence in critical analysis through negotiation and interpretation of meaning. This involves *textual fluency*, which we have defined as the ability to critically evaluate and produce a wide variety of plurimodal texts and text types. However, taking into account Gee's definition of literacies development involving primary and secondary discourse as 'Discourse' and 'discourse' (see Chapter 3), in subject-discipline first-language contexts, learners bring very diverse primary discourse to the classroom. From there, they develop a growing command of secondary discourse related to the language of the subject discipline (e.g. the language of science, the language of mathematics). Herein lies the conundrum – foreign languages as linguistic systems do not have a secondary discourse in the same way as other disciplines. Learners themselves do not usually come equipped with a primary discourse repertoire in the language being learned. However, rather than being a disadvantage, instead this opens up – as has already been suggested – new possibilities for foregrounding *discourses* in the language classroom developed and analysed through a culturally conscious and linguistically rich repertoire of literature using multimodal texts

   Therefore, we suggest that a significant contribution of language teaching to pluriliteracies development consists in increasing *textual fluency in primary as well as secondary discourses of the target language.* In other words, literacies development in language learning encompasses basic, intermediate and disciplinary literacies (cf. Chapter 3.2) through the use of text, which result in growing command of relevant genres of primary and secondary discourses.

> [B]y teaching about Discourses, rather than teaching a Discourse, our students can become consciously aware of how their first language or D/discourse works. For this to happen, the students need to be engaged in an apprenticeship... in which they develop a 'meta-language' that can help them to see how the Discourses they already have work, how these Discourses relate to other Discourses, and how these Discourses relate to self and society. (MacKay, 2003, p. 20)

When textual fluency operates in tandem with cultural consciousness, opportunities evolve for developing an understanding of what Gee refers to as *Liberating literacies and Discourses*, and which have subsequently become known as critical literacies.

9.5.3   The Role of Genres as Pathways for Progression

Building on notions of textual fluency, we propose that pluriliterate language use manifests in the growing mastery of respective genres in primary and secondary discourses. This also entails an increasing capacity for semiotic translation, or, in other words, the ability to move along the plurimodal communication continuum (cf. Chapter 4.5). As Byrnes reflects:

> Learning to write and writing to learn language and content can be imagined simultaneously when language professionals embrace a fundamentally semiotic position regarding language as a system of meaning potentials and regarding the nature of wordings in particular instances of texts. (Byrnes, 2011, p. 150)

This idea is captured in Hallet's Genre Matrix (2016), which is based on the idea that in language education (both in first and other languages) there are three dominant macro-genres: narrative, expository and argumentative. By further subdividing these macro-genres into several more specific micro-genres and by adding the concept of 'mode', Hallet arrives at his matrix (Table 9.6).

Table 9.6 Hallet's Genre Matrix (adapted from Hallet, 2016)

Macro-genre	Genre	Oral mode	Written mode	Multimodal mode	Digital mode
Narrative texts	Recount	Talking to friends at school: *My practicum in Australia*	Written account: *My practicum in Australia*	Portfolio: *My practicum in Australia*	Blog entry: *My practicum in Australia*
	Story	Phone call to my parents: *My friend's accident and helicopter rescue*	Written story: *My friend's accident and helicopter rescue*	A cartoon: *My friend's accident and helicopter rescue*	Social network post/collage: *My friend's accident and helicopter rescue* (Pinterest etc.)
	Anecdote	Talking to my friend: *An incident at the holiday camp*	An email to my friend: *An incident at the holiday camp*	Photo album: *An incident at the holiday camp*	A slide show for my family: *An incident at the holiday camp*
	Exemplum	Classroom presentation: *The story of the life of a pair of blue jeans*	A school magazine article: *The story of the life of a pair of blue jeans*	A flyer: *The story of the life of a pair of blue jeans*	Online presentation/website: *The story of the life of a pair of blue jeans*
	Vision	Telling my parents: *The first three months after my final school exam*	Diary entry: *The first three months after my final school exam*	An illustrated scenario: *The first three months after my final school exam*	Chat forum contribution/Prezi: *The first three months after my final school exam*
Expository (factual) texts	Description	Conversation: *A new apartment*	Estate agents expose: *A new apartment*	Estate agents brochure: *A new apartment*	Website presentation: *A new apartment*
	Report	Presentation: *Aborigines in contemporary Australia*	Written report: *Aborigines in contemporary Australia*	A poster: *Aborigines in contemporary Australia*	A multimedia collage/Padlet: *Aborigines in contemporary Australia*

	Explanation	Oral explanation: *How an electric bike works*	Written explanation: *How an electric bike works*	Illustrated magazine page: *How an electric bike works*	Wiki text: *How an electric bike works*
	Procedure	Instruction: *How to build a paper plane*	Instruction: *How an electric bike works*	Illustrated manual: *How an electric bike works*	Step-by-step YouTube video: *How an electric bike works*
	Protocol	Introducing rules for new members: *Ten dos and don'ts in the theatre club*	Written rules for new members: *Ten dos and don'ts in the theatre club*	A booklet for new members: *Ten dos and don'ts in the theatre club*	Social network group post: *Ten dos and don'ts in the theatre club*
Arguments	Exposition	A speech: *Abolish child labour!*	A letter to the president: *Abolish child labour!*	A pamphlet: *Abolish child labour!*	A website: *Abolish child labour!*
	Discussion	Peer discussion: *The pros and cons of prohibiting alias names on the internet*	Written discussion: *The pros and cons of prohibiting alias names on the internet*	A wall display: *The pros and cons of prohibiting alias names on the internet*	An overview of chat forum entries: *The pros and cons of prohibiting alias names on the internet*
	Argument	Debate: *A limited mobile phone account*	Parent-child mail exchange: *A limited mobile phone account*	Object-related discussion (using phone to demonstrate): *A limited mobile phone account*	Parent-child WhatsApp exchange: *A limited mobile phone account*
	Persuasion	An election campaign speech	An election campaign leaflet	An election campaign party flyer	An election campaign newsletter/video ad

Whilst we believe that the matrix is a highly useful tool, in that it allows for differentiated teaching and learning by visualising the wide array of available genres in their various modes as they relate to texts being studied, it does not address the question of how to conceptualise progressions or learning pathways for these genres. However, if we superimpose a dynamic understanding of cognitive discourse functions (CDFs; cf. Chapter 4) and how they can be rank-shifted to function as vital parts of more complex types or genres, we can conceptualise learning progressions within genre use (Figure 9.4). For example: a book review composed by a lower-secondary learner might include all the necessary components/moves of the genre but will not reflect the conceptual understanding or the linguistic sophistication of a book review composed by an upper-secondary learner.

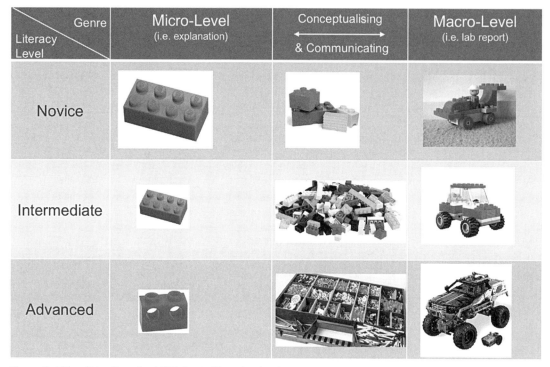

Literacy Level \ Genre	Micro-Level (i.e. explanation)	Conceptualising & Communicating	Macro-Level (i.e. lab report)
Novice			
Intermediate			
Advanced			

Figure 9.4 Visualising the role of CDFs in pluriliteracies development

From this perspective, deeper learning in the language classroom could lead to improved linguistic performance in terms of fluency, syntactical and lexical complexity, accuracy and task adequacy. In sum, those performance gains will indicate growing command of a given genre and thus increased meaning-making potential.

Again, we believe that it is extremely important to reiterate that we cannot separate language from content: learners will only be able to advance their ability to communicate knowledge adequately if we help them increase their understanding of the content they are trying to communicate. Therefore, we have to reconceptualise ways in which texts relating to topics and themes provide opportunities for learners to engage in deep practice, deep understanding and the development of a growth mindset. Skill development must be tied to growing understanding, which requires clear articulation of what we want our learners to understand and communicate in the language classroom. This will require language teacher engagement in new ways of designing, monitoring and evaluating classroom tasks which build on progression through genre use, textual fluency and appropriate levels of functional language use. In short, a grammar-oriented, competence-based syllabus focussing on the development of four language skills is no longer adequate on its own for developing a pluriliteracies approach to deeper learning.

We turn now to considering the kinds of emerging strategies which provide some initial guidance for classroom practice.

9.6 Strategies to Deepen the Language Learning Experience

The following eight strategies, which have emerged from the research in pluriliteracies subject discipline classrooms, can be adopted and adapted for the language classroom (Figure 9.5). Each will be considered in turn before concluding this chapter.

Figure 9.5 Deeper learning strategies

9.6.1   Deepening Textual Understanding

As highlighted throughout, understanding text is a highly individual process which depends on many factors, such as learners' prior knowledge, their strategic competence or motivation and engagement, and their own identities and discourses. In order to make sure that all learners fully understand the texts they are asked to read, listen to or watch, special attention needs to be paid to anticipating the potential knowledge demands of any text. An analysis of these issues provides a rich source of material for task design. Seven key aspects are briefly listed below, all of which will require further context-related consideration.

Salient features of text requiring attention to inform task design and analysis

Concepts

- Explore the full potential of texts in terms of conceptual knowledge.
- Focus on increasing conceptual understanding as well as learner engagement in complex tasks and producing outputs.
- Use concept maps to promote understanding – they challenge learners to actively deconstruct and reconstruct a text, thereby inviting them to connect the dots themselves and crucially to specify (through labelling) the nature of the connection.

Note: Hattie (2017) reports effectiveness of concept mapping in an updated list of factors related to student achievement. His findings confirm concept mapping prevents learners from simply copying and pasting information from a text. Instead, it challenges learners to visualise and language their understanding – even more so, when concept mapping is done collaboratively with a partner. Concept maps make understanding visible, reveal gaps in understanding and provide important clues for follow-up activities.

Lexis

- Emphasise the use of words in context (e.g. Lewis' *Lexical Approach*).
- Pay attention to how words are used in combination to make meaning – for example, develop learner understanding through an emphasis on collocations and ways to record, learn and use lexical elements (such as lexical notebooks or digital quiz cards).
- Move away from new introducing lexical elements in isolation and 1:1 word equations (word L1 = word L2).
- Explore Lewis's ten principles of organising lexis (situation, notion, collocation, narration, metaphor, cascades, register/politeness, etc.).

Table 9.7   Collocation box (based on Lewis, 2007)

Verb	Adjective	Noun
to deal with	a minor, major	problem
to tackle	a pressing, urgent	
to solve	an immediate, long-term	

We have developed an activity we call 'lexical harvesting', which we recommend can be applied to all texts: once learners have a basic understanding of the content of a text, they are invited to go through that text again, paying special attention to how certain ideas are expressed and what collocations, phrases etc. are being used to express them. Next, they are asked to record the most useful collocations into their lexical notebook by using collocation boxes (see Table 9.7). This not only raises awareness of collocations and chunks but shifts the focus from the content to *how that content is languaged* by the author.

Linguistic elements

- Analyse the text for linguistic features used at the word or sentence level and the style (these impact on learners' ability to process text).
- Analyse texts for complex sentence structures, use of nominalisations and academic vocabulary. These pose different challenges compared to texts in colloquial language. Literary texts often present additional difficulties by using figurative and highly connotative language.

Text structure

- Teach learners how to understand the structure of complex texts (i.e. by transforming them into flow charts, rewriting segments of a novel using a different point of view, etc.) to increase their ability to cope with text variety.
- Be aware of text structures which present difficulties for learners – for example:
  - Learners struggle to understand how ideas are organised in texts.
  - Texts with a linear or chronological structure are typically easier to understand than non-linear ones.
  - Literary texts are often structured in a highly complex way with different points of view, a range of different characters and storylines and many confusing details.

Underlying ideological and cultural concepts/assumptions

- Learners need to know how to uncover, analyse and evaluate the ideological and cultural assumptions underlying the texts they work with.
- Critical readers need to learn how to become responsive as well as responsible readers.
- Learners need to develop the skills to:
  1. make observations about a text;
  2. establish connections among observations;
  3. make inferences based on observations and connections;

4. draw conclusions from the inferences; and

5. consider values the text embodies and possibly endorses (DiYanni, 2017).

- Learners need to develop an understanding of text as a 'complex set of discursive strategies that is situated in a special cultural context' (Fürsich, 2009).

- Reading for understanding increasingly encompasses reading from multiple sources:

Competent readers must coordinate diverse – and sometimes contradictory – information and perspectives from multiple texts, accounting for authors' intent, evaluating evidence presented in the text, and judging the relevance and useful-ness of each text for the task at hand. (Goldman et al., 2016, p. 4)

- Deeper learning language classrooms use models of reading which expand comprehension from single to multiple sources, both for *factual* as well as *literary* texts.

Note: *Facing Ferguson: News Literacy in a Digital Age*[1] is an excellent set of free online teaching materials that demonstrate exemplary ways of promoting media literacy to advanced students, by teaching how to detect and analyse explicit as well as implicit biases; to verify breaking news; analyse the power of images and the role of social media; and discuss the role of citizen watchdogs.

Purpose and meaning

- Factual texts are usually less challenging than texts that offer conflicting or biased information.
- Literary texts often consist of multiple layers of meaning (e.g. plot or surface level, discourse or deeper level).
- Intertextual understanding, especially when themes are implicit rather than explicit, can only be discovered by looking at a text in its entirety and through its relation to other texts.

Specificities of genre and mode

- Textual fluency encompasses five semiotic modes (spoken language, written language, visual, audio, gestural and spatial). Learners need guidance in how meaning is created and expressed through each of the modes.
- It is increasingly important for learners to understand how semiotic modes work individually or jointly to create holistically produced meanings (Siefkes, 2015).

---

[1] www.facinghistory.org/resource-library/facing-ferguson-news-literacy-digital-age

- Learners need support in understanding how *intermodal relations* play a significant role in the creation of plurimodal meaning. An intermodal relation is present when 'one mode has a definable influence on the formal, semantic, and/or stylistic properties of another mode in a specific text' (Siefkes, 2015, p. 115).

Taking the example of films, as integral to the language curriculum: film analysis tends to focus on plot level, often neglecting genre but especially mode specificities. Siefkes sees film as a 'specific type of intermodal text with high complexity, including spoken and written language … moving images, kinesics (gesture, body posture, facial expression, proxemics), sound and music' (2015, p. 127). Deeper understanding of a movie and its effects on the viewer primarily result from an understanding of intermodal relations and how these are planned and created by the producers.

Similarly, TV shows encompass not only the question of how genres operate within larger cultural systems or how to interpret the textual meanings of genres by situating them within their social contexts, but how a given genre accrued particular meanings for particular audiences in a historically specific instance. In other words, 'we need to ask what a genre means for specific groups in a particular cultural instance' in order to understand 'how the use of genre categories is shaped by – and shapes cultural power relations' (Mittel, 2004, p. 5).

9.6.2 Increasing Content Relevance

In Chapter 5.2 we discussed the significance of student engagement on deeper learning. Citing Priniski's Relevance Continuum, we reported factors and variables which can increase personal meaningfulness and help learners move from rather ephemeral situational interest to more individual investment. Moreover, we argued that one important function of mentoring learning is for teachers to communicate relevance and encourage learners to discover and explore personal connections to the content in order to boost engagement. As emphasised throughout earlier sections, for language learning to be 'subject' learning, the relevance of text topics shared with and for learners is fundamental to designing Deeper Learning Episodes. Finding ways of negotiating relevance does not require special skills or specific tools, but requires culturally responsive teaching of growth mindsets and creating safe yet challenging spaces for learners. Establishing personal relevance is well suited for the transfer stage of Deeper Learning Episodes. An example is provided for reflection.

A Deeper Learning Episode on Shakespeare's Sonnet 130 might begin with learners discussing ideals of beauty and their inherent risks to teenager health after critically analysing TV adverts. This will not only prepare them for a deeper understanding of the ideals expressed in the sonnet and the turnaround in the heroic couplet, but also show them how these concepts have been relevant through the ages. Asking learners to write a contemporary version of the sonnet will lead to a deeper understanding of the genre in terms of structure and rhyme, and challenge learners to analyse the specific lexical choice made in the poem itself and find ways of 'translating' the imagery into colloquial English. The sequence might end with learners preparing a TV show where they discuss the dangers of falling prey to unhealthy ideals of beauty conveyed by the media and photoshopped models, and ways to avoid these dangers. One of the fictional guests of that show might be Billie Eilish, who steadfastly refuses to succumb to shallow ideas of beauty by refusing to wear skimpy clothes or expose her skin when on tour.

9.6.3   Developing Cultural Consciousness

The need to address ways in which *cultural consciousness* can be brought to the fore emphasises ways in which we not only acknowledge but value differences that are inherent in cultural identities and experiences that are forever present in any classroom. The invisibility of difference contributes to inequitable classroom literacy practices which impact on language and learning opportunities. In the language classroom, the use of text, the selection and choice, the analysis and reinterpretation, all hold untapped potential. These militate against cultural and linguistic outsiders or 'overhearers' of a language curriculum (Foley, 2018) which is of increasingly limited relevance for the real world.

There are two strategies which require significant attention. The first relates to the *selection of text*; the second to the tasks facilitating reflexive reading through a cultural lens. In terms of text selection, a recent national syllabus for thirteen-year-old learners recommended the topic of 'house and home'. The textbook suggested learning vocabulary connected with rooms in a house; its size; including garden and garages; the neighbourhood; and the inhabitants. It targeted writing or spoken tasks for comparisons and descriptions. At the surface level, this is meaningless. It is anodyne and is no-one's reality – for a three-year old or a thirty-three-year old. The topic does not reflect the intricacies and diversity of life outside the classroom. However, when educators with their learners make shared decisions about text selection, the context for learning can radically change direction. For example, when text selection focusses on exploring similarities and differences between transitory or temporary homes, urban and rural communities, social housing and homelessness, then learners are invited to engage in meaning making which can be drawn from social realities or imaginary worlds, from the media to literary works and from stories to personal accounts.

The second strategy is fundamental since it concerns ensuring text 'accessibility' for diverse learners. This strategy should not be confused with selecting text only according to linguistic level of difficulty. Clearly the linguistic level is important – but only in so much as it relates to the concepts within. It is the nature and progression of tasks which guide learners through using text, develop their literacies skills, raise their cultural consciousness and make visible ways in which language works to convey meaning, as they develop discourses which lead towards deeper understanding.

With regard to the actual reading process, there are a number of strategies to mentor the development of cultural consciousness in language learners:

1. **Use of analytical tools:** In order to objectively observe and classify cultural differences, learners need specific categories and tools. In recent training courses with upper-secondary language teachers, we developed deeper learning sequences where students learn how to apply the cultural frameworks of Hofstede and Hall to analyse and re-enact critical incidents.

2. **Perspective shifting through empathetic and cultural reading:** According to Bennett's Model of Intercultural Sensitivity, the development of intercultural communicative competence of individuals is marked by moving from ethnocentrism, where one's own culture is viewed as the only real one, towards stages of ethnorelativism, where one's own culture is viewed as just one of a number of equally complex worldviews (Bennett, 1993). Reid stresses that ethnorelativism 'does not come naturally hand in hand with foreign language education' and argues that learners may even become more ethnocentric if cultural issues are excluded from language classrooms (Reid, 2013, p. 48). Freitag-Hild (2018) recommends empathetic and cultural reading to facilitate the development of cultural learning processes: during *empathetic reading* activities, learners assume the perspective of literary characters to better understand their respective situations and behaviour. *Cultural reading* activities teach learners how to read texts as part of a cultural discourse to understand how a given text relates and responds to other fictional or non-fictional texts. There are a number of excellent, freely available short films that teachers can use to facilitate empathetic reading/watching: Steph Green's *New Boy* is based on the eponymous short story by Roddy Doyle. It depicts a young African boy's eventful first day of school in Ireland. *Majorité Opprimée* by Eleonore Pourriat narrates the story of a man exposed to sexism and sexual violence in a society dominated by women.

3. **Transcultural learning:** Transculturality refers to 'a number of characteristics that are shared by modern cultures: inner differentiation, polyphony, cultural complexity hybridity, external networking and entanglements with other cultures. Cultures and identities can be described as "transcultural" if traditional

categories of, i.e. national, cultural, religious communities, are deliberately questioned, broken up or transgressed.' (Freitag-Hild, 2018, pp. 170–1). Netflix' *Never Have I Ever* (2020) is a coming-of-age comedy about the complicated life of a first-generation Indian American teenage girl who clearly possesses a transcultural identity. Caught between her traditional Indian upbringing and the values of American high school life, fifteen-year-old Devi has to find out who she really wants to be.

9.6.4   Increasing Learner Agency and Accountability

In Chapter 5.2 we presented a study by Hospel and Galand that established a link between autonomy support and learner engagement. The work stresses the importance of psychological freedom and choice of learners to determine and self-regulate their learning behaviours. In Deeper Learning Episodes there are spaces for differentiated and individualised learning pathways (see Sections 9.6.5 and 9.6.6). In terms of deeper learning, however, we believe that a degree of learner agency should be coupled with a high degree of learner accountability. For example, normalising classroom practices which include using (digital) portfolios to document research and creating concept maps for findings (online, along with digital or analogue lexical stash cards, which contain newly discovered words, images, translations and information on collocation etc.) will go some way to encouraging and modelling how learners can act responsibly and purposefully. It will also demonstrate that time spent away from the textbook might be time well spent in terms of increased relevance, agency and accountability. Moreover, involvement with the nature of (content) texts selected for in-depth study is critical in terms of student voice, individual investment, developing cultural consciousness and textual fluency.

9.6.5   Differentiating Learning Pathways

Differentiated learning is fundamental to the founding principles upon which pluriliteracies approaches are based. Guidance from Universal Design for Learning – one approach among many – identifies 'inflexible, "one-size-fits-all" curricula as the primary barrier to fostering expert learners'. The authors argue that in learning environments, 'individual variability is the norm, not the exception' (CAST 2011, p. 4). Three primary principles for differentiated instruction are presented, based on research into learner variability. Whilst the three principles are commonly agreed, ways of operationalising them so that they become owned by teachers and learners will require very careful analysis and planning. The three principles can be summarised as ensuring that all learners have access to:

1. multiple means of representation (i.e. differentiated access pathways for individual learners);

2. multiple means of action and expression (i.e. various ways of constructing knowledge and demonstrating understanding); and

3. multiple means for meaning making and languaging through choices which are values driven, foster interest, sustain effort and encourage self-regulation.

9.6.6 Individualising Learning Pathways

In Chapter 8.1 we introduced the concept of *task alignment* and stressed its essential role in creating Deeper Learning Episodes. In fact, aligning disciplinary core constructs, knowledge activity domains and the mechanics of deeper learning with learner needs, strengths and interests is a prerequisite in designing Deeper Learning Episodes. Increasing learner autonomy, accountability and choice will contribute greatly to individualising learning. However, none of these ideas offer a way of adjusting the difficulty or conceptual complexity of the content to the needs of a learner. This is the unique and most valuable and practical feature of our dynamic approach to CDFs, presented in Chapter 4.7. Being able to up- or downscale both the underlying cognitive structure of a CDF as well as the language used to express and demonstrate understandings (i.e. explain X at Level I, II or III) offers a novel approach to individualising knowledge construction and communication. Thus, our approach offers a practical way of linking content with language learning in ways that are 'developmentally learnable and educationally teachable', which according to Byrnes are key requirements for the development of meaning-based language learning curricula (Byrnes, 2014, p. 98).

9.6.7 Providing Opportunities for Deep Practice

The automatisation of skills via instructed strategy use is of paramount importance in language learning. As has already been mentioned, this is why we need to rethink and re-evaluate the role of practice in language learning and find ways of designing tasks which make up Deeper Learning Episodes in such a way that challenging and complex tasks are complemented with episodes of deep practice and reflection (see Chapter 4.3). This implies that we need to find novel ways of breaking down complex tasks into smaller units which can then be mastered through practice. Also, we need to acknowledge that enhancing skills requires repetition and reflection and that both of these require time, sometimes even more time than we are willing to grant our learners.

> [C]urricula must make sure that the particular slice of lived reality that their diverse pedagogical task instantiate and incorporate in instruction are not isolated, unmotivated 'busy-work' activity. The role attributed to 'practise' in L2 writing development rightly recognizes that good writing abilities are long in coming. But 'not all practice is made equal'. The most obvious way to offer worthwhile opportunities for practise is by

consistently and continuously linking all modalities that are otherwise used to plan instruction, particularly the reading-speaking-writing connection. (Byrnes, 2011, p. 149)

There is an identified need for further research into the effects of deep practice on skill acquisition and its effects on performance in the language classroom. Should these results confirm what Berg's (Berg, 2020) and Connolly's (Connolly, 2019) research indicates for CLIL classrooms, then providing learners with opportunities and sufficient time for *deep* practice can no longer be considered an optional 'ingredient' in language learning but must take centre stage.

9.6.8   Scaffolding Development

In Chapter 6.2 we proposed a reconceptualisation of scaffolding as mentoring learning which is both dynamic (because it spans every phase of learning-teaching) and multi-dimensional (because it targets every domain of learning). To successfully mentor language learning, teachers will need to anticipate potential pitfalls for their learners and provide support whilst designing Deeper Learning Episodes. Whilst this might seem an obvious statement, the issue is one of how to best prepare learners to meet with unknowns; to construct tasks which scaffold learners to develop their own strategies for dealing with unknowns; and finally to design tasks which focus on challenging learners without compromising the conceptual and linguistic level required to achieve deeper – rather than surface – learning.

The guide to genre writing provided by the Berlin Senate Administration offers specific, comprehensive scaffolding at two different levels for all the major text types commonly taught in language classrooms. These materials are exemplary because they offer sample texts, writing frames and clear instructions for learners about which steps to take when writing a specific text type, as well as checklists for autonomous learning self-evaluation.[2]

Whilst students are engaged in Deeper Learning Episodes, teachers need to monitor progress and provide ongoing feedback and support if needed to make sure that learners master the tasks at their respective levels. In such contexts, it is of paramount importance to understand that 'from an SLA perspective, feedback should be guided by an interest in acquisition for growth, most especially growth in the capacity to mean, not primarily for improving accuracy' (Byrnes, 2014, p. 91).

Byrnes emphasises that in order to successfully mentor deeper learning, language teachers need to embrace a deeper learning mindset which guides their decisions as to how to deploy the various strategies we have outlined. That mindset first

---

[2] https://bildungsserver.berlin-brandenburg.de/fileadmin/bbb/unterricht/faecher/sprachen/englisch/pdf/HANDREICHUNG_ONLINE-FINAL_06.05.16.pdf, https://bildungsserver.berlin-brandenburg.de/fileadmin/bbb/unterricht/unterrichtsentwicklung/Individualisierung_des_Lernens/2018_Materialien_zum_selbststaendigen__standardorientierte_Lernen__in_der_gymnasialen_Oberstufe_Englisch_Text_production.pdf

and foremost needs to be grounded in an understanding of language as a complex adaptive system (Five Graces Group, 2009).

Complexity arises in systems via incremental changes based on locally available resources, rather than via top-down direction or deliberate movement toward some goal (see, e.g., Dawkins, 1985). Similarly, in a complex systems framework, language is viewed as an extension of numerous domain-general cognitive capacities such as shared attention, imitation, sequential learning, chunking and categorisation (Bybee, 1998b; Ellis, 1996). Language is emergent from ongoing human social interactions, and its structure is fundamentally moulded by the pre-existing cognitive abilities, processing idiosyncrasies and limitations, and the general and specific conceptual circuitry of the human brain. Because this has been true in every generation of language users from its very origin, in some formulations, language is said to be a form of cultural adaptation to the human mind, rather than the result of the brain adapting to process natural language grammar (Christiansen, 1994; Christiansen & Chater, 2008; Deacon, 1997; Schoenemann, 2005). These perspectives have consequences for how language is processed in the brain. *Specifically, language will depend heavily on brain areas fundamentally linked to various types of conceptual understanding, the processing of social interactions, and pattern recognition and memory.* It also predicts that so-called 'language areas' should have more general, pre-linguistic processing functions (even in modern humans) and, further, that the homologous areas of our closest primate relatives should also process information in ways that makes them predictable substrates for incipient language. Further, it predicts that the complexity of communication is to some important extent a function of social complexity. Given that social complexity is, in turn, correlated with brain size across primates, brain size evolution in early humans should give us some general clues about the evolution of language (Schoenemann, 2006). Recognising language as a complex adaptive system allows us to understand change at all levels (Five Graces Group, 2009, 17–18).

Consequently, language learning should be viewed as facilitating growth in meaning making. Since this growth is a highly individualistic process, we posit that language learning understood as pluriliteracies learning is not compatible with the traditional focus on the teaching of universal grammar elements or standardised vocabulary instruction in one-size-fits-all approaches.

We are well aware that some of the ideas presented in this chapter are in their early stages of development. Whilst we have attempted to present clear theoretical unpinning for language teaching as subject teaching, we also realise that transforming these into regular practice will require a strong determination to change classroom practices and patience to experiment and explore how these might be practised with learners. There is a clear need now for practitioner enquiry, class-based or near-practice research for co-design to provide the professional community of educators with worked-through examples of how these ideas may be disseminated, critiqued and developed. The following section provides two such examples, which may serve to inspire teachers and their learners to explore potential in ways which they themselves own, direct and critique.

9.7   Deeper Learning Episodes in the Language Classroom: Emerging Exemplars

There is clearly now an urgent need to develop classroom materials which model the principles discussed in this chapter. We believe that this will encourage language educators to experiment with changing practices in a move towards exploring and evaluating their own lived experiences in their own contexts, demonstrating their own interpretations of a pluriliteracies approach to language learning as a subject discipline. The following Deeper Learning Episodes were 'prototypes' designed to meet the criteria of high-fidelity tasks (see Chapter 8) which focus on: increasing the depth of understanding of relevant topics through applying a set of analytical frameworks (e.g. how to analyse prosody, how to construct convincing arguments, how to analyse movie scenes); and developing and mastering skills through deep practice, offering learners ways to reflect on their own learning and use and give feedback in order to revise drafts of their work. In essence, the Deeper Learning Episodes simultaneously offer learners opportunities to:

1. become deeply engaged with texts in a foreign language through DL strategies;
2. language understanding to build/deepen their conceptual knowledge; and
3. demonstrate growth in understanding or make their learning visible and accessible for (peer or teacher) feedback, reflection and revision.

9.7.1   Promoting Oral Language Skills: Phonological Chunking and Prosody Training

Focus principles: Chunking is an essential process in learning. Chunking supports and accelerates retrieval from long-term memory and reduces cognitive load. That process is especially important for language learning. Lewis's Lexical Approach emphasises the importance of lexical chunks (e.g. lexical phrases, collocations, frames) that learners need to have at their disposal in order to communicate fluently and adequately. According to Lewis, fluency is based on 'the acquisition of a large store of fixed and semi-fixed prefabricated items' which serve as the foundation 'for any linguistic novelty or creativity' (Lewis, 2002, p. 15). Lewis' approach has been very influential in language teaching and his ideas have greatly affected the way language support is conceptualised and provided in the classroom. However, little attention has been paid to the concept of *phonological chunking*, which is only briefly mentioned in Lewis' book *Implementing the Lexical Approach*. Phonological chunking is based on the idea that spoken language is governed/organised through musical signals to a large extent. In speech, rhythm and melody are important carriers of information. They function as roadside markers and offer the listener important cues for understanding. Prosodic signals provide cohesion and contrast by not only signalling to the informed listener when to expect new information, but also offering cues as to how these new pieces of information are related to previous ones. In short, understanding prosodic principles of a foreign language is of great importance for developing listening skills. In addition, we posit that prosodic competence, the ability of a speaker to deliberately apply prosodic knowledge to their own repertoire, can significantly affect a speaker's intelligibility. This is why we argue that prosody training should become an important component of deeper learning in the language classroom. Not only will it increase learners' awareness and knowledge of prosody and its importance for speech production, it can also boost intelligibility. Above all, it will offer learners an efficient way to form chunks via the process of phonological chunking and to automatise and accelerate the retrieval of those chunks.

We suggest the following four interweaving steps for experimenting prosodic training:

1. Learners listen to or watch an authentic spoken dialogue and check for understanding, harvesting the text for relevant new collocations and phrases.
2. Learners analyse the dialogue for phonological chunks using the prosody pyramid (Gilbert, 2008).
3. Learners practise emulating the dialogue in a setting that will guarantee a high number of repetitions.
4. Learners continue the dialogue, using the prosody pyramid to increase intelligibility and record their versions.

Sample Deeper Learning Episode

In a recent teacher training seminar, we developed a Deeper Learning Episode based on a *Stranger Things* Episode (Season 3 Episode 1)[3]. We selected this episode because of the relevance of the topic concerning growing up, falling in love, negotiating boundaries with parents etc. and the likelihood of this being listed

---

[3] The relevant scenes can be found on YouTube. Enter the search terms 'Stranger Things: Mike & Eleven make out', 'Hopper "heart to heart" talk', 'Hopper's awkward talk with Eleven and Mike' and/or 'Hopper's heart to heart Speech'.

in language learning curricula. Moreover, being enabled to discuss such issues of interest and sensitivity in a foreign language is of great relevance to learners.

This Deeper Learning Episode seeks to provide learners with very relevant and authentic input and enable them to collect and automatise relevant chunks, phrases and collocations. In so doing, they will be demonstrating how they can talk effectively about this topic whilst improving their active command of colloquial language as primary discourse.

1. **Promoting engagement/deepening understanding:**
   a. Explain why the shop Joyce works in is closing.
   b. Explain what Hopper is complaining about.
   c. Define 'heart to heart'.
   d. Go through the transcript of the scene and collect phrases and collocations that seem especially relevant.
   e. Record them in your lexical notebook or your personal Quizlet stash.
2. **Awareness raising: working with the prosody pyramid:** [4]
   a. Listen to the dialogue and divide each sentence into thought groups. Use '/' to mark the end of a thought group.
   b. Listen again and mark the syllables that are connected/pronounced together.
   c. Listen again and mark the most important syllable of each thought group by ticking the box above it.
   d. Now look at the whole sentence again. Mark the most important word of each sentence by colouring it.
   e. Compare your results to those of your partner and make corrections if necessary.
3. **Active pronunciation/fluency training:**
   a. Practise the dialogue with your partner. Pay special attention to sentence melody and rhythm. When in doubt watch the scene again.
   b. Whole-class activity: *double circle*. Form a double circle so that people in both circles are facing each other. Practise the dialogue with your partner. After each turn, the outer circle turns clockwise so you will be facing a new partner each turn. When you have talked to everyone, switch roles and start again.
4. **Creative tasks:**
   a. Hopper takes Joyce's advice and talks to Eleven.
      1. Prepare a dialogue between Hopper and Eleven. Use a collocation dictionary to find out if you use the right combination of words.

---

[4] For this task, learners are provided with a transcript of the relevant scene.

2. Divide the sentences into groups and mark the stress by finding the focus word and peak syllable.
3. Practise your dialogue with your partner until it feels right.
4. Act out the dialogue in front of the class.

b. After their conversation, Eleven wants to talk to Mike about it. She calls to tell him all about their 'heart to heart'. Draft their phone conversation, apply the prosody pyramid, practise the dialogue and record it.

9.7.2   Arguing along the Mode Continuum

Focus on argumentation: Language learners are often advised to come up with better arguments, more relevant to their maturity than their linguistic level ('I like it because I like it' syndrome). Although we have no doubts concerning the good intentions of such advice, we question its efficiency. In our experience, learners need to understand exactly what constitutes a 'good argument' and the steps they can take and language structures they can employ to argue effectively and convincingly. The following Deeper Learning Episode was designed to address these issues.

1. **Promoting engagement/deepening understanding:**
   a. Learners listen to a *Post Reports* podcast episode about social tracking apps and how they transform parent-child relationships.[5]
   b. After an initial listen, learners work in teams of three to create a concept map. One team member focusses on how the tracking app works, the second team member on the advantages tracking offers and the third team member concentrates on the negative effects of social tracking.
   c. Using the transcript of the show, each team member also harvests the text for valuable key words, collocations and phrases relevant to their task and together the team builds a lexical stash on Quizlet (or any other suitable app) as well as a digital lexis quiz on Socratic or Kahoot.
   d. The team then records a short video in which they formulate a joint position on where they stand concerning social tracking.
   e. The teacher will then ask the class to develop a way of rating the quality of these arguments. This will lead to Task 2.
2. **Awareness-raising: building blocks of better arguments:**
   a. Learners watch a YouTube video to learn more about the seven building blocks of effective arguments.[6]

---

[5] *Post Reports* podcast, 6 November 2019: www.stitcher.com/podcast/the-washington-post/post-reports/e/65107269?autoplay=true

[6] www.youtube.com/watch?v=DmKGMOFON0g

b. In follow-up activities, learners analyse how these building blocks are used in selected TED talks on the topic. In a follow-up plenary session, learners collect the most relevant information with support from their teacher to create criteria for effective arguments. The teacher provides additional words and phrases that might be used for each of the seven building blocks.

3. **Deep practice:** Equipped with a deeper understanding, the learners go back to their recorded videos from Task 1 and apply their new knowledge by recording an improved version of the video, which is put on a secure learning platform so that other groups can provide feedback for the final version of the video.

4. **Demonstrating understanding:** Learners are now asked to write a comment on the use of social tracking apps.

a. In order to understand the difference between arguing in the oral/colloquial mode and arguing in the written/academic mode, learners analyse the linguistic features that are used in comments/articles to present and connect arguments. In a follow-up plenary session, learners collect the most relevant information with support from their teacher to create criteria for effective written arguments. The teacher provides additional words and phrases that might be used for each of the seven building blocks.

b. Learners write comments using the Team-pair-solo method:
   i. first, they write an article together in teams, which then receives feedback form another group;
   ii. next, learners will incorporate that feedback in pairs; before
   iii. they compose the final draft of their article alone.

9.7.3 Postscript

There is no conclusion to this chapter, since we feel the way ahead is unfolding. What we do know is that in our contemporary world, traditional language teaching which focusses on linguistic systems and the development of 'controlled' communicative competence is no longer appropriate. We also wish to emphasise that this chapter has not been about dismissing the role of grammatical systems and lexical expansion, textbooks and curricula, but rather making the case that these need to be re-situated into an alternative paradigm so that language learning *is* subject learning and so that subject learning is relevant, challenging and of value to each and every individual. The principles have been articulated and will be further iterated and reiterated under scrutiny, but nonetheless we feel the time is right for transforming theoretical principles into critical classroom practices that are owned and developed by those who matter. We must also take account of increasing diversity in our classrooms in terms of cultural, economic, language and religious identities – which requires us to continually assess the context of our teaching. However, when language teachers can bring the wealth of their own knowledge, experiences and values to visibly connect with those of their learners, the foundations for language as subject teaching and learning are laid. We look forward to continuing inclusive practitioner-led developments in the quest for deeper learning in the languages classroom.

10 Closing Comments: The Road Ahead

Our personal journey, which would eventually lead to this book, started with our desire to address shortcomings in CLIL theory and practice as identified by state-of-the-art research since around 2010 outlined in Chapter One. Primarily, we wanted to understand why so many learners seemed to have difficulties expressing their understanding of subject content in adequate ways, especially in writing. The only conclusion we could reach back then was that those research findings indicated gaps in student learning or, as we would learn in the process, that learning did not go deep enough. If learners can't explain their understanding properly, the chances are they haven't fully understood. Somehow, many learners seemed to be stuck at a superficial level of learning and unable to 'connect the dots' in order to develop conceptual knowledge, which in turn is a prerequisite for transfer of learning.

CLIL has always been about the relationship between content and language and ways of integrating them. But once we began to understand the actual role of language in learning – more specifically, its role in the formation of conceptual knowledge – we realised a number of things: first, we began to see why integration is of such paramount importance. This is because languaging (as reflected action) is how we internalise conceptual knowledge; it's how we learn. Second, if that is indeed the case – and there is strong evidence to support it – then the idea of languaging being an essential component of deeper learning is not limited to learning in and through a foreign language. It goes far beyond CLIL and encompasses every kind of learning in any kind of subject, in any kind of language.

Finding out that deeper learning is strongly and directly linked to domain-specific ways of knowledge construction made us realise that we needed to move beyond CLIL to explore the concept of pluriliteracies as an educational paradigm for the twenty-first century. This in turn helped us understand that we needed to move far beyond the *mechanics* of deeper learning to define the *drivers* of deeper learning, which would eventually lead us to develop the Pluriliteracies Teaching for Deeper Learning model described in this book.

We believe that the principles, experiences and guiding questions we have introduced have the potential to make a significant contribution to transforming classroom learning into deeper learning ecologies or learnscapes, thus preparing our children for lifelong learning and helping them acquire the competences required to nurture and sustain democratic societies.

However, we are fully aware that designing, scaffolding and mentoring deeper learning episodes must be complemented by ways of assessing for deeper learning commensurate with the requirements and practical realities of the classroom. It is fair to say that the Mohan et al. (2010) article heavily influenced our thinking as we set out on our journey. Mohan et al. argue for the introduction of an integrated assessment of content and language (IALC), reporting that there has been little actual research on IALC assessment because appropriate theory, analysis and practices are not widely known. Citing Byrnes, they propose that 'the assessment of content requires a language-based theory of knowing and learning that addresses characteristics of literate language use in all modalities' (Mohan et al., 2010).

Our pluriliteracies model is based on a functional understanding of language as a process of meaning making. This idea is best captured in the following definition:

> SLF [Systemic Functional Linguistics] sees *language as a means for learning about the world*. It models *learning as a process of making meaning*, and *language learning as building one's meaning making potential* to make meaning *in particular contexts*. Knowledge is viewed as meaning, a resource for understanding and acting on the world. *All knowledge is constituted in semiotic systems with language as the most central.* (Mohan et al., 2010, p. 221; our emphasis)

However, our work has led us to conclude that we might need to revise a basic tenet: we believe that the notion of language learning as a means of building one's potential to make meaning in particular contexts might be misleading. Instead we would propose that it is pluriliteracies development (i.e. the dynamic and evolving development of subject-specific literacies in several subjects and languages) that enables learners to make meaning in particular contexts.

We would suggest, therefore, that the adage of 'every teacher is a language teacher' deserves critical reflection. Rather, we propose that the concept of deeper learning be complemented by the notion of *deeper teaching*. Deeper teaching involves an understanding of the mechanics and drivers of deeper leaning, which in turn require mentoring learning for personal growth.

This suggestion has far-reaching consequences for all teachers, educators and trainers. It encompasses developing practices which are principled, disruptive, manageable and classroom-oriented, embedded in raising awareness of pluriliteracies – not only for those teaching in bilingual contexts, but in any contexts and at any level. It demands subject teachers understand how and why successfully learning a subject rests on the transparent teaching and learning of subject literacies, which naturally include languaging activities as a means to promoting understanding.

Accordingly, we describe learning progression in pluriliteracies as the individual extension of every learner's meaning making potential. Extended meaning making potential results from deepening conceptual understanding of content knowledge (in terms of conceptual depth and breadth). Extended meaning making also potentially develops in line with the growing command of subject-specific procedures, skills and strategies (i.e. subject-specific ways of knowledge construction) as well as adequate ways of communicating knowledge. In this sense, progression involves the growing mastery of the four major activity domains of 'doing, organising, explaining and arguing' in school subjects and their corresponding genres. Assessment for deeper learning would therefore have to assess/evaluate progress in those four activity domains and include:

- command of genres and genre moves in continuous and non-continuous texts;
- depth of content information provided in each of these moves as an indicator of the development of conceptual understanding;
- quality of language use at the discourse, sentence and lexico-grammatical level;
- the mastery of subject-specific skills and strategies; and
- learner's ability to reflect on their learning process.

Whilst significant moves in thinking for assessment have led to reconsidering assessment practices, especially formative ones, how we set about pluriliteracies assessment in practical ways is in its early stages of development.

For example, in her doctoral research study, Connolly (2019) employs a dynamic understanding of one of the key cognitive discourse functions (CDFs; see Chapter Two) to assess the quality of learners' *written explanations* in the CLIL chemistry classroom. Her framework for assessing subject-specific explanations is built on classroom data which confirms that *literacy development results from both conceptual as well as communicative sophistication* (see Figure 10.1).

In a similar fashion, Berg (2020) also focussed on learner *explanations* and how they can be improved in real classroom settings. She developed and validated a rating scale to assess the quality of *oral explanations* in the CLIL geography classroom (see Figure 10.2).

Whilst we believe that those frameworks and descriptor bands are both valid and highly innovative tools for IALC, we also realise that they may be too complex to be applied in their current form by teachers to assess their students' learning.

However, we are convinced that such ratings scales and descriptor bands can be simplified for everyday use. That being the case, similar scales and bands can be developed for all CDFs and their subject-specific use. That way it might be possible to map the whole spectrum of subject-specific meaning making. Once the importance of assessing and providing feedback on our learners' meaning making skills is realised and operationalised, we will succeed in properly assessing learner understanding and contribute to learner growth.

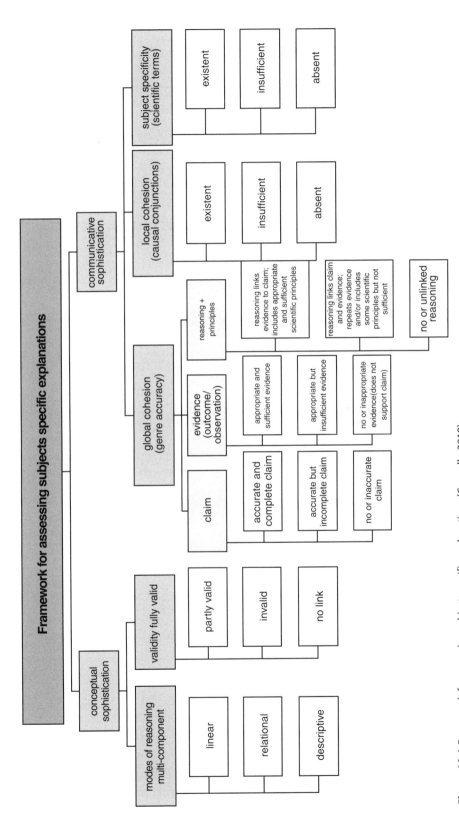

Figure 10.1 Framework for assessing subject-specific explanations (Connolly, 2019)

Indicator	Definition	Score						
		3 Points	2,5 Points	2 Points	1,5 Points	1 Point	0,5 Points	0 Points
Conceptual Depth and Structure of explanation	Describes depth and elaboration of explanation by identifying the causal coherence, namely whether the student a) simply lists multiple singular ideas through addition (1) b) combines singular ideas in a causal relationship (2) c) relates multiple causes to one or more effects (3).	Aspects are integrated into theoretical cause and effect framework. Multiple causes and effects are connected to a deep learning "why" explanation. Entails "what", and "how" explanations.	Explanation shows many aspects that are mostly connected, but still not embedded into a cause and effect framework.	Explanation shows simple causal structures and aspects/ ideas are brought into relation. Structure appears more coherent. because aspects are not listed but often related/ connected to each other, making it a deeper learning "how" explanation.	Addition of aspects/ ideas that are partly connected or brought into causal relation, still more a description/ list than a "how"-explanation.	Addition of aspects/ideas that are not connected or brought into causal relation, making it a shallow "what"-explanation without reasoning. More like a description or a list.	Explanation is unistructural and entails one (short explanation) or two aspects (longer explanation) that are however only added up and not related to each other.	No explanation identifiable, no connection to topic.
Linking of explanation	Describes the degree of linking in the oral material. Linking is displayed through use of conjunctions and expressions (linking words, see list) that structure the text logically, create smooth transitions of sentences and connect the different ideas.	Sentences consistently well linked (every sentence 1) through linking words with a lot of variation.	Sentences mostly linked with a lot of variation.	sentences are mostly linked, but with a limited range of linking words and repetitions.	Sentences are partly linked, partly not. but with more than 1or 2 different linking words.	Sentences only linked to very limited degree. Mostly repetitions/ same 1 or 2 linking words used.	Ideas not connected with linking words but there is an intro sentence OR one linking and no intro sentence.	No linking of sentences.
Evidence	Evidence refers to the way in which an explanation entails support for the claims that are made, such as in the form of giving examples to illustrate a point and indicating the student's understanding of content.	In relation to texts' length, speaker always gives full evidence that is always connected to claims.	In relation to texts' length, speaker mostly gives evidence that is always connected to claims.	In relation to texts' length, speaker mostly gives evidence, but sometimes not connected to claims.	Some instances where speaker gives evidence, but not sufficient compared to texts' length/ unconnected to claim/incomplete.	One evidence but insufficient in relation to texts' length or not connected to specific claim.	Uses evidence but is "empty" or doesn't fit the idea.	There are no evidence/ examples provided in the text.

Indicator	Definition	Score						
		3 Points	2,5 Points	2 Points	1,5 Points	1 Point	0,5 Points	0 Points
Use of Subject-Specific Terms	The explanation entails subject-specific terms (and expressions) that should be used in the correct context and display the content knowledge of the students.	Subjects-specific terms are used thoroughly and correctly, no terminology missing at all.	Terms are mostly used, all correctly, but still bits of terminology missing.	Terms mostly used, limited number is used incorrectly or missing, but mostly correct and used when necessary.	Limited number of terms used, but mostly correctly.	Limited number of terms used, partly correctly, but mostly incorrectly or missing.	If one or two are used on a long text but incorrectly.	No correct use of subject-specific terms or no use at all.
Use of specifying verbs	Use of specifying verbs indicates deeper understanding. These verbs are specific and clear and the opposite of general verbs, e.g. „get". They further specify a point/ Process etc.	Specifying verbs are used thoroughly and whenever possible.	Specifying verbs are mostly used, only one or two instances where they are lacking.	Specifying verbs are partly used; making the whole explanation more complex.	In between 1 and 2 points, Specific verbs are still limitedly used, but those used have a high quality.	Specific verbs are use limitedly and at certain points, more general verb use.	One specific verb is used.	No specifying verb use at all.

Figure 10.2 Descriptors for subject-specific explanations (Berg, 2020)

In the beginning of the book we said that the idea of deeper learning requires us to rethink what we know about teaching and learning. We believe that this also applies for assessment. In our understanding, assessment is integral to understanding and personal growth and cannot be positioned as external to learning. If learners demonstrating their understanding is as vital to deeper learning, as we have argued in this book, then assessing demonstrations of understandings at different points in time informs learners (and teachers) about where they stand and where they need to go. It is fundamental for learner progression. It is fundamental for meaningful *learning partnerships* embedded in the here and now. In short, as we have tried to demonstrate throughout, deeper learning involves 'unleashing the potential of every student'.

> Learning is rooted in relationships; and supportive relationships can unleash the potential of every student... the future of teaching may ultimately centre in deeper relationships built between teachers and students, developed through creative, collaborative, socially connected and relevant *learning experiences*. (Fullan & Langworthy, 2014, p. 14)

The road ahead points firmly in the direction of working together with classroom teachers, their learners and teacher educators in order to engage in critical action and reflection; to build practice-based, accessible guidance; to create a dynamic, principled repertoire of materials; to disseminate case studies across diverse contexts; to constantly question and develop the founding, applied principles; and to grow iterative shared understandings, adaptation and ownership of Pluriliteracies Teaching for Deeper Learning.

Bibliography

Agustín Llach, M. P. (2017). Teaching language through literature: The Waste Land in the ESL classroom. *ODISEA. Revista de Estudios Ingleses*, 8. https://doi.org/10.25115/odisea.v0i8.90

Alderson, J. C. (2000). *Assessing Reading* (1st ed.). Cambridge University Press. https://doi.org/10.1017/CBO9780511732935

Alexander, R. J. (2005). Talking to learn: oracy revisited. In C. Conner (ed.), *Teaching Texts*, (pp. 75–93). National College for School Leadership.

Alexander, R. J. (2017). Primary education: evidence with vision. In Academy of Social Sciences (ed.), *Making the Case for the Social Sciences: Education*, (pp. 18–9). AcSS.

Alexander, R. J. (2018). Developing dialogue: genesis, process, trial. *Research Papers in Education*, 33(5), 561–98.

Alptekin, C. (2002). Toward intercultural communicative competence in ELT. *ELT Journal*, 56(1), 57–65.

Anderson, J. R. (1983). *The architecture of cognition*. Harvard University Press.

Anderson, J. R., Corbett, A. T., Koedinger, K. R., & Pelletier, Ray. (1995). Cognitive tutors: lessons learned. *Journal of the Learning Sciences*, 4(2), 167–207. https://doi.org/10.1207/s15327809jls0402_2

Anderson, L. W., & Krathwohl, D. R. (eds.). (2001). *A Taxonomy for Learning, Teaching, and Assessing: A Revision of Bloom's Taxonomy of Educational Objectives*. Longman.

Australian Curriculum Assessment and Reporting Authority (2014). *National Report on Schooling in Australia 2012*. ACARA. www.acara.edu.au/reporting/national-report-on-schooling-in-australia/national-report-on-schooling-in-australia-2012

Assessment Reform Group. (1999). *Assessment for Learning: Beyond the Black Box*. Qualifications and Curriculum Authority.

Azkarai, A., & Imaz Agirre, A. (2016). Negotiation of meaning strategies in child EFL mainstream and CLIL settings. *TESOL Quarterly*, 50(4), 844–70. https://doi.org/10.1002/tesq.249

Bak, T. H. & Mehmedbegovic (2017). Healthy linguistic diet: the value of linguistic diversity and language learning across the lifespan. *Multilingualism*. www.meits.org/policy-papers/paper/healthy-linguistic-diet

Balsamo, A. (2010). Working the paradigm shift: educating the technological imagination. In D. Araya & M. A. Peters (eds.), *Education in the Creative Economy: Knowledge and Learning in the Age of Innovation* (pp. 423–46). Peter Lang.

Bandura, A. (1997). *Self-Efficacy: The Exercise of Control*. Freeman.

Bandura, A. (2006). Adolescents' development from an agentic perspective. In F.

Pajares & T. Urdan (eds.), *Self-Efficacy Beliefs of Adolescents* (pp. 1–45). Information Age Publishing.

Banegas, D. (2012). Integrating content and language in English language teaching in secondary education: models, benefits, and challenges. *Studies in Second Language Learning and Teaching*, 2(1), 111–36.

Banks, F., Leach, J., & Moon, B. (1999). New understandings of teachers' pedagogic knowledge. In J. Leach & B. Moon (eds.), *Learners and Pedagogy*. Paul Chapman Publishing.

Barwell, R. (2005). Integrating language and content: issues from the mathematics classroom. *Linguistics and Education*, 16(2), 205–18. https://doi.org/10.1016/j.linged.2006.01.002

Barwell, R. (2016). A Bakhtinian perspective on language and content integration: encountering the alien word in second language mathematics classrooms. In T. Nikula, E. Dafouz, P. Moore, & U. Smit (eds.), *Conceptualising Integration in CLIL and Multilingual Education* (pp. 101–20). Multilingual Matters. https://doi.org/10.21832/9781783096145-008

Bateman, B. E. (2002). Promoting openness toward culture learning: ethnographic interviews for students of Spanish. *The Modern Language Journal*, 86(3), 318–31. https://doi.org/10.1111/1540-4781.00152

Beacco, J.-C., Fleming, M., Goullier, F., Thürmann, E., Vollmer, H. J., Sheils, J. (2016). *The Language Dimension in All Subjects: A Handbook for Curriculum Development and Teacher Training*. Council of Europe. https://rm.coe.int/ a-handbook-for-curriculum-development-and-teacher-training-the-languag/16806af387

Becher, T., & Trowler, P. (2001). *Academic Tribes and Territories: Intellectual Enquiry and the Culture of Disciplines*, (2nd ed.). Open University Press.

Becker, C., Blell, G. & Rössler, A. (eds.), (2016). *Web 2.0 und komplexe Kompetenzaufgaben im Fremdsprachenunterricht*. Peter Lang.

Bernstein, B. (2000). *Pedagogy, Symbolic Control and Identity: Theory, Research and Critique*. Taylor and Francis.

Berg, N. (2020). *Listening for Literacies – Effekt von fachspezifischem Hör-Verstehenstraining auf die Entwicklung der mündlichen Sachfachliteralität im bilingualen Geographieunterricht*. Johannes Gutenberg-Universität.

Biesta, G. (2015). What is education for? On good education, teacher judgement, and educational professionalism. *European Journal of Education*, 50(1), 75–87. https://doi.org/10.1111/ejed.12109

Biggs, J. B., & Tang, C. (2003). *Teaching for Quality Learning at University: What the Student Does*. McGraw-Hill Education

Blell, G. and Rössler, A. (2016). *Web 2.0 und Komplexe Kompetenzaufgaben im Fremdsprachenunterricht*. Peter Lang.

Blown, E. J. & Bryce, T. G. K. (2017). Switching between everyday and scientific language. *Research in Science Education*, 47(3), 621–53.

Boaler, J., & Dweck, C. S. (2016). *Mathematical Mindsets: Unleashing Students' Potential through Creative Math, Inspiring Messages and Innovative Teaching*. Jossey-Bass.

Boekaerts, M. (1999). Self-regulated learning: where we are today. *International Journal of Educational Research*, 31(6), 445–57.

Borg, S. (2018). Teachers' beliefs and classroom practices. In P. Garrett, & J. M. Cots (eds.), *The Routledge Handbook of Language Awareness*, (pp. 75–91). Routledge.

Borland, J. (2007). A smarter web – new technologies will make online search more intelligent – and may even lead to a 'Web 3.0'. *MIT Technology Review*. www.technologyreview.com/s/407401/a-smarter-web/

Bower, K., Coyle, D., Cross, R., & Chambers, G. N. (eds.). (2020). *Curriculum Integrated Language Teaching: CLIL in Practice*. Cambridge University Press.

Broady, E. (2004). Sameness and difference: the challenge of culture in language teaching. *The Language Learning Journal*, 29(1), 68–72. https://doi.org/10.1080/09571730485200131

Brooks, R., Brooks, S. & Goldstein, S. (2012). The power of mindsets: nurturing student engagement, motivation, and resilience in students. In A. L. Christenson & C. Wylie (eds.), *Handbook of Research on Student Engagement* (pp. 541–62). Springer.

Broudy, H. S. (1977). Types of knowledge and purposes of education. In R. C. Anderson, R. J. Spiro, & W. E. Montague (eds.), *Schooling and the Acquisition of Knowledge* (pp. 1–17). Erlbaum.

Brown, J. S. & Thomas, D. 2011. *A New Culture of Learning: Cultivating the Imagination for a World of Constant Change*. CreateSpace Independent Publishing Platform.

Brown, N. J. S. & Wilson, M. (2011). A model of cognition: the missing cornerstone of assessment. *Educational Psychology Review*, 23(2), 221–34.

Brumfit, C., & Carter, R. (eds.). (1986). *Literature and Language Teaching*. Oxford University Press.

Bruton, A. (2013). CLIL: some of the reasons why... and why not. *System*, 41, 587–97.

Buttjes, B., & Byram, M. (1991). *Mediating Languages and Cultures: Towards an Intercultural Theory of Foreign Language Education*. Multilingual Matters.

Bygate, M. (ed.), (2018). *Learning Language Through Task Repetition*. John Benjamins Publishing Company.

Byrnes, H. (2002). Towards academic-level foreign language abilities: Reconsidering foundational assumptions, expanding pedagogical options. In B. L. Leaver & B. Shektman (eds.), *Developing Professional-Level Language Proficiency* (pp. 34–58). Cambridge University Press.

Byrnes, H. (2005). Reconsidering the nexus of content and language: a mandate of the NCLB legislation. *Modern Language Journal*, 89, 277–82.

Byrnes, H. (2011). Beyond writing as language learning or content learning. Construing foreign language writing as meaning-making. In R. M. Manchon (ed.). *Learning-to-Write and Writing-to-Learn in an Additional Language* (pp. 133–57). John Benjamins.

Byrnes, H. (2014). Theorizing language development at the intersection of 'task' and L2 writing. In H. Byrnes & R. M. Manchon, (eds.). *Task-Based Language Learning – Insights from and for L2 writing* (pp. 79–103). John Benjamins.

Carter, R. (2007). Literature and language teaching 1986–2006: A review. *International Journal of Applied Linguistics*, 17(1), 3–13. https://doi.org/10.1111/j.1473-4192.2007.00130.x

Carter, R. and McRae, J. (eds.), (1996). *Language, Literature and the Learner: Creative Classroom Practice*. Longman.

CAST (2011). *Universal Design for Learning Guidelines Version 2.0*. Author.

Cazden, C. B., & Snow, C. E. (1990). English plus: issues in bilingual education. In *American Academy of Political and Social Science Annals* (Vol. 508). Sage Publications, Inc.

Cazden, C. B., Cope, B., Fairclough, N., Gee, J. et al. (New London Group) (1996). A pedagogy of multiliteracies: designing social futures. *Harvard Educational Review*, 66(1), 60–92.

Cenoz, J., Genesee, F., & Gorter, D. (2014). Critical analysis of CLIL: taking stock and looking forward. *Applied Linguistics*, 35, 243–62. https://doi.org/10.1093/applin/amt011

Chamot, A. U. & Harris, V. (eds.). (2019). *Learning Strategy Instruction in the Language Classroom: Issues and Implementation*. Multilingual Matters.

Chi, M. T. H. & VanLehn. K. A. (2012). Seeing deep structure from the interactions of surface features. *Educational Psychologist*, 47(3), 177–88. https://doi.org/10.1080/00461520.2012.695709

Chiriac, S. E. and Ghitiu-Bratescu, A. (2011). Linking globalisation, sustainable development and knowledge transfer: a network based approach. *Journal of Doctoral Research in Economics*, 3(1), 12–22.

Christodoulou, D. (2017). *Making Good Progress?: The future of Assessment for Learning*. Oxford University Press.

Claro, S., Paunesku D., Dweck, C. (2016). Growth mindset tempers the effects of poverty on academic achievement. *Proceedings of the National Academy of Sciences of the United States of America. PNAS*, 113(31), 8665–8.

Claxton, G. (2013). School as an epistemic apprenticeship: the case of building learning power. In *School as an Epistemic Apprenticeship: The Case of Building Learning Power. 32nd Vernon-Wall Lecture*, (pp. 1–27). British Psychological Society.

Cochran-Smith, M. (2003). The Unforgiving complexity of teaching: avoiding simplicity in the age of accountability. *Journal of Teacher Education*, 54(1), 3–5. https://doi.org/10.1177/0022487102238653

Coffin, C. (2006a). Mapping subject-specific literacies. *National Association for Language Development in the Curriculum Quarterly*, 3(3), 13–26.

Coffin, C. (2006b). *Historical Discourse: The Language of Time, Cause and Evaluation*. Continuum.

Coffin, C. (2006c). Learning the language of school history: the role of linguistics in mapping the writing demands of the secondary school curriculum. *Journal of Curriculum Studies*, 38(4), 413–29.

Coffin, C., & Donohue, J. (2014). *A Language as Social Semiotic-Based Approach to Teaching and Learning in Higher Education*. John Wiley & Sons Ltd.

Cohen, A., D. & Macaro, E. (2007). *Language Learner Strategies: Thirty Years of Research and Practice.* Oxford University Press.

Commission of the European Communities. (1996). *Teaching and Learning: Towards the Learning Society: White Paper on Education and Training.* Office for Official Publications of the European Communities.

Connolly, T. (2019). *Die Förderung vertiefter Lernprozesse durch Sachfachliteralität: Eine vergleichende Studie zum expliziten Scaffolding kognitiver Diskursfunktionen im bilingualen Chemieunterricht am Beispiel des Erklärens.* Johannes Gutenberg University of Mainz.

Cooney, C. (n.d.). Using a project-based learning approach to support language learning. *Association for Language Learning.* www.all-languages.org.uk/language-futures/using-project-based-learning-approach-support-language-learning/

Council of Europe (ed.). (2018). *Context, Concepts and Model.* Council of Europe Publishing.

Council of Ministers of Education (Canada). (1997). *Common Framework of Science Learning Outcomes K to 12: Pan-Canadian Protocol for Collaboration on School Curriculum.* Council of Ministers of Education, Canada.

Counsell, C. (2018). Taking the curriculum seriously. *Impact: Journal of the Chartered College of Teaching.* https://impact.chartered.college/article/taking-curriculum-seriously/

Costa, L. & Kallick, B.O. (2008). *Learning and Leading with Habits of Mind: 16 Essential Characteristics for Success.* ASCD.

Coyle, Da. (2009). *The Talent Code: Greatness Isn't Born, It's Grown, Here's How.* Bantam.

Coyle, D. (2007). Content and language integrated learning: towards a connected research agenda for CLIL pedagogies. *International Journal of Bilingual Education and Bilingualism,* 10(5), 543–62. https://doi.org/10.2167/beb459.0

Coyle, D. (2008). CLIL—a pedagogical approach from the European perspective. In N. H. Hornberger (ed.), *Encyclopedia of Language and Education* (pp. 1200–14). Springer US. https://doi.org/10.1007/978-0-387-30424-3_92

Coyle, D. (2013). Listening to learners: an investigation into 'successful learning' across CLIL contexts. *International Journal of Bilingual Education and Bilingualism,* 16(3), 244–66.

Coyle, D. (2018). The place of CLIL in (bilingual) education. *Theory Into Practice,* 57(3), 166–76. https://doi.org/10.1080/00405841.2018.1459096

Coyle, D., & Al Bishawi, R. (2016). *The TePL Initiative, Final Report.* University of Aberdeen.

Coyle, D. & Chopey-Paquet, M. (2020). Enacting Pluriliteracies Teaching for Deeper Learning (PTDL) in a language classroom. 'A big, big shift'. Research report. *University of Edinburgh & International School of Geneva.*

Coyle, D., Halbach, A., Meyer, O., & Schuck, K. (2018). Knowledge ecology for conceptual growth: teachers as active agents in developing a pluriliteracies approach to teaching for learning (PTL). *International Journal of Bilingual Education and Bilingualism,* 21(3), 349–65.

Coyle, D., Hood, P., & Marsh, D. (2010). *CLIL – Content and Language Integrated Learning.* Cambridge University Press. https://doi.org/10.1080/13670050.2017.1387516

Dale, L. (2020). *On Language Teachers and CLIL: Shifting the Perspectives.* PhD thesis. Amsterdam University of Applied Sciences Centre for Applied Research in Education

Dale, L., Oostdam, R., & Verspoor, M. (2018a). Searching for identity and focus: towards an analytical framework for language teachers in bilingual education. *International Journal of Bilingual Education and Bilingualism,* 21(3), 366–83. https://doi.org/10.1080/13670050.2017.1383351

Dale, L., Oostdam, R., & Verspoor, M. (2018b). Towards a professional development tool for teachers of English in bilingual streams: the dynamics of beliefs and practices. *International Journal of Bilingual Education and Bilingualism,* 1–18. https://doi.org/10.1080/13670050.2018.1556244

Dalton-Puffer, C. (2004). Academic language functions in content and language integrated classrooms: defining and hypothesizing. *Vienna English Working Papers,* 13, 23–48.

Dalton-Puffer, C. (2007). *Discourse in Content and Language Integrated Learning (CLIL) Classrooms* . John Benjamins Pub. Co.

Dalton-Puffer, C. (2011). Content-and-language integrated learning: from practice to principles? *Annual Review of Applied Linguistics,* 31, 182–204. https://doi.org/10.1017/S0267190511000092

Dalton-Puffer, C. (2013). A construct of cognitive discourse functions for conceptualizing. *European Journal of Applied Linguistics,* 1(2), 1–38. https://10.1515/eujal-2013–0011

Dalton-Puffer, C. (2016). Cognitive discourse functions: specifying an integrative interdisciplinary construct. In T. Nikula, E. Dafouz, P. Moore, & U. Smit (eds.), *Conceptualising Integration in CLIL and Multilingual Education* (pp. 29–54). Multilingual Matters. https://doi.org/10.21832/9781783096145–005

Dalton-Puffer, C. (2017). Cognitive Discourse Functions as joint concern in language and content pedagogy. *University of Cambridge Talks.cam.* http://talks.cam.ac.uk/talk/index/69626

Dalton-Puffer, C. (2018). Postscriptum: research pathways in CLIL/immersion instructional practices and teacher development. *International Journal of Bilingual Education and Bilingualism,* 21(3), 384–7. https://doi.org/10.1080/13670050.2017.1384448

Dalton-Puffer, C., Llinares, A., Lorenzo, F., & Nikula, T. (2014). 'You can stand under my umbrella': immersion, CLIL and bilingual education. A response to Cenoz, Genesee & Gorter (2013). *Applied Linguistics,* 35(2), 213–8.

Dalton-Puffer, C., Nikula, T., & Smit, U. (eds.) (2010). *Language Use and Language Learning in CLIL Classrooms.* John Benjamins Pub. Co. https://doi.org/10.1093/applin/amu010

Dann, R. and Hanley, C. (2018). Re-examining the curriculum. *Research Intelligence,* 138.

Darn, S. (2006). Content and language integrated learning (CLIL): a European overview. *Education Resources Information Center.* https://eric.ed.gov/?id=ED490775

Davison, C., & Williams, A. (2001). Integrating language and content: Unresolved issues. In B. Mohan, C. Leung, & C. Davison (eds.), *English as a Second Language in the Mainstream: Teaching, Learning and Identity* (pp. 51–70). Longman.

De Graaff, R. (2016). Integrating content and language in education: best of both worlds? In T. Nikula, E. Dafouz, P. Moore, & U. Smit (eds.), *Conceptualising Integration in CLIL and Multilingual Education* (pp. xiii–xvi). Multilingual Matters. https://doi.org/10.21832/9781783096145-003

Deardorff, D. K. (2006). The identification and assessment of intercultural competence as a student outcome of internationalization at institutions of higher education in the United States. *Journal of Studies in International Education*, 10(3), 241–66.

Deci, E. L., & Ryan, R. M. (2000). The 'what' and 'why' of goal pursuits: human needs and the self-determination of behavior. *Psychological Inquiry*, 11(4), 227–68.

Dede, C. (2014). *The Role of Digital Technologies in Deeper Learning. Students at the Center: Deeper Learning Research Series. Jobs For the Future.*

Deller, S. (2005). Teaching other subjects in English (CLIL), *In English*, Spring 2005, 29–31.

DeKeyser, R. (2007). *Practice in a Second Language: Perspectives from Applied Linguistics and Cognitive Psychology.* Cambridge University Press.

Department of Education and Science (DES), (1975). *A Language for Life (The Bullock Report).* HMSO.

Deppeler, J. M., Loreman, T., Smith, R., & Florian, L. (eds.) (2015). Inclusive pedagogy across the curriculum. In *International Perspectives on Inclusive Education*, (Vol. 7, p. iii). Emerald Group Publishing Limited. https://doi.org/10.1108/S1479-363620150000007006

Detterman, D. K., & Sternberg, R. J. (1993). *Transfer on trial: Intelligence, Cognition, and Instruction.* Ablex Publishing.

Dettmer, P. (2005). New blooms in established fields: four domains of learning and doing. *Roeper Review*, 28(2), 70–8. https://doi.org/10.1080/02783190609554341

Diehr, B. & Suhrkamp, C. (2015). Die Entwicklung literaturbezogener Kompetenzen in der Sekundarstufe I: Modellierung, Abschlussprofil und Evaluation. In W. Hallet, C. Surkamp & U. Krämer, (eds.). *Literaturkompetenzen Englisch. Modellierung – Curriculum – Unterrichtsbeispiele* (pp. 21–40). Friedrich Verlag.

diSessa, A. A., Wagner, J. F. (2005). What coordination has to say about transfer. In J. Mestre (ed.), *Transfer of Learning from a Modern Multidisciplinary Perspective* (pp. 1–51). Information Age Publishing.

DiYanni, R. Reading responsively, reading responsibly. An approach to critical reading. In R. DiYanni, & A. Borst, (2017). *Critical Reading Across the Curriculum.* (Vol. 1). John Wiley & Sons.

Dobbs, C. L. et al. (2016). Layering intermediate and disciplinary literacy work: lessons learned from a secondary social studies teacher team. *Journal of Adolescent and Adult Literacy*, 60(2), 131–9.

Doiz, A., Lasagabaster, D., & Sierra, J. M. (2012). Globalisation, internationalisation, multilingualism and linguistic strains in higher education. *Studies in Higher Education*, 39(9), 1404–21.

Doiz, A., Lasagabaster, D., & Sierra, J. M. (2014). *Motivation and Foreign Language Learning From Theory to Practice*. Benjamins.

Dudley, P. (2013). The general rationale and underlying principles of lesson study. In *Lesson Study: Making a Difference to Teaching Pupils with Learning Difficulties*, (pp. 15–33). Bloomsbury Academic. https://doi.org/10.5040/9781472593306

Duit, R., & Tesch, M. (2010). On the role of the experiment in science teaching and learning—visions and the reality of instructional practice. In M. Kalogiannakis, D. Stavrou, & P. Michaelidis (eds.), *Proceedings of the 7th International Conference on Hands-on Science*, (pp. 17–30). http://www.clab.edc.uoc.gr/HSci2010

Dweck, C. S. (2006). *Mindset: The New Psychology of Success*. Random House.

Dweck, C. S., Walton, G. M., & Cohen, G. L. (2014). *Academic Tenacity: Mindsets and Skills that Promote Long-Term Learning*. Bill & Melinda Gates Foundation.

Edelson, D. C. (2009). Geographic Literacy in U.S. by 2025. *ArcNews*. www.esri.com/news/arcnews/spring09articles/geographic-literacy.html

Education Week. (2016). *The Journey to a Growth Mindset: Carol Dweck's Live Keynote Presentation*. Online video clip. www.youtube.com/watch?v=kuq91hqUvBg

Eerikainen, L. M. (2015). *Notebooking with iPads – ELLs in Science Class and Beyond*. Unpublished MEd dissertation, University of Aberdeen.

Engle, R. A., Lam, D. P., Meyer, X. S. & Nix, S. E. (2012). How does expansive framing promote transfer? Several proposed explanations and a research agenda for investigating them. *Educational Psychologist*, 47(3), 215–31. https://doi.org/10.1080/00461520.2012.695678

Eppler, M. J., Burkhard, R. A. (2004). *Knowledge Visualization: Towards a New Discipline and its Fields of Application*. Institute for Corporate Communication.

European Commission (2001). *Making a European area of lifelong learning a reality*. European Commission. http://eur-lex.europa.eu/LexUriServ/LexUriServ.do?uri=COM:2001:0678:FIN:EN:PDF

European Commission, & Directorate-General for Education and Culture. (2012). *EU High Level Group of Experts on Literacy: Final report, September 2012*. Publications Office. http://bookshop.europa.eu/uri?target=EUB:NOTICE:NC3212307:EN:HTML

Fang, Z., & Coatoam, S. (2013). Disciplinary literacy: what you want to know about it. *Journal of Adolescent & Adult Literacy*, 56(8), 627–32. https://doi.org/10.1002/JAAL.190

Fendler, L. & Muzafar, I. (2008). The history of the bell curve. *Educational Theory*, 58(1), 63–82. https://doi.org/10.1111/j.1741-5446.2007.0276.x

Fields, R. D. (2008). White matter matters. *Scientific American*, 298(3), 42–9.

Five Graces Group (2009). Language is a complex adaptive system: position paper. *Language Learning*, 59(1), 1–26. https://doi.org/10.1111/j.1467-9922.2009.00533.x

Florian, L. (2014). What counts as evidence of inclusive education? *European Journal of Special Needs Education*, 29(3), 286–94.

Florian, L. (2015). Conceptualising inclusive pedagogy: the inclusive pedagogical approach in action. In J. M. Deppeler, T. Loreman, R. Smith, & L. Florian (eds.), *International Perspectives on Inclusive Education* (Vol. 7, pp. 11–24). Emerald Group Publishing Limited. https://doi.org/10.1108/S1479-363620150000007001

Flynn, P., Thompson, K., & Goodyear, P. (2018). Designing, using and evaluating learning spaces: the generation of actionable knowledge. *Australasian Journal of Educational Technology*, 34(6), i–v. https://doi.org/10.14742/ajet.5091

Foley, Y., & Pratt, L. (2020). Using critical literacy to 'do' identity and gender. In R. Arshad, T. Wrigley, & L. Pratt (eds.), *Social Justice Re-examined: Dilemmas and Solutions for the Classroom Teacher* (pp. 72–91). UCL Institute of Education Press.

Freitag-Hild, B. (2018). Teaching culture – intercultural competence, transcultural learning, global education, in: C. Suhrkamp & B. Viebrock, (eds.), *Teaching English as a Foreign Language. An introduction* (pp. 159–75). J.B. Metzler.

Frenzel, A. C., Pekrun, R., Goetz, T., Daniels, L. M., Durksen, T. L., Becker-Kurz, B., & Klassen, R. M. (2016). Measuring teachers' enjoyment, anger, and anxiety: the teacher emotions scales (TES). *Contemporary Educational Psychology*, 46, 148–63.

Fullan, M., & Langworthy, M. (2013). *Towards a New End: New Pedagogies for Deep Learning.* Collaborative Impact.

Fullan, M., & Langworthy, M. (2014). *A Rich Seam: How New Pedagogies Find Deep Learning.* Pearson.

Fürsich, E. (2009). In defense of textual analysis. *Journalism Studies*, 10(2), 238–52.

Galton, M. (2008). *Creative Practitioners in Schools and Classrooms.* University of Cambridge Faculty of Education.

García, O. (2009). *Bilingual Education in the 21st Century. A Global Perspective.* Wiley Blackwell.

García, O., Bartlett, L. and Kleifgen, J. A. (2007). From biliteracy to pluriliteracies. In P. Auer & L. Wei (eds.), *Handbook of Applied Linguistics*, (Vol. 5, pp. 207–28). Mouton-De Gruyter.

Gay, G. (2010). *Culturally Responsive Teaching – Theory, Research and Practice*, (2nd ed.). Teachers College Press.

Gee, J. P. (1989). What is Literacy? *Journal of Education*, 171, 18–25.

Gee, J. P. (1996). *Social Linguistics and Literacies: Ideology in Discourses*, (2nd ed.). Taylor & Francis.

Genesee, F., & Hamayan, E. (2016). *CLIL in Context: Practical Guidance for Educators (Cambridge Teacher).* Cambridge University Press.

Gentner, D., Loewenstein, J., Thompson, L., & Forbus, K. D. (2009). Reviving inert knowledge: analogical abstraction supports relational retrieval of past events. *Cognitive Science*, 33(8), 1343–82.

Gerstein, J. (2013). Schools are doing Education 1.0; talking about doing Education 2.0; when they should be planning Education 3.0. *User Generated Education.* https://usergenerat ededucation.wordpress.com/2013/ 03/22/schools-are-doing-education-1-0-talking-about-doing-education-2-0-when-they-should-be-planning-education-3-0/

Gilbert, J. B. (2008). *Teaching Pronunciation: Using the Prosody Pyramid.* Cambridge University Press.

Gillis, V. (2014). Disciplinary literacy: adapt not adopt. *Journal of Adolescent & Adult Literacy* 57(8), 614–23.

Goldman, S. R., Britt, M. A., Brown, W., Cribb, G., George, M. A., Greenleaf, C., Lee, C. D., Shanahan, C. & Project READI (2016). Disciplinary literacies and learning to read for understanding: a conceptual framework for disciplinary literacy, *Educational Psychologist*, 51(2), 219–46. https://doi.org/10.1080/0 0461520.2016.1168741

Goldstein, S., & Brooks, R. (2007). *Understanding and Managing Classroom Behavior: Creating Resilient, Sustainable Classrooms.* Wiley.

Gonzalez, M. G. (2016). *CLIL and Writing: A Double Challenge.* Unpublished doctoral dissertation. University of Vallodolid.

Gowin, D. B. (1981). *Educating.* Cornell University Press.

Graz Group (2015). *The Graz Group Model: Mapping Pluriliteracies Development. A Pluriliteracies Approach to Teaching for Learning.* European Centre for Modern Languages. https://pluriliteracies.ecml.at/

Greenberg, D. L. and Verfaellie, M. (2010). Interdependence of episodic and semantic memory: evidence from neuropsychology. *J Int. Neuropsychol. Soc.*, 16(5), 748–53.

Grellet, F. (1981). *Developing Reading Skills.* Cambridge University Press.

Gunckel, K. L., Covitt, B. A., & Anderson, C. W. (2009). Learning a secondary discourse: shifts from force-dynamic to model-based reasoning in understanding water in socio-ecological systems. Paper presented at Learning Progressions in Science (LeaPS), June 2009, Iowa City, IA. Michigan State University. http://education.msu.edu/projects/ leaps/proceedings/Gunckel.pdf

Hallet, W. (2012). *Kompetenzaufgaben im Englischunterricht: Grundlagen und Unterrichtsbeispiele.* Klett/Kallmeyer.

Hallet, W. (2016). *Genres im Fremdsprachlichen und Bilingualen Unterricht: Formen und Muster der Sprachlichen Interaktion.* Klett/Kallmeyer.

Halliday, M. A. K. & Martin, J. R. (1993). *Writing Science: Literacy and Discursive Power.* University of Pittsburgh Press.

Halliday, M. A. K., & Matthiessen, C. M. I. M. (2004). *An Introduction to Functional Grammar.* Arnold.

Harrison-Greaves, J. (2016). Slow education leads to rich and balanced learning. *BERA.* www.bera.ac.uk/blog/ slow-education-leads-to-rich-and-balanced-learning

Harrop, E. (2012). Content and language integrated learning (CLIL): limitations and possibilities. *Encuentro*, 21, 57–70.

Harte, W. & Paul Reitano, P. (2016). 'Doing geography': evaluating an independent geographic inquiry assessment task in an initial teacher education program. *Journal of Geography*, 115(6), 233–43. https://doi.org/10.1080/00221341.2016.1175496

Hassan, X., Macaro, E., Mason, D., Nye, G., Smith, P. & Vanderplank, R. (2005). *Strategy Training in Language Learning – A Systematic Review of Available Research*. EPPI-Centre, Social Science Research Unit, Institute of Education, University of London.

Hattie, J. & Clarke, S. (2019). *Visible Learning: Feedback*. Routledge.

Hattie, J., & Timperley, H. (2007). The power of feedback. *Review of Educational Research*, 77(1), 81–112. http://dx.doi.org/10.3102/003465430298487

Hattie, J. & Yates, G. (2013). *Visible Learning and the Science of How We Learn*. Routledge.

Heemsoth, T., & Heinze, A. (2016). Secondary school students learning from reflections on the rationale behind self-made errors: a field experiment. *Journal of Experimental Education*, 84(1), 98–118.

Higgins, S., Xiao, Z., & Katsipataki, M. (2012). *The Impact of Digital Technology on Learning: A Summary for the Education Endowment Foundation*. Education Endowment Foundation.

Hipkins, R., Denny, M., Shanks, L., & White, K. (2010). *Designing Effective Extended Learning Episodes—The Alfriston College Experience*. Teaching & Learning Research Initiative.

Hoa, N. T. P.; Huong, N. T. (2015). Inert knowledge in tertiary teacher training and how to activate it. *VNU Journal of Science: Education Research*, 31(4), 54–65.

Holland, D., Lachicotte, W., Skinner, D. and Cain, C. (1998). *Identity and Agency in Cultural Worlds*, Harvard University Press.

Hood, P. & Tobutt, K. (2015). *Teaching Languages in the Primary School*, (2nd ed.). Sage Publications.

Hornberger, N. H. (2002). Multilingual language policies and the continua of biliteracy: an ecological approach. *Language Policy*, 1, 27–51.

Hornberger, N. H. (2003). *Continua of Biliteracy: An Ecological Framework for Educational Policy, Research and Practice in Multilingual Settings*. Multilingual Matters.

Hospel, V., & Galand, B. (2016). Are both classroom autonomy support and structure equally important for students' engagement? A multilevel analysis. *Learning and Instruction*, 41, 1–10. https://doi.org/10.1016/j.learninstruc.2015.09.001

Hsieh, P., Sullivan, J. R. & Guerra, N. S. (2007). A closer look at college students: self-efficacy and goal orientation. *Journal of Advanced Academics*, 18(3), 454–76.

Huang, L. S. (2017). Three Ideas for Implementing Learner Reflection. *Faculty Focus*. www.facultyfocus.com/articles/teaching-and-learning/three-ideas-implementing-learner-reflection/

Huettner, J., & Smit, U. (2014). CLIL (content and language integrated learning). *International Journal of Applied Linguistics*, 18, 146–65.

International Commission on Education for the Twenty-first Century, Delors, J., & Unesco (eds.), (1996). *Learning, the Treasure Within: Report to UNESCO of the International Commission on Education for the Twenty-first Century*. Unesco Pub.

International Society for Technology in Education (ed.). (2008). *National educational technology standards for students*, (2nd ed.). International Society for Technology in Education.

International Society for Technology in Education (ed.). (2016). *The 2016 ISTE Standards for Students*. International Society for Technology in Education. www.iste.org/standards/standards/for-students–2016

Iran-Nejad, A., & Stewart, W. (2010). Understanding as an educational objective: from seeking and playing with taxonomies to discovering and reflecting on revelations. *Research in the Schools*, 17(1), 64–76.

Irvine, J. (2017). A comparison of revised Bloom and Marzano's New Taxonomy of Learning. *Research in Higher Education*, 33. https://files.eric.ed.gov/fulltext/EJ1161486.pdf

Jackson, N. (2019). *Exploring Learning Ecologies*. Chalk Mountain.

Jackson, Yvette. (2011). *The Pedagogy of Confidence – Inspiring High Intellectual Performance in Urban Schools*. Teachers College Press.

Jaekel, N. (2015). *Use and Impact of Language Learning Strategies on Language Proficiency: Investigating the Impact of Individual Difference Variables and Participation in CLIL Streams*. Unpublished doctoral dissertation. Ruhr-University Bochum.

Jahnke, I. & Norberg, A. (2013). Digital didactics: scaffolding a new normality of learning. In *Open Education 2030 – Contributions to the JRC-IPTS Call for Vision Papers*, 129–34. http://blogs.ec.europa.eu/openeducation2030/category/vision-papers/higher-education/

Janks, H. (2014). The importance of critical literacy. In J. Z. Pandya & J. Avila (eds.), *Moving Critical Literacies Forward – A New Look at Praxis Across Contexts*. (pp. 32–44). Routledge.

Janks, H., Dixon, K., Ferreira, A., Granville, S., & Newfield, D. (2014). *Doing Critical Literacy: Texts and Activities for Students and Teachers*. Routledge.

Jetton, T. L. & Shanahan, C. (2012). *Adolescent Literacy in the Academic Disciplines: General Principles and Practical Strategies*. Guilford.

Jones, S. (2006). *Girls, Social Class, and Literacy: What Teachers Can Do to Make a Difference*. Heinemann.

Kale, D., Little, S., & Hinton, M. (2011). Reconfiguration of knowledge management practices in new product development – the case of the Indian pharmaceutical industry. In K. A. Grant, (ed.), *Case Studies in Knowledge Management Research* (pp. 102–19). Academic Publishing International Ltd.

Kapp, K. (2014). *The Gamification of Learning and Instruction Fieldbook: Ideas into Practice*. Wiley.

Kelso, J. A. S. (1995). *Dynamic Patterns: The Self-Organization of Brain and Behavior (Complex Adaptive Systems)*. MIT UP.

Kern, R. (2000). *Literacy and Language Teaching*. Oxford University Press.

Knapp, A., & Aguado, K. (2015). *Fremdsprachen in Studium und Lehre: Chancen und Herausforderungen für den Wissenserwerb / Foreign Languages in Higher Education: Opportunities and Challenges for the Acquisition of Knowledge.* Peter Lang.

Konu, A. I., & Lintonen, T. P. (2006). School well-being in grades 4–12. *Health Education Research*, 21(5), 633–42.

Koutsompou, V. (2015). The use of literature in the language classroom: methods and aims. *International Journal of Information and Education Technology.* 5(1), 74–9.

Kramsch, C. (1993). Teaching language along the cultural faultline. In D. L. Lange & R. M. Paige (eds.), *Culture as the Core: Perspectives on Culture in Second Language Learning,* (pp. 205–32). Connecticut Information Age Publishing

Lam, S., Wong, B. P. H., Yang, H., & Liu, Y. (2012). Understanding student engagement with a contextual model. In S. L. Christenson, A. L. Reschly, & C. Wylie (eds.), *Handbook of Research on Student Engagement* (pp. 403–19). Springer US. https://doi.org/10.1007/978-1-4614-2018-7_19

Lambert, D. (2016) Geography. In D., Wyse, L. Hayward, and J. Pandya, (eds.), *The Sage Handbook of Curriculum, Pedagogy and Assessment* (pp. 391–408). Sage Publications

Lambert, D., & Biddulph, M. (2015). The dialogic space offered by curriculum-making in the process of learning to teach, and the creation of a progressive knowledge-led curriculum. *Asia-Pacific Journal of Teacher Education*, 43(3),

210–24. www.ucl.ac.uk/ioe/case-studies/2016/jan/curriculum-making-geography-education

Lantolf, J. P, and Poehner, M. E. (2014) *Sociocultural Theory and the Pedagogical Imperative in L2 Education: Vygotskian Praxis and the Research/Practice Divide.* Routledge.

Lasagabaster, D., & Sierra, J. M. (2010). Immersion and CLIL in English: more differences than similarities. *ELT Journal*, 64, 367–75.

Laurillard, D. (2013). *Teaching as a Design Science: Building Pedagogical Patterns for Learning and Technology.* Routledge Taylor and Francis Group.

Lea, M. R., & Street, B. V. (2006). The 'Academic Literacies' Model: Theory and Applications. *Theory Into Practice*, 45(4), 368–77. https://doi.org/10.1207/s15430421tip4504_11

Lee, C. D., Goldman, S. R., Levine, S., & Magliano, J. P. (2016). Epistemic cognition in literary reasoning. In J. Green, W. Sandoval, & I. Bråten (eds.) *Handbook of Epistemic Cognition,* (pp. 165–83). Routledge.

Leisen, J. (2005). Wechsel der Darstellungsformen. Ein Unterrichtsprinzip für alle Fächer. *Der fremdsprachliche Unterricht Englisch*, 78, 9–11.

Leung, C., & Morton, T. (2016). Language competence, learning and pedagogy in CLIL – deepening and broadening integration. In T. Nikula, E. Dafouz, P. Moore, & U. Smit (eds.), *Conceptualising Integration in CLIL and Multilingual Education* (pp. 235–48). Multilingual Matters. https://doi.org/10.21832/9781783096145-014

Levy, F., & Murnane, R. (2004). *The New Division of Labor: How Computers Are Creating the Next Job Market.* Princeton University Press.

Lewis, M. (2002). *Implementing the Lexical Approach. Putting Theory into Practice.* Thomson Heinle.

Lin, A. M. Y. (2016). *Language Across the Curriculum & CLIL in English as an Additional Language (EAL) Contexts: Theory and Practice.* Springer.

Little, D. (n.d.). Learner autonomy and second/foreign language learning. *LLAS.* https://www.llas.ac.uk/resources/gpg/1409

Llinares, A., Morton, T., & Whittaker, R. (2012). *The Roles of Languages in CLIL.* Cambridge University Press.

Llinares, A. & Whittaker, R. (2006). Linguistic analysis of secondary school students' oral and written production in CLIL contexts: studying social science in English. *Vienna English Working Papers*, 15, 28–32.

Lomas, T., Medina, J. T., Ivtzan, I., Rupprecht, S., Hart, R., & Eiroa-Orosa, F. R. (2017). The impact of mindfulness on well-being and performance in the workplace: an inclusive systematic review of the empirical literature. *European Journal of Work and Organisational Psychology*, 26, 1–22.

Long, M. H. (1991). Focus on form: A design feature in language teaching methodology. In K. De Bot, R. Ginsberg, & C. Kramsch (eds.), *Foreign language research in cross-cultural perspective*, (39–52). John Benjamins.

Lorenzo, F., Casal, S. & Moore, P. (2010). The effects of content and language integrated learning in European education: key findings from the Andalusian Bilingual Sections Evaluation Project. *Applied Linguistics*, 31(3), 418–42.

Lorenzo, F., & Dalton-Puffer, C. (2016). Historical literacy in CLIL: telling the past in a second language. In T. Nikula, E. Dafouz, P. Moore, & U. Smit (eds.), *Conceptualising Integration in CLIL and Multilingual Education* (pp. 55–72). Multilingual Matters. https://doi.org/10.21832/9781783096145-006

Lüftenegger, M., Schober, B., van de Schoot, R., Wagner, P., Finsterwald, M., & Spiel, C. (2012). Lifelong learning as a goal – do autonomy and self-regulation in school result in well prepared pupils? *Learning and Instruction*, 22(1), 27–36. https://doi.org/10.1016/j.learninstruc.2011.06.001

Luke, A. (2000). Critical literacy in Australia: a matter of context and standpoint. *Journal of Adolescent and Adult Literacy*, 43(5), 448–61.

Lyster, R. (2007). *Learning and Teaching Languages through Content: A Counterbalanced Approach.* John Benjamins.

Lyster, R. (2014). Using form-focused tasks to integrate language across the immersion curriculum. *System*, 54, 4–13.

Lyster, R. (2018). *Content-Based Language Teaching.* Routledge. https://doi.org/10.4324/9781315103037

Macaro, E. (2006). Strategies for language learning and for language use: revising the theoretical framework. *The Modern Language Journal*, 90(3), 320–37.

Macaro, E. (2010). *The Continuum Companion to Second Language Acquisition.* Continuum.

MacKay, T. (2003). *Gee's Theory of D/discourse and ESL*. University of Manitoba. https://umanitoba.ca/faculties/education/media/MacKay-2003.pdf

Mandell, N. (2008). Thinking like a historian: a framework for teaching and learning. *OAH Magazine of History*, 22(2), 55–9. https://doi.org/10.1093/maghis/22.2.55

Markauskaite, L., & Goodyear, P. (2017). *Epistemic Fluency and Professional Education: Innovation, Knowledgeable Action and Actionable Knowledge*. Springer. https://doi.org/10.1007/978-94-007-4369-4

Martin, J. R. (1992). *English text: System and Structure*. Benjamins.

Martin, J. R., & Rose, D. (2008). *Genre Relations: Mapping Culture*. Equinox.

Martin, J. R., & White, P. R. R. (2005). *The Language of Evaluation: Appraisal in English*. Palgrave.

Marton, F. & Saljo, R. (1976). On qualitative differences in learning. 1 – Outcome and process. *British Journal of Educational Psychology*, 46, 4–11.

Marzano, R. J., & Kendall, J. (2008). *Designing and Assessing Educational Objectives: Applying the New Taxonomy*. Corwin Press.

Marzano, R. J. (2017). *The New Art and Science of Teaching*. Solution Tree.

May, S. (2014). *The Multilingual Turn*. Routledge.

McConachie, S. M., Petrosky, A. R., & Resnick, L. B. (2009). *Content Matters: A Disciplinary Literacy Approach to Improving Student Learning*. Jossey-Bass.

Mehan, H. (Bud), & Cazden, C. B. (2015). The Study of classroom discourse: early history and current developments. In L. B. Resnick, C. S. C. Asterhan, & S. N. Clarke (eds.), *Socializing Intelligence Through Academic Talk and Dialogue* (pp. 13–34). American Educational Research Association. https://doi.org/10.3102/978-0-935302-43-1_2

Mercer, N. (2000). *Words and Minds: How We Use Language to Think Together*. Routledge.

Merino, J. A., & Lasagabaster, D. (2018). CLIL as a way to multilingualism. *International Journal of Bilingual Education and Bilingualism*, 21(1), 79–92. https://doi.org/10.1080/13670050.2015.1128386

Meyer, O. (2010). Towards quality-CLIL: successful planning and Teaching strategies. *Puls*, 33, 11–29.

Meyer, O., & Coyle, D. (2017). Pluriliteracies teaching for learning: conceptualizing progression for deeper learning in literacies development. *European Journal of Applied Linguistics*, 5(2), 199–222. https://doi.org/10.1515/eujal-2017-0006

Meyer, O., Coyle, D. & Halbach, A. (2015). *A Pluriliteracies Approach to Teaching for Learning: Putting a Pluriliteracies Approach into Practice*. European Centre for Modern Languages. http://pluriliteracies.ecml.at/Portals/4/publications/pluriliteracies-Putting-apluriliteracies-approach-into-practice.pdf

Meyer, O., Coyle, D., Halbach, A. Ting, T., & Schuck, K. (2015). A pluriliteracies approach to content and language integrated learning: mapping learner progressions in knowledge construction and meaning-making. *Language, Culture, and Curriculum*, 28(1), 41–57.

Meyer, O., Imhof, M., Coyle, D., Banerjee, M. (2018). Positive learning and pluriliteracies: growth in higher education and implications for course design, assessment and research. In O. Zlatkin Troitschanskaia, G. Wittum, & A. Dengel (eds.): *Positive Learning in the Age of Information. A Blessing or a Curse?*, pp. 235–66. Springer.

Miles, D., Ward, M., & Geography Teacher's Association of Victoria. (2008). *Geography it's essential: Its place in the Victorian curriculum (2007-).* Geography Teacher's Association of Victoria.

Milton, M. (2017). Literacy and inclusion: current perspectives. In M. Milton (ed.), *International Perspectives on Inclusive Education* (Vol. 11, pp. 3–18). Emerald Publishing Limited. https://doi.org/10.1108/S1479-363620170000011001

Mittel, J. (2004). *Genre and Television. From Cop Shows to Cartoons in American Culture.* Routledge.

Mohan, B. A. (1986). *Language and Content.* Addison-Wesley.

Mohan, B. A., Leung, C., & Davison, C. (2001). *English as a Second Language in the Mainstream : Teaching, Learning, and Identity.* Longman.

Mohan, B. A., Leung, C., & Slater, T. (2010). 11. Assessing language and content: a functional perspective. In A. Paran & L. Sercu (eds.), *Testing the Untestable in Language Education* (pp. 217–40). Multilingual Matters. https://doi.org/10.21832/9781847692672-013

Mohan, B. A. & van Naerssen, M. (1997). Learning through language. *Forum,* 35(4), 22–9.

Moje, E. B. (2004). Powerful spaces: tracing the out-of-school literacy spaces of Latino/a youth. In K. Leander and M. Sheehy (eds.), *Spatializing Literacy Research and Practice* (pp. 15–38). New York: Peter Lang.

Moje, E. B., Dillon, D. R., & O'Brien, D. G. (2000). Re-examining the roles of the learner, the text, and the context in secondary literacy. *Journal of Educational Research,* 93, 165–80.

Morcom, V. (2015). Scaffolding social and emotional learning within 'shared affective spaces' to reduce bullying: a sociocultural perspective. *Learning, Culture and Social Interaction,* 6, 77–86. https://doi.org/10.1016/j.lcsi.2015.04.002

Mortimer, E. F., & Scott, P. H. (2003). *Meaning making in secondary science classrooms.* Open University Press.

Morton, T. (2018). What does research on content and language integrated learning (CLIL) tell us about EAL? *EAL Journal,* 6, 56–62

Morton, T., & Llinares, A. (2017). Content and language integrated learning (CLIL): type of programme or pedagogical model? In A. Llinares & T. Morton (eds.), *Language Learning & Language Teaching* (Vol. 47, pp. 1–16). John Benjamins Publishing Company. https://doi.org/10.1075/lllt.47.01mor

Mulcahy, D., Cleveland, B. & Aberton, H. (2015) Learning spaces and pedagogic change: envisioned, enacted and experienced. *Pedagogy, Culture & Society,* 23:4, 575–95, https://doi.org/10.1080/14681366.2015.1055128

Murdoch, I. (1950). The novelist as metaphysician. *BBC Genome Radio Times 1923–2009.* https://genome.ch.bbc.co.uk/727f653d2f444b70b1ef4069edae5cfc

NASBE Study Group on Student Engagement (2015). *A State of Engagement.* www.nasbe.org/wpcontent/uploads/StudentEngagementStudyGroupReport_March-2015_FINAL1.pdf

National Research Council (2007). *Taking Science to School: Learning and Teaching Science in Grades K-8.* The National Academies Press. https://doi.org/10.17226/11625.

National Research Council (U.S.), Pellegrino, J. W., Hilton, M. L., (eds.) (2012). *Education for Life and Work: Developing Transferable Knowledge and Skills in the 21st Century.* The National Academies Press.

Nault, D. (2006). Going global: rethinking culture teaching in ELT contexts. *Language, Culture and Curriculum*, 19(3), 314–28. https://doi.org/10.1080/07908310608668770

Nelson, M. D., Tarabochia, D. S., & Koltz, R. L. (2015). PACES: a model of student well-being. *Journal of School Counseling*, 13(19). www.jsc.montana.edu/articles/v13n19.pdf

Neuner, G. (1996). The role of sociocultural competence in foreign language teaching and learning. *Language Teaching*, 29(4), 234–9. https://doi.org/10.1017/S0261444800008545

Nicol, R. & Sangster, P. (2019). You are never alone: understanding the educational potential of an 'urban solo' in promoting place-responsiveness, *Environmental Education Research*, 25(9), 1368–85. https://doi.org/10.1080/13504622.2019.1576161

Nieveen, N., & van der Hoeven, M. (2011). Building the curricular capacity of teachers: insights from the Netherlands. In P. Picard & L. Ria (eds.), *Beginning Teachers: A Challenge for Educational Systems – CIDREE Yearbook 2011.* 49–64. ENS de Lyon, Institut Français de l'Éducation

Nikula, T. (2010). Effects of CLIL on a teacher's classroom language use. In C. Dalton-Puffer, T. Nikula, & U. Smit (eds.), *AILA Applied Linguistics Series* (Vol. 7, pp. 105–24). John Benjamins Publishing Company. https://doi.org/10.1075/aals.7.06nik

Nikula, T., Dafouz, E., Moore, P. & Smit, U. (2016a). *Conceptualizing Integration in CLIL and Multilingual Education.* Multilingual Matters.

Nikula, T., Dalton-Puffer, C., Llinares, A., & Lorenzo, F. (2016b). More than content and language: the complexity of integration in CLIL and bilingual education. In T. Nikula, E. Dafouz, P. Moore, & U. Smit (eds.), *Conceptualising Integration in CLIL and Multilingual Education* (pp. 1–26). Multilingual Matters. https://doi.org/10.21832/9781783096145-004

Ning, K., & Downing, K. (2010). The reciprocal relationship between motivation and self-regulation: a longitudinal study on academic performance. *Learning and Individual Differences*, 20, 682–6.

Novak, Joseph D. (2002). Meaningful learning: the essential factor for conceptual change in limited or inappropriate propositional hierarchies leading to empowerment of learners. *Science Education* 86. 548–71.

O'Keefe, P. A., Ben-Eliyahu, A., & Linnenbrink-Garcia, L. (2013). Shaping achievement goal orientations in a mastery-structured environment and concomitant changes in related contingencies of self-worth. *Motivation and Emotion*, 37(1), 50–64. https://doi.org/10.1007/s11031-012-9293-6

OECD (2017). *PISA 2015 Results (Volume III): Students' Well-Being.* OECD Publishing. http://dx.doi.org/10.1787/9789264273856-en

OECD (2019). *OECD Future of Education and Skills 2030: OECD Learning Compass 2030: A Series of Concept Notes.* www.oecd.org/education/2030-project/contact/OECD_Learning_Compass_2030_Concept_Note_Series.pdf

Ormrod, J. E. (2011). *Educational Psychology: Developing Learners.* Pearson.

Ortega, L. (2008). *Understanding Second Language Acquisition.* Routledge.

Pane, D. M. (2009). Third space: blended teaching and learning. *Journal of the Research Center for Educational Technology (RCET)*, 5(1), 64–92.

Panos, A. (2017). Towards translingual and transcultural practice: explorations in a white-majority, rural, Midwestern elementary classroom. *Journal of Multilingual and Multicultural Development*, 38(5), 422–37. https://doi.org/10.1080/01434632.2016.1186679

Parsi, A. (2015). Student engagement's three variables: emotion, behavior, cognition. *Getting Smart.* www.gettingsmart.com/2015/03/student-engagements-three-variables-emotion-behavior-cognition/

Paul Hamlyn Foundation & Innovation Unit. (2012). *Learning futures: A vision for engaging schools.* www.innovationunit.org/sites/default/files/Learning_Futures_Engaging_Schools.pdf

Paunesku, D., Walton, G .M., Romero, C., Smith, E., Yeager, D. S., Dweck, C. S. (2015). Mind-set interventions are a scalable treatment for academic underachievement. *Psychological Science*, 26(6), 784–93.

Pérez Cañado, M. L. (2016). From the CLIL craze to the CLIL conundrum: addressing the current CLIL controversy. *Bellaterra Journal of Teaching & Learning Language & Literature*, 9(1), 9–31.

Persson, T., af Geijerstam, Å., & Liberg, C. (2016). Features and Functions of Scientific Language(s) in TIMSS 2011. *Nordic Studies in Science Education*, 12(2), 176–96. https://doi.org/10.5617/nordina.2425

Pietarinen, J., Soini, T., & Pyhältö, K. (2014). Students' emotional and cognitive engagement as the determinants of well-being and achievement in school. *International Journal of Educational Research*, 67, 40–51. https://doi.org/10.1016/j.ijer.2014.05.001

Pink, D. H. (2009). *Drive: The Surprising Truth about What Motivates Us.* Riverhead Books.

Plonsky, L. (2019). Language learning strategy instruction: recent research and future directions. In A. U. Chamot & V. Harris (eds.) *Learning Strategy Instruction in the Language Classroom* (pp. 3–21). Multilingual Matters. https://doi.org/10.21832/9781788923415-007

Polias, J. (2016). *Apprenticing Students into Science: Doing, Talking, and Writing Scientifically.* Lexis Education.

Priniski, S. J., Hecht, C. A. & Harackiewicz, J. M. (2018). Making learning personally meaningful: a new framework for relevance research. *The Journal of*

Experimental Education, 86(1), 11–29. https://doi.org/10.1080/00220973.2017.1380589

Prichard, C., & Moore, J. (2016). The Balance of Teacher Autonomy and Top-Down Coordination in ESOL Programs. *TESOL Quarterly*, 50(1), 190–201. https://doi.org/10.1002/tesq.278

Putra, G. B. S. & Tang, K.-S. (2016). Disciplinary literacy instructions on writing scientific explanations. A case study from a chemistry classroom in an all-girls school. *Chemistry Education Research and Practice*, 17, 569–79.

Raitbauer, M., Fürstenberg, U., Kletzenbauer, P., & Marko, K. (2018). Towards a cognitive-linguistic turn in CLIL: unfolding integration. *LACLIL*, 11(1), 87–107. https://doi.org/10.5294/laclil.2018.11.1.5

Reid, E. (2013). Models of intercultural competences in practice. *International Journal of Language and Linguistics*, 1(2), 44–53. https://doi.org/10.11648/j.ijll.20130102.12

Renoult, L. et. al. (2012). Personal semantics: at the crossroads of semantic and episodic memory. *Trends in Cognitive Sciences*, 16(11), 550–8.

Renoult, L., Tanguay, A., Beaudry, M., Tavakoli, P., Rabipour, S., Campbell, K., Moscovitch, M., Levine, B., & Davidson, P. S. R. (2016). Personal semantics: is it distinct from episodic and semantic memory? An electrophysiological study of memory for autobiographical facts and repeated events in honor of Shlomo Bentin. *Neuropsychologia*, 83, 242–56. https://doi.org/10.1016/j.neuropsychologia.2015.08.013

Renshaw, P. D. (2013). The social, cultural and emotional dimensions of scaffolding. *Learning, Culture and Social Interaction*, 2(1), 56–60.

Resnick, L. B., & Schantz, F. (2015). Talking to learn: the promise and challenge of dialogic teaching. In L. B. Resnick, C. S. C. Asterhan, & S. N. Clarke (eds.) *Socializing Intelligence Through Academic Talk and Dialogue* (pp. 441–50). American Educational Research Association. https://doi.org/10.3102/978-0-935302-43-1_34

Ritchhart, R., Church, M. and Morrison, K. (2011) *Making Thinking Visible: How to Promote Engagement, Understanding, and Independence for All Learners*. Wiley.

Rodgers, C. R. (2006) Attending to student voice: the impact of descriptive feedback on learning and teaching. *Curriculum Inquiry*, 36(2), 209–37. https://doi.org/10.1111/j.1467-873X.2006.00353.x

Rogers, R. R. (2001). Reflection in higher education: a concept analysis. *Innovative Higher Education*, 26(1), 37–57.

Rose, D., & Martin, J. (2012). *Learning to Write, Reading to Learn: Genre, Knowledge and Pedagogy in the Sydney School*. Equinox.

Ruiz de Zarobe, Y. & Cenoz, J. 2015. Way forward in the twenty-first century in content-based instruction: moving towards integration. *Language, Culture and Curriculum*, 28(1), 90–6.

Sadovnik, A. R. (2001). Basil Bernstein (1924–2000). *Prospects*, 31(4), 607–20. https://doi.org/10.1007/BF03220044

Sani, A. & Hashim, C. N. (2016). Evaluating the students' level of cognitive engagement to achieve English language curriculum objectives at international Islamic school, Gombak. *Advances in Research*, 8(2). https://dx.doi .org/10.9734/AIR/2016/29456

Savignon, S. J., & Sysoyev, P. V. (2002). Sociocultural strategies for a dialogue of cultures. *The Modern Language Journal*, 86(4), 508–24. https://doi .org/10.1111/1540-4781.00158

Scardamalia, M., & Bereiter, C. (2006). Knowledge building: theory, pedagogy, and technology. In K. Sawyer (ed.), *Cambridge Handbook of the Learning Sciences* (pp. 97–118). Cambridge University Press.

Scarino, A. & Liddicoat, A. J. (2016). Reconceptualising learning in transdisciplinary languages education. *L2 Journal*, 8(4), 20–35.

Schatzki, T. R., Cetin, K., & von Savigny, E. (eds.). (2001). *The Practice Turn in Contemporary Theory*. Routledge.

Schleppegrell, M.J. (2004). *The Language of Schooling: A Functional Linguistics Perspective*. Erlbaum.

Schmenk, Barbara. (2009). Kulturelle und soziale Aspekte von Lernstrategien und individuellem Strategiegebrauch. *Fremdsprachen Lehren und Lernen*, 38, 70–88.

Schwartz, D., Bransford, J., & Sears, D. (2005). Efficiency and innovation in transfer. In J. Mestre (ed.), *Transfer of Learning from a Modern Multidisciplinary Perspective* (pp. 1–51). Information Age Publishing.

Segalowitz, N. (2003). Automaticity and second languages. In C. J. Doughty & M. H. Long (eds.), *The Handbook of Second Language Acquisition* (pp. 382–408). Blackwell Publishing Ltd. https://doi.org/10.1002/ 9780470756492.ch13

Seixas, P. (n.d.). Historical thinking concepts. *The Historical Thinking Project*. https://historicalthinking.ca/historical-thinking-concepts

Selingo, J. J. (2017). Why can't college graduates write coherent prose? *Washington Post*. www.washingtonpost .com/news/grade-point/wp/2017/08/11/ why-cant-college-graduates-write/

Senatsverwaltung für Bildung, Jugend, und Wissenschaft (2016). *Textsortenspezifisches Schreiben im Englischunterricht der Sekundarstufe 1. Materialien zum selbstständigen Lernen*. https://bildungsserver.berlin-brandenburg.de/fileadmin/bbb/ unterricht/unterrichtsentwicklung/ Individualisierung_des_Lernens/ HANDREICHUNG_ONLINE-FINAL_06.05.16.pdf

Shanahan, T. and Shanahan, C. (2008). Teaching disciplinary literacy to adolescents: rethinking content-area literacy. *Harvard Educational Review*, 78(1), 40–59.

Shanahan, T. and Shanahan, C. (2012). What is disciplinary literacy and why does it matter? *Topics in Language Disorders*, 32(1), 7–18.

Shernoff, D. J., Kelly, S., Tonks, S. M., Anderson, B., Cavanagh, R. F., Sinhaa, S., & Abdi, B. (2016). Student engagement as a function of environmental complexity in high school classrooms. *Learning and Instruction*, 43, 52–60.

Shulman, L. S., & Shulman, J. H. (2004). How and what teachers learn: a shifting perspective. *Journal of Curriculum Studies*, 36(2), 257–71.

Shulman, L. S. (2005). Signature pedagogies in the professions. *Daedalus*, 134(3), 5259.

Shires, L. (2018). Using theories of task design in curriculum planning. *Impact Journal of the Chartered College of Teaching.* https://impact.chartered.college/article/theories-task-design-curriculum-planning/

Shor, I. (1992). *Empowering Education: Critical Teaching for Social Change.* Chicago University Press.

Short, D. J. (1996). *Integrating Language and Culture in the Social Studies. A Final Report to the U.S. Department of Education, Office of Educational Research and Improvement.* https://eric.ed.gov/?q=Short+Integrating+language+1996&ff1=autShort%2c+Deborah+J.&id=ED415685

Siefkes, M. (2015). How semiotic modes work together in multimodal texts. *10plus1: Living Linguistics*, 1, 113–31.

Sinnema, C., & Aitken, G. (2013). Emerging international trends in curriculum. In M. Priestley & G. J. J. Biesta (eds.), *Reinventing the Curriculum: New trends in Curriculum Policy and Practice.* Bloomsbury Academic.

Skehan, P. (1998). *A Cognitive Approach to Language Learning.* Oxford University Press.

Skidmore, D (2000). From pedagogical dialogue to dialogical pedagogy. *Language and Education*, 14(4), 283–96. https://doi.org/10.1080/09500780008666794

Smith, F., F. Hardman, K. Wall, & M. Mroz. (2004). Interactive whole class teaching in the national literacy and numeracy strategies. *British Educational Research Journal*, 30(3), 403–19.

Solomon, J. (1983). Learning about energy: how pupils think in two domains. *European Journal of Science Education*, 5(1), 49–59.

Spivack, N. (2007). Web 3.0: the third generation web is coming. *Lifeboat Foundation.* https://lifeboat.com/ex/web.3.0

Stern, H. H. (1992). *Issues and Options in Language Teaching.* Oxford University Press.

Stigler, J. W., & Hiebert, J. (1999). *The Teaching Gap; Best Ideas from the World's Teachers for Improving Education in the Classroom.* The Free Press.

Stoll, L., & Louis, K. S. (2007). *Professional Learning Communities: Divergence, Depth and Dilemmas.* Open University Press/McGraw Hill.

Street, B. V. (1994). Cross cultural perspectives on literacy. In J. Maybin (ed.), *Language and Literacy in Social Practice* (pp. 139–50). Open University.

Street, B. V. (1995). *Social Literacies: Critical Approaches to Literacy in Development, Ethnography, and Education.* Longman.

Suhrcke, M., & de Paz Nieves, C. (2011). *The Impact of Health and Health Behaviours on Educational Outcomes in High-income Countries: A Review of the Evidence.* World Health Organization Europe.

Swain, M. (2006) Languaging, agency and collaboration in advanced language proficiency. In H. Byrnes (ed.),

Advanced Language Learning: The Contribution of Halliday and Vygotsky (pp. 95–108). Continuum.

Tedick, D. J., & Cammarata, L. (2012). Content and language integration in K-12 contexts: student outcomes, teacher practices, and stakeholder perspectives. *Foreign Language Annals*, 45(1), 28–53. https://doi.org/10.1111/j.1944-9720.2012.01178.x

Tillema, H., Westhuizen, G. J. V. D., & Merwe, M. P. V. D. (2015). Knowledge building through conversation. In H. Tillema, G. J. van der Westhuizen, & K. Smith (eds.), *Mentoring for Learning: 'Climbing the Mountain'* (pp. 1–19). SensePublishers. https://doi.org/10.1007/978-94-6300-058-1_1

The Douglas Fir Group. (2016). A transdisciplinary framework for SLA in a multilingual world. *The Modern Language Journal*, 100(1), 19–47.

Tough, P. (2013). *How Children Succeed: Grit, Curiosity, and the Hidden Power of Character*. Houghton Mifflin Harcourt.

Toulmin, S. (1958). *The Uses of Argument*. Cambridge University Press.

Tulving, E. (1972). Episodic and semantic memory. In E. Tulving & W. Donaldson, *Organization of Memory*. Academic Press.

Tulving, E. (2002). Episodic memory: from mind to brain. *Annual Review of Psychology*, 53, 1–25.

Ulmanen, S., Soini, T., Pietarinen, J., & Pyhältö, K. (2016). The anatomy of adolescents' emotional engagement in schoolwork. *Social Psychology of Education*, 19, 587–606. https://doi.org/10.1007/s11218-016-9343-0.

United Nations Educational, Scientific and Cultural Organization (2013).

Intercultural Competences: Conceptual and Operational Framework. UNESCO.

United Nations General Assembly (2000). *United Nations Millennium Declaration*. 55/2. United Nations General Assembly Oceana Publications.

Unsworth, L. (2004). Comparing school science explanations in books and computer-based formats: the role of images, image/text relations and hyperlinks. *International Journal of Instructional Media*, 31(3), 283–301.

Van Lier, L. (1996). *Interaction in the Language Curriculum: Awareness, Autonomy, and Authenticity*. Longman.

Van Lier, L. (2008). Ecological-semiotic perspectives on education linguistics. In B. Spolsky & F.M. Hult (eds.), *The Handbook of Educational Linguistics*, (pp. 596–605). Blackwell.

Van Lier, L. (2010). Telling ELT tales out of school. The ecology of language learning: practice to theory, theory to practice. *Procedia – Social and Behavioral Sciences*, 3, 2–6.

Van Liehr, L. (2011). Research in and around the language classroom: qualitative and quantitative approaches. *Modern Language Journal*, 95,(s1), 1–3.

Veel, R. (1997). Learning how to mean – scientifically speaking: Apprenticeship into scientific discourse in the secondary school. In F. Christie & J. R. Martin (eds.), *Genre and Institutions. Social Processes in the Workplace and School*, 161–95. Continuum.

Verloop, N., van Driel, J., & Meijer, P. (2001). Teacher knowledge and the knowledge base of teaching. *International Journal of Educational Research*, 35(5), 441–61.

Vertovec, S. (2007). Super-diversity and its implications, *Ethnic and Racial Studies*, 30, 1024–54.

Visible Learning (n.d.) Hattie ranking: 252 influences and effect sizes related to student achievement. *Visible Learning.* https://visible-learning.org/hattie-ranking-influences-effect-sizes-learning-achievement/

Vollmer, H. J. (2008). Constructing tasks for content and language integrated learning and assessment. In O. Eckerth & S. Siekmann (eds.), *Task-based Language Learning and Teaching – Theoretical, Methodological, and Pedagogical Perspectives*, 227–90. Peter Lang.

Vollmer, H. J. (2011). Schulsprachliche Kompetenzen: Zentrale Diskursfunktionen. Osnabrück University. www.home.uni-osnabrueck.de/hvollmer/VollmerDF-Kurzdefinitionen.pdf

Walqui, A. (2006). Scaffolding instruction for English language learners: a conceptual framework. *The International Journal of Bilingual Education and Bilingualism*, 9(2), 159–80.

Wang, M. T., & Degol, J. (2014). Motivational pathways to STEM career choices: using expectancy-value perspective to understand individual and gender differences in STEM fields. *Developmental Review*, 33, 304–40.

Wang, M. T., Fredricks, J. A., Ye, F., Hofkens, T. L., & Linn, J. S. (2016). The math and science engagement scales: scale development, validation, and psychometric properties. *Learning and Instruction*, 43, 16–26.

Weinburgh, M. H & Silva, C. (2012). An instructional theory for English language learners: the 5 R Model for enhancing academic language development in inquiry based science. In B. J. Irby, G. Brown, R. Lara-Alecio (eds) & J. Koch (sect. ed.), *Handbook of Educational Theories* (pp. 293–304). Information Age Publishing Inc.

Wells, G. (1999). *Dialogic Inquiry: Towards a Socio-cultural Practice and Theory of Education*. Cambridge University Press.

Wertsch, J. (1998). *Mind as Action*. Oxford University Press.

Whitty, G. (2010). Revisiting school knowledge: some sociological perspectives on new school curricula. *European Journal of Education*, 45, 28–45. https://doi.org/10.1111/j.1465-3435.2009.01422.x

Widdowson, H. G. (1983). Talking shop: literature and ELT. *ELT Journal*, 37, 30–5.

Wiggins, G. & McTighe, J. (2005). *Understanding by Design*, (2nd ed.). ASCD.

Wise, A. F. & O'Neill, K. (2009). Beyond more versus less. A reframing of the debate on instructional guidance. In S. Tobias, & T. M. Duffy, (eds.), *Construtivist Instruction: Success or Failure?* (pp. 82–105) Routledge.

Wolff, D. (2009). Strategien im bilingualen Sachfachunterricht. *Fremdsprachen Lehren und Lernen (FLuL)*, 38, 137–57.

Wollenschläger, M., Hattie, J., Machts, N., Möller, J., & Harms, U. (2016). What makes rubrics effective in teacher-feedback? Transparency of learning goals is not enough. *Contemporary Educational Psychology*, 44–45, 1–11. http://dx.doi.org/10.1016/j.cedpsych.2015.11.003

Young, M. (2019). Conceptualising the Curriculum. *Research Intelligence*, 138, 14–5.

Young, M. & Muller, J. (2010). Three educational scenarios for the future: lessons from the sociology of knowledge. *European Journal of Education*, 45(1), 11–27.

Zee, M., & Koomen, H. M. Y. (2016). Teacher self-efficacy and its effects on classroom processes, student academic adjustment, and teacher well-being: a synthesis of 40 years of research. *Review of Educational Research*, 86(4), 981–1015. https://doi.org/10.3102/0034654315626801

Zimmerman, B. J. (2000). Attaining self-regulation: a social cognitive perspective. In M. Boekaerts, P. R. Pintrich & M. Zeidner (eds.), *Handbook of Self-Regulation* (pp. 13–39). Academic Press.

Zlatkin-Troitschanskaia, O., Pant, H. A., Lautenbach, C., Molerov, D., Toepper, M., & Brückner, S. (2017). *Modeling and Measuring Competencies in Higher Education: Approaches to Challenges in Higher Education Policy and Practice*. Springer VS.

Index